Insuring States in an Uncertain World

Of the sectors comprising global capital markets, insurance and reinsurance deserve more attention than they typically receive, not least in the fields of international relations and political economy. New social conventions and financial instruments arising from the invention of probabilistic calculation and the discovery of risk began to spread around the world five centuries ago. They disciplined speculative impulses, promoted economic development and integration, and fostered societal resilience after disasters. That the modern regulatory and redistributive state would evolve simultaneously with insurance markets is no coincidence. Today, leading states and a dynamic private sector are harnessing the insuring instinct as they experiment with innovative arrangements to address increasingly complex global risks. The logic of insurance opens promising pathways towards sustainable political collaboration on rising financial, technological, and environmental challenges. At a time when many global initiatives face deepening resistance, narratives drawn from the history of insurance and reinsurance suggest ways to move pragmatically beyond illusions of self-reliance in a profoundly interconnected world.

LOUIS W. PAULY is J. Stefan Dupré Distinguished Professor of Political Economy in the Department of Political Science and the Munk School of Global Affairs & Public Policy at the University of Toronto. He is a Fellow of the Royal Society of Canada and a recipient of the Distinguished Scholar Award in International Political Economy from the International Studies Association. His publications include *Opening Financial Markets* (1988), *Who Elected the Bankers?* (1997), *The Myth of the Global Corporation* (1998), and *Complex Sovereignty* (2005).

Insuring States in an Uncertain World

Towards the Collaborative Government of Complex Risks

LOUIS W. PAULY
University of Toronto

CAMBRIDGE
UNIVERSITY PRESS

CAMBRIDGE
UNIVERSITY PRESS

Shaftesbury Road, Cambridge CB2 8EA, United Kingdom

One Liberty Plaza, 20th Floor, New York, NY 10006, USA

477 Williamstown Road, Port Melbourne, VIC 3207, Australia

314–321, 3rd Floor, Plot 3, Splendor Forum, Jasola District Centre, New Delhi – 110025, India

103 Penang Road, #05–06/07, Visioncrest Commercial, Singapore 238467

Cambridge University Press is part of Cambridge University Press & Assessment, a department of the University of Cambridge.

We share the University's mission to contribute to society through the pursuit of education, learning and research at the highest international levels of excellence.

www.cambridge.org
Information on this title: www.cambridge.org/9781009662895

DOI: 10.1017/9781009662918

When citing this work, please include a reference to the DOI 10.1017/9781009662918

First published 2025

Printed in Great Britain by CPI Group (UK) Ltd, Croydon CR0 4YY

A catalogue record for this publication is available from the British Library

A Cataloging-in-Publication data record for this book is available from the Library of Congress

ISBN 978-1-009-66289-5 Hardback

For

Caryl Leslie Clark

♫

Contents

Preface and Acknowledgments

Long ago, I worked in the financial sector, first in commercial banking and later in a new division of the International Monetary Fund (IMF) focused on international capital markets. From my first day on Wall Street to my last day at the IMF, I was challenged to learn about various kinds of risk. We talked about credit risk, funding risk, liquidity risk, macroeconomic risk, political risk, systemic risk, and many others. But we never talked about uncertainty. I guess it was just generally assumed that what we couldn't know, measure, or manage was outside our zone of pressing interest. What I have come to understand since those days is that much of what really matters in our everyday lives lies between risks that can be estimated and uncertainties that can only dimly be imagined.

This book grew out of a long friendship and research collaboration with Edgar Grande. Without him, it would not exist. Chapter 3 in particular reflects insights he developed, sometimes with his students at the University of Munich and sometimes with his co-author, Ulrich Beck. Ten years before he died in 2015, Ulrich contributed a key chapter to a volume on the evolution of state sovereignty that Edgar and I edited and the University of Toronto Press published. Through Edgar and his wife, Brigitte, I was able to get to know Ulrich and his wife, Elisabeth Beck-Gernsheim, a distinguished sociologist in her own right.

I began outlining specific ideas for the book during sojourns in the Global Governance Department of the WZB Berlin Social Science Center, under the leadership of Michael Zürn, and in the School of Political Science and International Studies at the University of Queensland in Brisbane, thanks to an invitation from Chris Reus-Smit. I also benefited from time spent in the library and with colleagues at the Robert Schuman

Centre for Advanced Studies at the European University Institute, under the direction of Brigid Laffan and later Erik Jones. Much appreciated support came from all of these institutions as well as from the Canada Research Chair Program of the Social Sciences and Humanities Research Council of Canada.

I thank Emily Nacol and Steven Bernstein for reading and providing advice on early draft chapters. Steven went even further and added essential value just before I sent the final manuscript off to copy-editing. Peter Katzenstein, who has been a wise mentor and treasured friend for over forty years, read early and late chapters and, as usual, gave me trenchant and stimulating comments. His continuing work on the politics of risk and uncertainty is fundamental.

The results of myriad informal discussions with executives of Munich Re, Swiss Re, Allianz, Manulife, and Lloyds underpin Chapter 4. Although I am responsible for what I have written in this and other chapters, I am very grateful for the knowledge and experience shared by Volker Deville, Michael Menhart, Markus Wadé, Rainer Sachs, Li Xing, Roma Lechner, Robin Erswell, Bridget Hutter, and Gregory Belton. I have also benefited enormously from the in-person and on-line conferences that the Geneva Association, Artemis.bm, Reinsurance News, and SWIFT have allowed me to attend.

Chapter 5 rests on patient advice and guidance from Julia Schwartz and Ximena Vásquez-Maignan of the Office of the Legal Counsel of the Nuclear Energy Agency of the Organisation for Economic Co-operation and Development (OECD), Aurelia Radu, archivist of the OECD, Alain Quéré from Swiss Re, Markus König from Munich Re, Fred Dermarkar from Atomic Energy of Canada Limited, and Anthony Wetherall from the International Atomic Energy Agency. I could not have completed the research for this chapter without much-appreciated visiting-scholar passes from both the OECD and the International Atomic Energy Agency. My colleague Dani Nedal also gave me the benefit of his expertise on the history of commercial nuclear energy as the chapter was being revised. The lessons learned are my own, as are any remaining mistakes or misunderstandings. An early version of the chapter was presented at the annual meeting of the International Studies Association in San Francisco on May 2, 2024.

Chapter 6 reflects my continuing work over many years on the political economy of global finance. Related papers have included "Governing Global Risks: The Evolution of Policy Capacity in the Financial Sector," *Discussion Paper Series*, Global Governance Department, WZB Berlin

Social Science Center, May 2014 (SP IV 2014–103), as well as chapters contributed over seven editions to the *Global Political Economy* textbook published by Oxford University Press, initially edited by John Ravenhill and then by John and Erin Hannah. My interest was sparked long ago during time spent on the staff of the IMF. Mark Allen, Jacques de Larosière, Joseph Gold, Manuel Guitián, Jacques Polak, and Max Watson influenced my views profoundly, as did Sylvia Ostry and Louis Rasminsky back in Canada. Through Polak and Rasminsky it was a special privilege to have direct connections back to the seminal work of the Economic and Financial Organization of the League of Nations. Confidential interviews with many participants in the Basel Process associated with the Bank for International Settlements much later proved essential to shaping my views of a long and continuing evolution of transnational policy in this arena.

The final chapters grew out of a long collaboration with William D. Coleman and our joint work on the "Globalization and Autonomy" theme, which was supported as a Major Collaborative Research Initiative by the Social Sciences and Humanities Research Council of Canada. Many years later, that work informed papers entitled "Beyond Self-Reliance in a World of Global Risks and Deepening Uncertainty," which was presented at the 41st Pacific Trade and Development Conference in Seoul, Korea, 12 September 2023; "A New Multilateralism for the Twenty-First Century," *International Studies Perspectives* 22, no. 4 (2021): 6–8, edited by Mark Boyer and Cameron Thies; and "Darkness and Light in a Global Political Economy," *New Political Economy* 26, no. 2 (2021): 302–311, edited by Jacqueline Best.

For helping me frame the book, I am grateful for insights, constructive criticism, and encouragement received over many years from Emanuel Adler, Alan Alexandroff, Jacqueline Best, Mark Blyth, Tim Büthe, Gordon Clark, Patricia Clavin, Benjamin J. Cohen, Charles Collyns, Eugénia da Conceição-Heldt, Daniel H. Deudney, Andrew Filardo, Orfeo Fioretos, Randall Germain, Charles Goodhart, Erin Hannah, Virginia Haufler, Eric Helleiner, C. Randall Henning, Barry Herman, G. John Ikenberry, Harold James, Bruce Jentleson, Erik Jones, Miles Kahler, Bill Keller, John Kirton, Kathryn Lavelle, Matthias Matthijs, Henry Nau, William O'Connell, Jonathan Ostry, Tony Porter, Lucia Quaglia, Klaus Regling, Simon Reich, Chris Reus-Smit, Lawrence Schembri, Dirk Schoenmaker, Mark Schwartz, Leonard Seabrooke, Robert Skidelsky, Janice Stein, Geoffrey Underhill, Amy Verdun, Nicolas Véron, David Vines, William White, Ngaire Woods, Bernhard Zangl, and Michael Zürn.

Three anonymous referees read the draft manuscript. Their detailed recommendations for final revisions were very helpful and much appreciated. At Cambridge University Press, I owe Robert Dreesen a great debt. Long ago, in a Toronto pub, we brainstormed the essential idea for the book. Fortunately for me, he is both a creative author and patient editor. I am also very grateful to John Haslam for his continuing interest and encouragement, Jacqueline Larson and Simon Fletcher for painstaking efforts to improve my prose, and Sable Gravesandy and Vigneswaran Gurumurthy for managing the final production process.

My father, who has long shared much more than his name with me, continues to be the master of the gentle nudge. Four of his great-grandchildren came along while I was writing this book. Barrett, Oscar, Winifred, and Clark provide personal reasons for hope in uncertain times, as do their exemplary parents, Tessa, Brian, Reid, and Natalie. What is certain, though, is that I have been very lucky. My current streak began in London in the Fall of 1976, when I heard the music of the spheres. The proof is that a pianist who became a distinguished musicologist heard it too. She has shared every season with me since then. I dedicate this book to her.

Introduction: Insurance, Then and Now

It was hardly unusual in May for a strong south wind to blow through the mountain passes leading into the town. At 10.00 p.m. on the tenth of the month, a small fire broke out in a nearby stable. Because of the wind, 150 houses extending to the middle of the town were ablaze within thirty minutes. By midnight, the firestorm had killed eight people and destroyed or damaged 793 buildings – two-thirds of the town's housing stock. Two thousand people, nearly half of the town's population, were left homeless.

When the smoke finally cleared, some called it a miracle that the death toll had not been much higher. The survivors nevertheless faced a monumental recovery challenge. How would they finance the massive cost of rebuilding the town? Most of the households involved (634) had no insurance. Forty percent of the others were underinsured, and few had any kind of coverage for the contents of their homes. The most exposed private insurance company found itself on the hook for one-quarter of all covered losses, which may well have forced it into bankruptcy had the regional government not agreed to absorb over a third of them. The owners of most of the insured buildings had purchased coverage from a public insurer authorized by that same government. Unfortunately, those policies had been badly mispriced. In the end, premium income and reserves proved wholly inadequate, and fiscal deficits mounted at both the town and regional levels of government.

The disaster would have left widespread misery in its wake no matter what. But a better and more comprehensive insurance system might have eased the pain, accelerated rebuilding, and promoted resilience. The town's citizens now demanded such a system, and their leaders were pressed to deliver it soon.

The year was 1861 and the town was Glarus, an emerging industrial center in the eastern part of Switzerland, 70 kilometers southeast of Zürich.[1] The scale of its catastrophe soon made Glarus famous, but the event was hardly unique in pointing to the need for better economic and political instruments to help modern societies, increasingly industrialized, financialized, and concentrated, manage risks. Among others, great fires had destroyed much of London in 1666 and Hamburg in 1842. The famous Chicago fire came ten years after the one in Glarus. The only uncertainty across all of them involved timing. By the late nineteenth century, the danger of fire in tightly packed communities posed a well-understood risk, and the myriad challenges of resilient recovery could and should have been readily anticipated. Why were so many so unprepared?

The Glarus disaster brought into clear view key elements of the protection systems that modern societies needed. In its aftermath, the role of public authorities changed, reliance on techniques for mobilizing private capital rose significantly, and the interaction of markets and states across established borders became deeper and more intricate. The disasters in Glarus and elsewhere in the late nineteenth century spawned new demands for citizens and firms to take more responsibility for their own lives and to lengthen their planning horizons. They stimulated financial innovations that promoted postcrisis resilience, which often opened new social cleavages. They spawned adaptive networks of private insurance and reinsurance provision as well as new expectations that governments would support those networks in novel ways for the common good. In time, and often in the wake of even more damaging catastrophes, national governments around the world would seek to use the practices and technical language of insurance to facilitate structural political changes and also to rationalize limits on claims to fiscal support.

That same language would increasingly be used to frame agreements between and among governments that underlined mutual interests in the transformation of public authority without directly breaching established constructions of political autonomy. At the same time, an expansion of private and cross-border financial networks soon provided vast

[1] The case is highlighted in Harold James, Peter Borscheid, David Gugerli, and Tobias Straumann, *The Value of Risk: Swiss Re and the History of Reinsurance* (Oxford: Oxford University Press, 2013). Also see the detailed historical website built by Swiss Re: https://history.swissre.com/.

new sources of capital for insurance and reinsurance. Evolving insurance practices as well as insurance metaphors justifying deeper forms of integration gradually pushed forward consequential transnational experiments in risk assessment, disaster prevention, and emergency management. Today those practices and metaphors transcend political and conceptual frontiers and intimately link private and public sectors around the world. As humanity confronts more encompassing risks and deeper sources of uncertainty, future decisions to travel along the collaborative path they have opened will not come automatically. Both reasonable as well as pragmatic social and political choices will be required, not unlike the choices facing the leaders and residents of Glarus in the spring of 1861.

Of the sectors that make up what is commonly referred to as global finance, the insurance and reinsurance industries that began to grow rapidly during the late nineteenth century have arguably attracted the least attention in the fields of international relations and political economy. And what attention they have received has often justifiably focused on market weaknesses, high premiums charged, inadequate protection offered, and the questionable fairness of ultimate coverage.

I am seeking larger lessons from the history of insurance and its normative foundations. That means first understanding how this vital sector of contemporary capital markets developed after the discovery of risk and the inception of probabilistic reasoning. Intrigued by how the incipient industry and its justifying rhetoric used political ideas and adapted to changing political conditions, my aim is to examine the possibilities and the limits of transposing lessons from that history to the modern global political sphere where our species confronts many risks apparently no longer manageable within established territorial boundaries.

At its most basic level, insurance revolves around efforts to smooth the peaks and valleys of life. But it also forms a key element in the modern quest for risk reduction, crisis prevention, and burden sharing across diverse groups of people unrelated to one another. It is no coincidence that the governments of states have been engaged in that same quest, as their constituents have looked to them for protection from dangers and help in coping with the vagaries of life. In fact, many governments have lately adapted the ideas and practices of insurance to justify policies aimed both at indemnifying citizens and sustaining their confidence in the future. In light of the evident challenges posed for all governments by vast contemporary sources of risk and uncertainty, my overarching objective is to explore the roles that techniques and metaphors drawn from the history of insurance and reinsurance might now be playing in the quiet reconstitution of world order.

New social conventions and financial instruments arising from the discovery of risk began to spread around the world five centuries ago. They rationalized speculative impulses and fostered resilience by spreading the burdens of economic loss and providing resources for recoveries after disaster. They also often concentrated the gains resulting from novel processes of financial intermediation. It's no coincidence that the modern state would emerge simultaneously with insurance and reinsurance markets. The social tensions of industrialization and what came to be called globalization demanded new political and economic buffers. Their interaction and incompleteness are part of a long and continuing story.

Today, states collectively face the challenge of adapting and designing anew politically tolerable instruments for governing some risks collaboratively, if they are to be governed at all. Market-led innovations in this direction typically give priority to efficient risk management. But when markets break down, other sources of support for resilience and recovery must be found.[2] In their absence, social and political structures can quickly become brittle, and then collapse in moments of crisis.

Since the end of World War II, the potential social costs of a widening array of risks, some measurable and some only plausibly imaginable, have loomed ever larger. In the midst of disasters, public authorities – often in complex alliances with private centers of effective power – have sometimes responded constructively and collectively. They have signaled explicit or implicit understandings about the practical necessity of mutual support and solidaristic adjustment. Those understandings have underpinned experiments aimed at recovery in the aftermath of emergencies and at the prevention of future emergencies. As we shall see, insurance practices and metaphors have proven to be most useful up to the point where plausible risk meets uncertainty. But even after that point, the notion of solidarity underpinning them has sometimes helped concentrate minds. Perhaps we have lately been more lucky than smart when systemic conditions have forced political and business leaders to gaze into the abyss, as happened when the global financial crisis of 2008

[2] That phenomenon has spawned a large and rapidly expanding body of research, some of which I refer to later. For an accessible and popular introduction to the core psychological and social issues involved, see Brian Klaas, *Fluke: Chance, Chaos, and Why Everything We Do Matters* (New York: Simon & Schuster, 2024).

reached its most perilous moment. The reasonable urge not to push our luck lies behind the next generation of political experiments to transcend the impulse of self-reliance.

Risks that cannot be contained within national silos are clearly expanding. Some are connected, for example, with international financial intermediation, nuclear energy production, and the rapid development of artificial intelligence and digital technologies. Others are linked to the deterioration of natural environments, genetic engineering, and the spread of lethal pathogens. Emerging plans to govern such risks set the stage for new experiments in global political collaboration. Some of the most ambitious combine attention to complex public and private interests with the seemingly anodyne practices of insurance and related metaphors. They promise to aggregate capital, craft new social balances, and justify deeper cross-border and cross-generational transfers of opportunities, burdens, and responsibilities. Critical debates on the benefits and costs of such plans remain vital.

After the global wars of the twentieth century, pooling risks and sharing burdens – the basic logic of insurance – motivated the design of collaborative international institutions targeted at specific problems of collective action. Without abridging the legal doctrine of state sovereignty, they were intended to breach radical notions of political autonomy, share prosperity, and promote mutual security and social stability. These days, many of them appear to have reached the limits of their capacities. To be sure, some productive adjustments have occurred in the missions of organizations such as the International Monetary Fund, the World Bank, the World Trade Organization, and the World Health Organization, but their shortcomings in the twenty-first century cannot be ignored. Even so, they were not primarily responsible for various recent disasters – from the global financial crisis of 2008 to the Great Recession and trade conflicts that followed to the COVID-19 pandemic. They also did not cause the increasingly visible damage from climate change, biodiversity loss, and fragile technological networks. While some commentators see them as useful scapegoats, the organizations themselves are trying to adapt their mandates and increase their resources in light of changing risk parameters. But the world soon needs much more ambitious political instruments to successfully manage more complex and long-term risks as well as better ways to cope with new generators of uncertainty.

Against the backdrop of history, I assess the political terrain that today's leaders have to traverse as they try to reform and design transformative governing arrangements on a global scale. The objective must be to share sustainably the burdens and benefits of change. My observation point is admittedly at a high altitude, or what the international relations scholar Barry Buzan calls the angle necessary to take in the big picture. I look back to highlight the conditions under which risk and the insurance techniques to manage it developed in the early stages of globalizing capitalism. After drawing analytical distinctions among the border-spanning risks encountered as that system advanced, I show how discrete insurance and reinsurance practices and related metaphors helped concentrate productive capital investment, propel innovations in the roles of government, facilitate societal resilience, and justify novel intergovernmental organizations. This leads to a brief exploration of the federalizing logic of insurance in the face of challenges that cannot be contained within national boundaries. I then provide detailed examples of how formal and informal public–private risk sharing experiments, some intergovernmental in form, confront the limits of complexity and time. Finally, without discounting the contemporary realities of great power rivalry and rising populist autocracy, I defend the idea that innovative collaborative policies – instinctive, pragmatic, and informed by the history of insurance and reinsurance – can help push those limits outward.

I

Risk, Uncertainty, and the Demand for Political Innovation

While statements of risk are intended to provide more certainty, they also convey uncertainty. They are at once expressions of knowledge and expressions of ignorance: uncertain knowledge claims about contingent future events that cannot be fully known.

—Richard V. Ericson, "Ten Uncertainties of Risk-Management Approaches to Security"

Border-spanning problems now frame our everyday lives. From climate change to the emergence of new technologies with unpredictable effects, our species is challenged to innovate in the ways we deal with the threats of harm that can begin in restricted domains but then spread uncontrollably. While doubts haunt us, our species' constructive instincts are also awakened by the idea of risk.

INSURANCE PRACTICES AND METAPHORS IN THE GOVERNANCE OF RISK

Human life has always been shrouded in a fog of uncertainty. Relatively recently in our history, however, the pragmatic logic of risk management began lifting some of that fog. Collective perceptions of the probability of prospective disasters formed the basis for new economic technologies. Although they did not promise immediate solutions to profound problems or guarantees of distributive justice, during the seventeenth century novel and functional social conventions and financial practices grounded in a particular worldview began to spread unevenly around the world.

Spreading from a European base, the fundamental idea of insurance rationalized and provided a moral foundation for constructive speculation in the cause of expanding commerce globally. Early innovative practices along this line encouraged efforts to reduce and manage the risks involved in maritime trade. They then helped strike new balances between profit making and burden sharing in one economic sector after another. Central to their evolution was the disciplined gathering of data and the systematic application of probabilistic reasoning. Eventually, they would become effective instruments through which governments, now often indirectly, could allocate values. As a burgeoning body of research would later assert, insurance became governance.

In retrospect, we can see such instruments taking the form of social and political experiments commonly categorized under the labels "insurance" and "reinsurance." They ranged from private cooperatives to organized markets and corporate enterprises to government-sponsored programs to international organizations. They traced the rise of an ethic of personal responsibility for risk control during the early stages of capitalism to the socialization of risk and the construction of related national and international institutions in the wake of global crises from the eighteenth century to the twenty-first. An important question today is whether new experiments in insurance-as-governance going well beyond those of the recent past are necessary to manage complex and mounting risks such as those that climate change and generative artificial intelligence pose.

But first I want to underline the intimate connection between insurance arrangements, even when they seem mundane, and fundamental social and political choices. In other words, I'm interested in "who gets what, when, and how," as Harold Lasswell subtitled his famous 1936 book, *Politics*. In such a context, governments can be compared and contrasted as providers of security, collective risk managers, and distributors of benefits and costs. An essentially functionalist approach develops naturally from such an intuition. As a standard textbook in the field put it, modern governments manage the key social functions of goal selection, decision making, resource mobilization, and policy design, implementation, and evaluation.[1] Over time, many governments of states have delegated some of these functions to other social actors, including insurance providers, even as they maintained the capacity to

[1] B. Guy Peters and Jon Pierre, *Comparative Governance* (Cambridge: Cambridge University Press, 2016).

reverse that delegation. Max Weber put his finger on that very capacity when he emphasized the essential enabling characteristic of the state: its monopoly over the legitimate use of force.

Six decades after Lasswell wrote his book, the political and legal theorist Thomas Morawetz made the conceptual link in modern governance theory to insurance systems explicit, especially for liberal states governing market-based social systems. He also highlighted its variability across particular cases. "Insurance recapitulates politics ... What options should we have? What arrangements should be compulsory? ... How much freedom should persons have? How much risk should they bear? How should responsibilities and rights be allocated between individuals and the state? How should the liberal idea of autonomy be reconciled with egalitarian ideals and goals?"[2]

All governments promise their constituents some degree of protection from dangers. If specific governments survive for any length of time, they have to somehow manage risks that won't simply disappear on their own. Although the distribution of associated burdens and benefits does not necessarily aspire to notions of fairness, it usually does hold the promise of stability. Along this line, politics and psychology merge everywhere, and governance metaphors drawn from the history of insurance become intuitive. Explicit or implicit promises to provide financial support after disasters may be politically attractive but can never be entirely guaranteed. Risks can't be entirely eliminated. Likewise, official declarations aimed at reinforcing personal responsibility and claiming never to provide bailouts can backfire. Imagine a Florida governor committed to an ideology of self-help and personal responsibility trying to get reelected after deciding in the wake of unusually destructive hurricanes not to provide any kind of last-resort public insurance option for constituents after private insurers have left the market.

The premiums paid for private insurance are today widely understood to be bets that essentially "pay off" after disasters. Paying taxes is an involuntary but analogous bet, even if the extent and reliability of protection that taxes provide can vary with specific governmental

[2] Thomas Morawetz, "Insurance: How It Matters as Psychological Fact and Political Metaphor," *Connecticut Law Journal* 6 no. 1 (1999): 9. In the field of international relations, a rich literature also exists on the uses and abuses of metaphors. See, for example, Michael P. Marks, *Metaphors in International Relations Theory* (New York: Palgrave Macmillan, 2011); Markus Kornprobst et al., eds., *Metaphors of Globalization* (London: Palgrave Macmillan, 2008); and Francis A. Beer and Christ'l De Landtsheer, eds., *Metaphorical World Politics* (Lansing: Michigan State University Press, 2004).

structures and many other factors. Whether the functions of risk management and disaster recovery are delivered publicly or privately in the modern era, the language and evolving practice of insurance provide an evidently useful social technology.

As Morawetz puts it for a contemporary audience, "The jerry-built structures of the state and private insurance hardly allow us to leave behind the dangers that we first meet in Hobbes's state of nature ... [But] insurance is a rich metaphor, notwithstanding the fact that it has rarely inspired novelists and dramatists." In practice, those structures can help ameliorate the effects of dangers we face, even if they cannot finally prevent us "from discovering the limits of our (or anyone's) control over our destiny, from knowing fear in a radically contingent world."[3]

Pushing those limits outward forms the core of a vital political project in our world today. Contemporary adaptations of insurance practices and metaphors are worth paying attention to as an emerging global society struggles to address multiplying risks, even as the fog of uncertainty appears to thicken.

PRAGMATISM IN THE MIDST OF UNCERTAINTY

Humanity today appears to be stumbling across an ill-defined terrain marked by both uncertainty and expanding risks, as well as by political limits that can seem insuperable. At the global level, great-power rivalries are resurgent. At the local level, populist or revolutionary movements unsettle established hierarchies in country after country. In between, it seems, some of us can sometimes agree on the identification of cross-border risks as well as on the design of shared rules and standards for managing them. But then we fail to put in place effective-enough or fair-enough policies to sustain and enforce them. Some of us assert that certain challenges require practices that definitively transcend the claims of nationalism underpinning the sovereign writs of existing states, but then we recoil from the full implications of that knowledge. Some of us have succeeded in building border-spanning economies, but we still oppose or have trouble imagining the transfer or pooling of adequate and effective authority to govern the intricate social interactions, shared interests, and unintended consequences of our success. Some of us know that government is the final source of security, however imperfect, in the face of uncertainty, but

[3] Morawetz, "Insurance," 9–10.

we cannot imagine how that function can reliably be delivered at the planetary level. The well-resourced pessimists among us prepare for disorder. The optimists call ever more assertively for "international cooperation."

I am with the pragmatists, who see no choice but to struggle patiently and hopefully on the ambiguous and unstable middle ground where risk and uncertainty are difficult to disentangle and where liberal hopes exist in tension with the persistent claims of illiberal nationalism. Reasonable historical interpretations and at least some recent developments justify such a temporizing disposition. In the context of risks that inexorably span borders and generations, humans are capable of engaging in a complex, dynamic, and adaptive process of pushing back many sources of uncertainty. However, there's no guarantee that we'll succeed. Daunting generators of conflict, inequality, and injustice stand in the way. Even so, there are visible signs of incremental progress.

Ever more precise assessments of global risks and evolving public and private practices of insurance and reinsurance describe their basic form in a system decisively shaped by the intersection of philosophical liberalism, national politics, and capitalist economics.[4] Since accepted governmental authority underpins the legitimacy of those practices, any examination of specific risks that cross boundaries or analysis of conceptual distinctions between "public" and "private" raises unavoidable political questions. My aims in this book are to provide a systematic structure for framing such questions and then to draw out key implications for future global policymaking.

Whether they assign priority to groups or individuals, political questions center on assessments of risk, on struggles to prevent disasters, and on the management of emergencies when such disasters nevertheless occur. Evolving practices and metaphors of insurance shed useful light on the search for answers. It is no coincidence that they first arose early in the 250-year struggle between the ideologies of nationalism and liberalism in the shaping of our current global economic order.

[4] An influential critical formulation by Lobo-Guerrero sees insurance as evolving in the context of a globalizing capitalism: "a complex technological construction, based on multiple assumptions, which brings together matters of politics, economics, society, and culture ... assumptions that frame the terms of *liberal* governance and influence the behaviour of *liberal* subjects in the everyday world." Luis Lobo-Guerrero, "Insurance, Subjectivity, and Governance," *International Relations* 33, no. 4 (2019): 606.

THE DIVERSITY OF RISKS IN A SYSTEM BOTH INTEGRATING AND FRAGMENTING

Social and political reactions to essentially liberal constructions of insurance, both in theory and in practice, include acquiescence, criticism, and resistance. Before we consider them, let's look at how and why insurance practices and insurance metaphors have arisen in the search for ideas and instruments to imagine and manage risks that transcend political boundaries and then to sustainably distribute the burdens and responsibilities of living with them. In doing so, we must explore their imperfections and ask if more promising alternatives might be feasible in a world that is simultaneously integrating and fragmenting.

Many types of risks actually span political frontiers. Over time, their management has come to be delegated to conventional insurance markets. Some, like disaster risks associated with hurricanes and other natural events, have lately evoked innovations involving international capital markets. In this book, I typically label such risks "cross-national" or "cross-border."

Beyond this category in much contemporary research, the terms *global* and *systemic* are often used interchangeably. This is a common source of confusion. "Systemic risk" refers specifically to the chance that a failure of one entity, such as a bank, firm, or municipality, will cascade to other entities it is connected to and cause the collapse of an entire industry, market, or society. In practice, the power to prevent such cascading failure has sometimes rested entirely within local or national boundaries. US authorities alone, for example, successfully managed systemic risk in 1984 by seizing Continental Illinois National Bank and Trust and preventing the collapse of markets that were just beginning to become intricately integrated across national borders. As we shall see later, in 2008 similar systemic risks were again managed, but only by the governments of the United States and other key nation-states acting collaboratively.

By way of distinction, *global risks*, like the risks associated with climate change, biodiversity loss, pandemics, and generative artificial intelligence, may be amenable to a degree of management or governance through insurance-like instruments. But the complexity of such risks and the fundamental uncertainty surrounding them suggests that they ultimately require intensely collaborative interventions resting on innovative forms of public authority spanning the planet – if they're to be governed at all.

RISK AND UNCERTAINTY IN CONTEMPORARY SOCIETY

Scholarly studies focusing on concepts of risk and uncertainty are legion, and we will encounter quite a few in this book. An award-winning study by the historian Jonathan Levy, for example, sees political struggles over bearing risk and its rewards as central to the history of capitalism in the United States.[5] Peter Katzenstein has sought to reorient the study of world politics away from predictable models of risk toward a more open-ended embrace of uncertainty.[6] Economists John Kay and Mervyn King similarly entreat investors and decision makers to pull back on commonplace notions that quantitative indicators of risk actually make the world more manageable.[7] Along this line, different social scientists have focused on proliferating sources of risk and uncertainty that defy containment within bounded markets or polities.

The sociologist Ulrich Beck, for example, placed a rather undifferentiated concept of global risks at the center of his field-opening studies. (I delve more deeply into that work later.) Like others we'll encounter, he drew much needed attention to the social implications of revolutionary technological developments, from the harnessing of nuclear fission to the expansion of discrete production systems releasing massive volumes of greenhouse gases into an atmosphere shared by all of humanity.[8] If he were still alive, he would likely put recent advances in artificial intelligence into the same category.

The dominant ways that people in the modern world conceive of and speak about such risks evoke core elements of a widely shared social imaginary as well as an intuitive sense of the structure of relations of power. The undeniable background condition of such impressions is uncertainty. What seems indisputable today is that perceptions of global risks in this context foster a vague but enveloping sense of dread. Although he often elided the distinction between risk and uncertainty, Beck and his sometime colleague Anthony Giddens sought to harness both notions to push all societies in the direction of self-interested collaboration, if only to preempt increasingly probable catastrophes. They

[5] Jonathan Levy, *Freaks of Fortune: The Emerging World of Capitalism and Risk in America* (Cambridge, MA: Harvard University Press, 2012).

[6] Peter J. Katzenstein, ed., *Uncertainty and Its Discontents* (Cambridge: Cambridge University Press, 2022).

[7] John Kay and Mervyn King, *Radical Uncertainty: Decision-Making Beyond the Numbers* (New York: W.W. Norton, 2020).

[8] See, for example, Ian Goldin, *Divided Nations* (Oxford: Oxford University Press, 2013).

hoped that *emancipatory catastrophism* would encourage global solidarity. As Beck ultimately concluded, "In a world of global crises and dangers produced by civilization, the old differentiations between internal and external, national and international, us and them, lose their validity and a new cosmopolitan realism becomes essential."[9]

Compelling as it is at first glance, such thinking underestimates the possibility that it will induce not progressive social development but excessive caution and even stultifying precautionary paralysis. For example, it seems to downplay the stimulus to innovation that a dominant stream within liberal thought associates with embracing both risk and uncertainty.[10] It also fails to take fully into account the need to disentangle the causes and effects of coincident crises, such as climate change and biodiversity loss.[11]

Remaining attentive to the complex political effects of uncertainty, my own sensibility is more pragmatic. In the fields of international relations and political economy, related debates framing the chapters that follow center on the contest between liberal aspirations and perennial struggles over power in an uncertain world.[12] Optimism can be justified, but only after clear-eyed observation and analysis of feasible collaborative responses to the daunting global challenges our species now confronts.

I examine the ground on which policies and instruments are actually developing as their essential objectives become clearer and the absence of action becomes ever less defensible. That ground was clearly exposed during the first half of the twentieth century by collaborative innovations

[9] Ulrich Beck, *Cosmopolitan Vision* (Cambridge: Polity, 2004), 14.

[10] Richard Ericson, "Governing through Risk and Uncertainty," *Economy and Society* 34, no. 4 (2005): 661.

[11] Here is the unstable terrain that a gathering body of research is organizing itself on around the evocative but vague term "polycrisis." The word was popularized by Adam Tooze, among other places in "Welcome to the World of the Polycrisis," *Financial Times*, October 29, 2022. Thomas Homer-Dixon, Ortwin Renn, and colleagues have erected an ambitious analytical scaffolding around the core idea in Michael Lawrence et al., "Global Polycrisis: The Causal Mechanisms of Crisis Entanglement," *Global Sustainability (Journal)* (2024). Of more direct relevance to this book is the taxonomy provided by Eric Helleiner in "Economic Globalization's Polycrisis," *International Studies Quarterly* 68, no. 2 (June 2024). Also see William White, "*Mitigating Global Warming Is Not Our Only Problem*," Toronto: Global Risk Institute (2023).

[12] The debate hinges on ever more subtle distinctions. Exemplary lodestars include G. John Ikenberry, *A World Safe for Democracy: Liberal Internationalism and the Crises of Global Order* (New Haven, CT: Yale University Press, 2020) and Jonathan Kirshner, *An Unwritten Future: Realism, Uncertainty, and World Politics* (Princeton: Princeton University Press, 2022).

informed by the history and logic of insurance. Robust intergovernmental institutions grew from earlier political experiments inspired essentially by confederal principles justifying only minimal burden-sharing obligations. I explore the contemporary limits of those principles and the possibilities of transcending them. Attention to actual experience across diverse issue areas, I conclude, indicates that serious political transformation is possible if we can harness the pragmatic intuitions and compromises underpinning more ambitious insurance-like experiments not only in the management of shared risks but also in collaborative government aimed at limiting sources of uncertainty.

The pioneering work of political scientist James Rosenau began sketching the same terrain by developing an insight often attributed to Herbert Simon. Late in his life, Rosenau, a leading analyst of the domestic politics of foreign policy, cast his gaze at the level of the system as a whole. He was among the first to introduce complexity theory to our fields as he described a world that was simultaneously integrating and fragmenting. On his optimistic days, he imagined that world being governed as a complex adaptive system "without government."[13] Along this line, he began thinking plausibly, realistically, and hopefully about the fluid contemporary meaning of state sovereignty and about the kinds of political arrangements that might come next as our species confronted the ambiguities of managing risk and coping with uncertainty in open and unstable physical, social, and political environments.[14]

Like Rosenau, I think such arrangements in practice can be understood as experiments aimed at shifting and sharing burdens posed by

[13] James N. Rosenau and Ernst-Otto Czempiel, eds., *Governance without Government*, (Cambridge: Cambridge University Press, 1992). Also see James N. Rosenau, *Turbulence in World Politics: A Theory of Change and Continuity* (Princeton: Princeton University Press, 1990); James N. Rosenau, "Governance in the Twenty-first Century," *Global Governance* 1, no. 1 (1995): 13–43; and, along the similar lines, Randall Germain, ed. *Susan Strange and the Future of Global Political Economy: Power, Control and Transformation* (Abingdon: Routledge, 2016).

[14] The distinction between "government" and "management" is commonly elided in much popular as well as academic commentary by invoking the word *governance*. In this book, *management* typically refers to the technical regulatory mechanics of private or governmental agents within markets that may be conceived as public or private. *Government* refers to authoritative oversight, supervision, and last-resort intervention to stabilize societies, which may be understood as local, national, regional, or international. A skeptic of what some colleagues depict as "private authority," except when it is formally or informally delegated by governments, I typically reserve *governance* for the activities of governments, most frequently the governments of states. For a nuanced and contrasting view, see Jessica F. Green, *Rethinking Private Authority* (Princeton: Princeton University Press, 2014).

risks that cannot be contained within national boundaries. In principle, they can reconstitute structures of government. Such a reconstitution, I conclude, is not only possible but likely when existing governments harness in innovative ways what the distinguished economic historian Harold James called the "insuring instinct."[15]

As we shall see, only a few centuries ago that instinct enveloped and transcended the psychological roles previously played in earlier human societies by luck, chance, destiny, and blind faith. It presaged the collective reimagining of what came to be widely understood as risks-to-be-managed through political and market mechanisms.[16] A remarkable and rapid process of social and political transformation ensued, even if fundamental uncertainties were never really displaced and, indeed, deepened over time. It is no coincidence that insurance markets and the modern state evolved simultaneously as institutions aimed at providing protection. It is also no coincidence that both are adapting as demands for protection change in character as well as scope.

Contemporary transformations of both state and market involve the development of new forms of political delegation. In a world reshaped by the vast expansion of global financial markets, for example, relationships among private insurers, reinsurers, and governmental actors have also changed. Such relationships reallocate values across time and space and constitute novel structures of *preventive governance*. More generally, they encourage *anticipatory collaboration* and challenge authorities with the capacity to decide and to build technical networks with the objective of preempting crises and facilitating resilience when disasters nevertheless occur.[17]

The process of building collaborative global governing structures in a rapidly changing world continues to feature instrumental experiments to manage the ever-more-complicated distribution of the benefits and

[15] Harold James, "The Insuring Instinct," in James et al., *The Value of Risk: Swiss Re and the History of Reinsurance* (Oxford: Oxford University Press, 2013), 1–20.

[16] Practical studies in finance have long been built on this foundation. See, for example, Howard Kunreuther et al., *The Future of Risk Management* (Philadelphia: University of Pennsylvania Press, 2020).

[17] André Broome and Leonard Seabrooke, "Recursive Recognition in the International Political Economy," *Review of International Political Economy* 28, no. 2 (2021): 369–381; Erin Lockwood, "Predicting the Unpredictable: Value-at-Risk, Performativity, and the Politics of Financial Uncertainty," *Review of International Political Economy* 22, no. 4 (2015): 719–756; John Berten and Matthias Kranke, "Anticipatory Global Governance: International Organisations and the Politics of the Future," *Global Society* 36, no. 2 (2022): 155–169.

costs of managing expansive risks. Not surprisingly, contestation over the common good deepens along the way. While one systemic crisis after another spawns partially constructive reactions from the political authorities actually underpinning contemporary markets, their own capacities for autonomous action are attenuated.[18] At the same time, slow-moving planetary threats with irreversible effects grow, and risk becomes more difficult to differentiate from uncertainty just as the systemic distribution of state power is becoming more dispersed.

Fundamental political questions are beginning to focus not only on whether leading states and the markets they influence can cope but also on whether others will follow. As in the past, crises, in and beyond markets, provide opportunities to adapt governing capacities and justify new governing instruments.[19] Ever since they first appeared, insurance practices and metaphors have helped construct instruments and justify ideas to manage crises. They have opened pathways to the transformation of essential governing structures. We are living in another such moment.

OVERVIEW OF THIS BOOK

Chapter 2 recounts the rise of the concept of risk and the early modern practice of insurance as it evolved from communal attempts, mainly in Europe between the seventeenth and nineteenth centuries, to discipline and commodify earlier forms of speculation. The processes eventually involved in risk assessment, pooling, and diversification were neither inevitable nor entirely capricious. Their evolution was complicated and indeterminate, and the chapter explores how accommodating structures of government developed in tandem.

It also digs into the rapidly expanding and increasingly complicated scholarship focused on the governance of risk *and* uncertainty as considerations of their consequences migrate over time and geographic space. Despite unavoidable technicalities, it notes how leading business firms around the world, not just in the insurance industry, came to base their strategies on sophisticated models that take for granted commonplace,

[18] For an exemplary critical study of direct relevance to this book, see Jean-Christophe Graz, *The Power of Standards: Hybrid Authority and the Globalisation of Services* (Cambridge: Cambridge University Press, 2019).

[19] Richard V. Ericson, Aaron Doyle, and Dean Barry, *Insurance as Governance* (Toronto: University of Toronto Press, 2003). Ian Bremmer puts the spotlight on this theme in *The Power of Crisis* (New York: Simon & Schuster, 2022).

even simplistic, notions of risk. Those strategies are nevertheless dynamic, and they shape larger structures within which firms and people interact. As collective impressions of risk and practices aimed at managing them become more complex, or as a shared sense of uncertainty rises, structural change can be gradual or abrupt. To employ the images made famous in Donald Mackenzie's study of finance theory, the models behind firm strategies are engines, not cameras. Sociologists are surely right that we need to understand how such models drive change in vital social and political structures.[20]

Chapter 3 sets out a conceptual framework for thinking systematically about old and new risks perceived to have a global dimension. It uses the complexity of those worldwide risks and the timeline of the disasters they portend to build the analytical scaffolding for understanding our current dynamic governing practices evolving to manage them in their diversity. It also sets out the scope conditions both for feasible insurance practices and for the utility of insurance metaphors. As risk complexity deepens and time horizons lengthen, the potential role of market mechanisms shrink, and collaborative government becomes necessary. The three chapters that follow set out illustrative cases of that evolving process.

The first case focuses on relatively simple risks and increasingly cross-border insurance and reinsurance markets. The second explores fascinating and intricate collective instruments engaging both private and public actors that have aimed over the past seven decades to insure more complex risks associated with the commercial production of nuclear energy. The third case examines the risks and sources of uncertainty associated with globalizing finance, which persistently call for innovative political instruments for threat assessment, disaster prevention, and emergency management.

The final chapters survey even more complex and long-term dilemmas that are top of mind these days when contemplating phenomena such as climate change, biodiversity loss, and microbial pandemics. Close observers commonly see them posing not risks but existential threats. To be sure, the domestic and international politics surrounding the assignment and acceptance of liability here are excruciatingly contentious. At the same time, the crucial task of designing effective, legitimate,

[20] Donald A. MacKenzie, *An Engine, Not a Camera: How Financial Models Shape Markets* (Cambridge, MA: MIT Press, 2006). Also see Michel Callon, ed., *The Laws of the Markets* (Oxford: Blackwell, 1998).

and sustainable global governing instruments may still be inspired by metaphors drawn from the history of insurance and reinsurance.

The insuring instinct remains irrepressible. The history and contemporary promise of insurance and reinsurance structures and networks do not promise near-term tranquility or infinite expansibility. Nor do the language and logic of insurance define ultimate solutions to all problems requiring collective action. Especially in an era of dramatic technological change, heightened political instability, and the constant possibility of military conflict, uncertainty remains undeniable. History nevertheless calls to mind pragmatic engagements with the principles and practices of insurance in similarly difficult circumstances. Political experiments aimed at harnessing the benefits of integration without entirely sacrificing the values of autonomy have sometimes developed. When they have succeeded. as in the formation of stable federations, they have pushed forward prior limits on managing risks and coping with uncertainty. Such experiments sustain the hope that human ingenuity has not yet reached its limit.

2

The Insuring Instinct in a Changing World

> We have to invent a new kind of polity, but we cannot yet imagine how it might work.
>
> —Susan Strange, *Mad Money*

Fairly recently in the history of our species, successful societies have come to accept the idea that psychological zones of risk can sometimes be carved out of uncertain circumstances. On that basis, those societies have built tools to limit anticipated dangers and manage outcomes when disasters occur. The concept of risk thus developed in tandem with novel practices for sharing and redistributing expected social burdens, that is, simultaneously with the emergence of insurance systems. Over time, buyers and sellers of insurance contracts conceptualized and steadily pushed outward the limits on their capacities to anticipate future developments and substitute risk for uncertainty.[1] The dynamics of government, though sometimes hidden, were always implicated, because citizens expect governments to provide protection.

This chapter connects the histories of risk, insurance, and modern government. It provides the scaffolding for examining the political implications of new risks and mounting sources of uncertainty that override established boundaries.

[1] Sylvain Maechler and Jean-Christophe Graz, "Is the Sky or the Earth the Limit? Risk, Uncertainty, and Nature," *Review of International Political Economy* 29, no. 2 (2022): 624–645.

THE IDEA OF RISK AND ITS EARLY APPLICATIONS

Throughout history, human beings have dealt with the potentially debilitating individual and collective consequences of uncertainty in two steps. The foundational step involved spontaneous cooperation among kinship groups followed by subsequent social enlargement, often via conquest. The next step entailed the construction of some form of government, typically combining military, administrative, and ideological/religious structures.[2] If those structures provided adequate security for a discrete group of people, they persisted. When organized and sanctified, such structures did not banish dangers, but they pushed back people's sense of uncertainty. Over the past five centuries, another method of achieving the same goal emerged. Although it didn't replace government, it added significantly to the social and political instruments available to cope with uncertainty and provide a sense of security. It rested on the invention and creative management of what came to be called risk.

These methods of social stabilization (i.e., cooperative kinship and government and then risk management) became intertwined and proved their utility in assuaging fear and bolstering people's confidence in the future. They thus supported the expansion of societies across time and space. The concept of risk, however, bequeathed us with an evolving sense that many sources of uncertainty can in fact be managed. If ancient human communities imagined no alternative to resignation in the face of the unknowable, modern ones came to resist the ideology of fatalism.

Many of our forebears believed that the ultimate causes of much suffering emanated from a realm absolutely beyond human control. Some sought solace in ideas of deserved destiny, reflecting a mysterious but imaginatively certain order. Most believed that ultimate safety came from overlords who were divinely sanctioned. Those kings or rulers might fail, or they might be corrupt. But everyone had to accept their

[2] Such assertions, often associated with European history, can be traced back to the fourteenth century or earlier, and well beyond Europe. See Giovanni Patriarca, "A Medieval Approach to Social Sciences: The Philosophy of Ibn Khaldūn," *Journal of Markets & Morality* 13, no. 1 (2010): 175–188; and Gabriel Martinez-Gros, ed., *Ibn Khaldūn: Political Thought* (Cambridge: Cambridge University Press, 2025). Pre-Confucian as well as Confucian political thought in China on political order and social harmony resonates, as do narratives dating back 1600 years in ancient Indian history. See Youngmin Kim, *A History of Chinese Political Thought* (Cambridge: Polity Press, 2018); Amrita Narlikar, Aruna Narlikar, and Amitabh Mattoo, *Strategic Choices, Ethical Dilemmas: Stories from the Mahabharat* (London/New York: Penguin Random House, 2023).

assigned places in the world – their designated positions in the great chain of being. If we put our trust in the higher forces controlling that chain, all would be well for us and our communities.[3] In short, throughout most of our history, societies organized beyond extended kinship groups dealt with the potentially debilitating physical, psychological, and social consequences of uncertainty by resigning themselves to the idea that forces beyond human control, both here and in an afterlife, ultimately and inexorably underwrote social purpose and political order.

In medieval Europe, these views on fateful resignation began to change with the gradual discovery of the individual, the ensuing struggle to strike new and durable social balances, and the eventual emergence of ideas about natural rights and obligations.[4] Thus began an epistemological revolution – a historic effort to reshape primitive structures of coercion, restrain doubt, and reconcile both faith and reason. This meant acknowledging and accepting individual and communal responsibilities more broadly, at least by dominant and privileged men. Doctrinal struggles among Christian sects and others, the unleashing of scientific discovery, the beginnings of industrialization, and imperial enlargement with new and more powerful technologies – all gradually set the stage for a widening if grudging acceptance of the idea that faith and doubt could be compatible. In this context, the modern concept of risk emerged in Europe.

In their seminal work together, Mary Douglas and Aaron Wildavsky argued that new thinking along this line was filtered through existing cultures and their underlying social structures.[5] Conflicts over issues of moral responsibility and accountability in avoiding or managing perceived dangers then spawned new vocabularies of political organization.[6] Similarly, Peter Bernstein linked the modern conception of risk to a revolutionary movement within natural philosophy in specific societies during the late Renaissance. He argued that a rather abrupt shift occurred from abstraction in a fixed and well-ordered universe to

[3] Arthur O. Lovejoy, *The Great Chain of Being: A Study of the History of an Idea* (Cambridge, MA: Harvard University Press, 1936), 64.

[4] Colin Morris, *The Discovery of the Individual, 1050–1200* (London: SPCK Publishing, 1972); Larry Siedentop, *Inventing the Individual: The Origins of Western Liberalism* (Cambridge, MA: Harvard/Belknap, 2014); Helena Rosenblatt, *The Lost History of Liberalism* (Princeton: Princeton University Press, 2018).

[5] Mary Douglas and Aaron Wildavsky, *Risk and Culture: An Essay on the Selection of Technical and Environmental Dangers* (Berkeley: University of California Press, 1982).

[6] Richard V. Ericson and Aaron Doyle, eds., *Risk and Morality* (Toronto: University of Toronto Press, 2003).

evidence-based experimental practices in a time of rapid social change.[7] Ian Hacking had earlier pinpointed the date of this movement to the mid-seventeenth-century propositions of Pascal and Fermat, which laid the groundwork for probabilistic reasoning.[8]

In her original 2016 treatise, Emily Nacol traced what happened next. She associated the development of techniques of estimating risks and their social consequences with the rise of Anglo-liberalism. She convincingly demonstrated how the work of Hobbes, Locke, Hume, and Smith in the seventeenth and eighteenth centuries built a coherent ideological foundation for new forms of economic and political organization.[9] Hopes for gain and fears of loss became tractable in the state-led commercial empire soon to reshape the world.

Contending social demands for the freedom to pursue opportunities for gain and limit the impact of loss simultaneously stimulated the development of key insurance practices. Nacol later described these as "a series of techniques and technologies that offer a kind of armor against probable harm."[10] From the very beginning, as I describe in Chapter 4 more fully, the merchant providers of these techniques and technologies of calculation evolved simultaneously with new forms of government. At their core, power struggles between actual polities turned, and continue to turn, on a shifting and variable balance between the ideals of individual and collective autonomy and the necessity of communal security. Personal freedom and social solidarity would never be easily reconciled anywhere, but the elaboration of risk and insurance practices promised to help make the ambiguities, hypocrisies, and ironies of modernity livable, and profitable – at least for some.

Looking back, we can see how the modern state's residual coercive authority manifested itself at the very point wherever and whenever novel notions of risk met their limit. Risks needed to be pooled and bound in legal contracts, which could be bought and sold, as well as mandated and expanded. The markets where much of this activity developed would ultimately depend on an irreducible and effective source of

[7] Peter L. Bernstein, *Against the Gods: The Remarkable Story of Risk* (New York: John Wiley, 1998).

[8] Ian Hacking, *The Emergence of Probability* (Cambridge: Cambridge University Press, 1975, 2006).

[9] Emily C. Nacol, *An Age of Risk* (Princeton: Princeton University Press, 2016).

[10] Emily C. Nacol, "Insurance and the Language of Risk in Early Modern Political Thought," in *The Routledge Companion to Media and Risk*, edited by Bishnupriya Ghosh and Bhaskar Sarkar (Abingdon: Routledge, 2020), 79–90.

nonmarket power that people accepted as legitimate. Underlying sources of uncertainty would remain, but they would not be debilitating. The broadening acceptance of scientific and technical rationality became intertwined with new understandings of risk transfer and burden sharing within and between "private" and ultimate "public" sectors. Risk models came to shape the behavior of firms and their clients, but they also had broader political consequences. Despite having come into existence to secure order and provide basic protection, certain states could choose *not* to be the insurer or coinsurer of *first* resort. But over time, most states surely took on the role as reinsurer of *last* resort.

With this function in mind in the modern era, some political communities elaborated new forms of society and state that today we commonly classify as liberal. They never entirely separated from their more primitive roots, but they rebuilt themselves on the basis of practical experiments in anticipating disasters, trying to preempt or manage them, and redistributing their associated burdens. Conceptions of probability gradually gave birth to practical economic tools aimed at risk management in a still uncertain world. They enabled public as well as private organizations to estimate the costs of potential future harms, arrange to reduce those costs, and design market-based instruments to share associated burdens while making explicit the scope of individual responsibility. Maintaining solidarity within market-based societies, or *risk societies* in sociological parlance, arguably became more difficult, but not less necessary.

THE SOCIOLOGY AND POLITICS OF RISK

Early in the twentieth century, Frank Knight promoted key conventions that are still in use by analysts of risk.[11] He accepted the now-common assertion that risk necessarily involves quantifiable probabilities. His followers continue likewise to insist that possible future harms that cannot be rigorously imagined remain in conceptual categories akin to "operational uncertainty," where some knowledge/data may someday be expected, or "radical uncertainty," where definitive knowledge/data will likely always be absent. Foregrounding various kinds of risks and downplaying uncertainty nevertheless remains conventional in much economic and financial analysis. Too often it ignores Knight's distinction.

[11] Frank Knight, *Risk, Uncertainty, and Profit* (Boston: Houghton, Mifflin, 1921); Dennis V. Lindley, *Understanding Uncertainty* (Hoboken: John Wiley & Sons, 2006).

It also tends to forget the related work of John Maynard Keynes, which emphasized the intersubjective nature of probability and the vital role of social conventions in coordinating expectations, sometimes promoting confidence and other times encouraging wishful thinking.[12]

By mid-century, sociologists had begun to consider the wider meaning of risk in the context of fundamental uncertainty. Against this background, Ulrich Beck asserted that human beings were now manufacturing new uncertainties, such as those associated with capitalist production systems. He argued that this phenomenon constituted modernity itself.[13] Beck depicted technology as the main driver of potential catastrophes threatening the internal organization of societies (and multilateral relations among them). He was trying to describe large-scale risks that were increasingly difficult to estimate in probabilistic terms.[14] He saw the more advanced of those societies devoting ever more extravagant energies "to ascertaining risks and communicating knowledge about them to secure the institutional environment and those who people it."[15] But the willingness to share risk-management burdens across established boundaries remained both rare and necessary. Since both the opportunities and the costs born of technological change and economic development now readily crossed those boundaries, Beck sensed the threat of ungovernability. In short, he highlighted the current manifestation of the persistent challenge liberal ideas and practices pose in a world still deeply marked by preliberal organizational structures designed mainly to cope with radical uncertainty.[16]

Charles Tilly drew a clearer image of the raw social material behind the rise of liberal societies and the limits of their evolving systems for governing risks. The memorable title of his work made it stark: "War-making and

12 Stephen C. Nelson and Peter J. Katzenstein, "Uncertainty, Risk, and the Financial Crisis of 2008," *International Organization* 68, no. 2 (2014): 361–392. Also see Robert Skidelsky, *Keynes: The Return of the Master* (New York: Public Affairs, 2009).

13 Ulrich Beck, *Risk Society: Toward a New Modernity* (London: SAGE, 1992); and *World Risk Society* (Cambridge: Polity Press, 1999).

14 Beck was in good company. So-called Bayesians grappled with the same issue by asserting that decision-makers in dynamic settings would and could update probability estimates on the basis of new information. From the start, however, the progenitor of such ideas insisted that this could describe optimal decision-making in only "small worlds." See Ken Binmore, "On the Foundations of Decision Theory," *Homo Oecon* 34 (2017): 259–273.

15 Richard V. Ericson, Aaron Doyle, and Dean Barry, *Insurance as Governance* (Toronto: University of Toronto Press, 2003), 33.

16 Mark Blyth, *Great Transformations* (Cambridge: Cambridge University Press, 2002).

State-making as Organized Crime."[17] In early modern Europe, Tilly claimed, wars made states, which eventually superseded most empires, city-states, and other structures of authority, and states made wars. In a nutshell, the extraction and gathering of resources adequate to the task of ensuring dominance in external struggles generated the modern state's internal institutions. Leaders of such states, in turn, then faced the task of legitimating their rule through new structures that promised more effectively to manage risks and cope with uncertainties. In many places, this meant replacing or supplementing religious political foundations with secular social formations distinguished from one another in terms of nationality. Likewise, as Hendrik Spruyt later asserted in this vein, there was nothing inevitable about that process, but it did culminate in the emergence of the nation-state.[18] Other forms of rule may well have become dominant in post-feudal Europe, but they did not. The global sinews of empire and the local ties of kinship and tribe never entirely disappeared or became irrelevant, but a novel system of political organization and efficient resource concentration manifested itself in what we now call the liberal nation-state.[19]

Elie Kedourie persuasively argued that the shift from imperial to statist rule, and the initial construction of the legitimating ideology of nationalism, definitively became clear in the aftermath of the French Revolution.[20] During the two centuries preceding that dramatic historical turn, the ideology of liberalism and its practice in markets profoundly shaped by states had also been developing, not only on the European continent, but most prominently in Great Britain and its colonies. The idea of individual rights and the practices of resource extraction and the slave trade eventually interacted with rising nationalism around the world. As a flexible political ideology, it later

[17] Charles Tilly, "War-making and State-making as Organized Crime," in *Bringing the State Back In*, edited by Peter Evans, Dietrich Rueschemeyer, and Theda Skocpol (Cambridge: Cambridge University Press, 1985), 169–191. On the historical and geographic limits of Tilly's image, see Christopher Blattman, *Why We Fight* (New York: Viking, 2022), 268.

[18] Hendrik Spruyt, *The Sovereign State and Its Competitors* (Princeton: Princeton University Press, 1996).

[19] Lauren Benton, *They Called It Peace: Worlds of Imperial Violence* (Princeton: Princeton University Press, 2024); Lauren Benton, *A Search for Sovereignty: Law and Geography in European Empires, 1400–1900* (Cambridge: Cambridge University Press, 2010). Also see Stephen M. Streeter, John C. Weaver, and William D. Coleman, eds., *Empires and Autonomy: Moments in the History of Globalization* (Vancouver: University of British Columbia Press, 2009).

[20] Elie Kedourie, *Nationalism* (New York: Praeger, 1960).

transcended the great twentieth-century struggle between socialism and capitalism. In some places, the character of the state it underpinned took a relatively inclusive, or "civic" form. In others, it was exclusionary or "ethnic."

Contemporary tensions between civic and ethnic nation-states can be traced back to their origins. New bargains gradually emerged between discrete rulers and ruled, and new forms of domination were extended overseas by states that never completely abandoned their imperial roots. Much later, as Tilly put it, "state-certifying organizations such as the League of Nations and the United Nations simply extended the European-based process [of political development] to the world as a whole."[21]

Tilly conceded that the state structures coming late to much of the world sometimes differed internally from the earliest "liberal" European states, such as France and Great Britain. In Germany and elsewhere,

> the most telling feature of the difference appears in military organization. European states built up their military apparatuses through sustained struggles with their subject populations and by means of selective extension of protection to different classes within those populations. The agreements on protection constrained the rulers themselves, making them vulnerable to courts, to assemblies, to withdrawals of credit services, and expertise.[22]

However, similar internal constraints on the modalities of official protection regimes did not necessarily develop in many states whose ostensible form was imported or imposed as European empires expanded and then dissolved.

At the core of what is now broadly perceived to be a globalizing system, diversely structured states in competition with one another continue to build societies, which differ in the arrangement, scope, and degree of their internal solidarity. Like all governments of human communities since ancient times, the essential task of those states is to manage the risks and cope with the uncertainties facing their societies. Tilly's extraction-protection racket provides an evocative image of a continuing process, but one that now confronts clear limits.

In the wake of eighteenth-century revolutions in Europe, the ideology of nationalism and its grafting onto and transformation of extant hierarchies in specific geographic locations came to play a fundamental role. The success of leading states in governing evident risks then reinforced

[21] Tilly, "War-making and State-making as Organized Crime," 185.
[22] Ibid., 186.

the claim that their legitimacy rested on the notion of a discrete "people." An admixture of liberalism, only in some states, tempered but never entirely transcended the appeal of nationalism, especially during emergencies. Even where claims of individual rights and responsibilities gained prominence, coping with uncertainty and effectively managing risks entailed continuing negotiation over the internal and external distribution of the costs and benefits involved. In this regard, the questions of exactly who belonged and who did not were always relevant and often fraught.

The imperial expansion and later retreat of certain nation-states led what we now call global capitalism.[23] Markets may be ancient, but capitalism is a relatively recent fusion of state power with the market economy.[24] Probabilistic reasoning, the invention of risk, and the ultimate failure of systemic efforts to completely overcome uncertainty – or to tame chance – simply redescribes in different language key elements in the (seemingly inexorable) rise of a capitalist system originally and mainly centered on liberal European states.

Even after the emergence of basic statistical techniques, it took centuries for practices of gathering data, defining risks, and then insuring them to be considered "liberal" and ethically distinguished from usury or blind speculation. Gambling taboos and prenationalist religious strictures proved hardy.[25] Even today, the phrase the word *anti-modernism* still applies to related nonstate hierarchies of power and authority, such as the Roman Catholic Church. Without entirely replacing such hierarchies – in fact, still relying on them to help reinforce social order – liberal market economies ultimately depended on reliable databases, statistical apparatuses, innovative financial instruments, and durable governing systems still grounded in the nation-state.

Theorists such as Beck and Giddens located the essence of modern capitalism at the point where liberal markets and states merged in the *first modernity*. It featured the collective bundling of social and economic

[23] Jeffry A. Frieden, *Global Capitalism* (New York: W. W. Norton, 2020). Also see Barry Buzan and George Lawson, *The Global Transformation* (Cambridge: Cambridge University Press, 2015), and Barry Buzan and Robert Falkner, *The Market in Global International Society* (Oxford: Oxford University Press, 2025).

[24] Michael Sonenscher highlights the role of public debt and war finance as well as the division of labor in signifying the new system. See *Capitalism: The Story Behind the Word* (Princeton: Princeton University Press, 2022).

[25] Also impeding developments were commonplace anti-Semitic concerns about impersonal credit markets. See Francesca Trivellato, *The Promise and Peril of Credit* (Princeton: Princeton University Press, 2019).

values at risk and translating them into legal claims that could be owned and traded. Although embedded in territorially bounded political foundations, its logic was inherently expansive. Early forms of insurance expressed that logic. They will be explored more fully in Chapter 4. For now, simply note that growing British maritime trade, despite the perils of shipping, initially prompted novel forms of pecuniary speculation that effectively pooled and transferred risks. The idea of adapting similar measures to spread the risks of urban fires beyond individual cities also arose around the same time from hard-won experience in Germany and Switzerland. Inventive actuarial tables likewise soon promoted precursors to life insurance in many places. Economic expansion and financial experimentation, combining liberal state and market energies, now marked the road ahead.

According to Beck, Giddens, and Lash, *second modernity* followed the intricate interplay of nation-state leaders' prudential interests, the ultimate erosion of inhibitions on speculation, the vaulting ambitions of pioneering financiers, and converging desires for social stability in the wake of systemic wars.[26] A decreasing tolerance for concentrated losses led naturally to the rapidly increasing acceptance of economic activities and political programs that expanded risk pools and fostered the diversification of associated investments. Across the Atlantic region in any case, nationalism and liberalism combined in diverse ways to provide the ideological underpinning for various versions of welfare programs intended to buffer and manage certain economic risks across the life cycle. Many societies then found themselves caught in tighter webs of interdependence as markets in risk-based financial instruments deepened within and among them.[27]

The essential project and quandary of what Giddens called the resulting "global society" and Beck referred to as "world risk-society" involved continuing to carve out of an inherently uncertain world discrete risks that could be collectively perceived, quantified, pooled, commodified, transferred, and managed by individuals across political frontiers. Ironically, extending the liberal-market project to the world evolved even as the ideology of nationalism became more deeply rooted in the wake of systemic wars. Beck decried this reality, and repeatedly

[26] Ulrich Beck, Anthony Giddens, and Scott Lash, *Reflexive Modernization*, (Cambridge: Polity Press, 1994). Anthony Giddens, *The Consequences of Modernity* (Cambridge: Polity Press, 1990); *Beyond Left and Right* (Cambridge: Polity Press, 1994).

[27] Robert O. Keohane and Joseph S. Nye, *Power and Interdependence* (Boston: Little, Brown, 1977).

criticized analysts of the consequent conundrum for their own *methodological* nationalism. Alas, the tension between liberalism and nationalism was hardwired from the start, and it remains so.

RISK SOCIETIES: THEIR RISE, EXPANSION, AND TRANSFORMATION

The invention of risk and the social transformation it inspired rank as monumental developments in human history. Novel methods of problem-solving arose from the idea of risk, along with new demands for collaboration. Probabilistic reasoning applied to quantitative data sets based on past events combined with impersonal market exchange reconstituted some societies. While such reasoning and activities gave states new instruments to steer those societies, they also stretched the boundaries around them. They had integrative effects, but also created new social divisions, within and across political frontiers.[28]

Debate on the causes and consequences of the ideational, social, and political upheavals coinciding around the time that risk and insurance arose in Europe have continued ever since then. The label once routinely used to signify that coincidence, "the Enlightenment," has become particularly contentious. The very idea that it marked a distinctively progressive moment in human history remains debatable.[29] Progressive for whom? that remains an especially important question. For my purposes, though, I want to emphasize how, by the end of the eighteenth century in Europe, a generalized sense of humanity's uncontrollable destiny had begun to erode.

Again, market societies gradually developed around the world as economic and political elites articulated a new faith in the power of probabilistic reasoning and then exported it to their colonies as well as to their neighbors. Eric Helleiner's work on the intellectual history of this process convincingly shows how supportive as well as critical commentary developed from indigenous roots in Asia, Africa, and South America.[30] With practical revolutions in shipping and maritime trade, the invention of risk and the development of insurance practices ultimately supercharged a global competition for land, slaves, gold, other

[28] Karl Polanyi, *The Great Transformation* (New York: Farrar & Rinehart, 1944).

[29] David Graeber and David Wengrow, *The Dawn of Everything* (London: Allen Lane, 2021).

[30] Eric Helleiner, *The Contested World Economy* (Cambridge: Cambridge University Press, 2023).

raw materials, and exotic goods. Merchants, their financiers, and their protectors began imagining how they might carve discrete and stable zones of risk from the uncertainty surrounding their expanding activities, which could, in principle, then be governed.

In some such zones, the probability of losses could be reasonably well estimated and then selectively transferred and redistributed. Early global capitalists, effectively licensed by their home states, gradually considered themselves to be "covering" some risks to the extent permitted by their financial capacities and reputations for reliability. From the start, the cover provided by insurance syndicates or individual agencies would be sanctioned indirectly or directly by the decisions and nondecisions, the evolving constitutive practices, and, ultimately, the fiscal capacities of the states governing or standing behind them. The most powerful of those states, such as Great Britain, thus played the key roles. The practices of insurance and reinsurance they licensed and supported were then and remain today reflective of their fundamental financial, social, *and* political priorities.[31]

When in later chapters we probe the constraints on well-established insurance practices increasingly posed by risks that cannot be narrowly contained, we need to remember that by their nature those practices have always faced analytical as well as ideological challenges. As Hacking made clear years after completing his seminal work on the emergence of probabilistic reasoning, the gathering and manipulation of certain sets of statistics at first seemed to give rise to notions of controllable destiny with a high degree of scientific plausibility.[32] The *ceteris paribus* assumptions of economists, the better statistics of actuaries, and the more refined calculations of mathematicians all appeared to align well with gathering Newtonian sensibilities concerning a world that could, in principle, be known – at least for a while. Individuals, investors, and government officials could make "rational" choices on seemingly firm psychological and political bases.

Over the past century, that understanding has come to be seen as simplistic, and even illusory. Prospect theorists have debunked the assumption of both individual and collective rationality.[33] The

[31] Jakob Arnoldi, *Risk: An Introduction* (Cambridge: Polity Press, 2009); John Adams, *Risk* (London: UCL Press, 1995).

[32] Ian Hacking, *The Taming of Chance* (Cambridge: Cambridge University Press, 1990).

[33] Essential psychological foundations for analysis along this line were set in place by seminal studies in prospect theory. See Daniel Kahneman and Amos Tversky, "Prospect Theory: An Analysis of Decision under Uncertainty," *Econometrica* 47, no. 2 (1979):

discovery of quantum mechanics has further complicated the analysis of decision-making under uncertainty.[34] Even so, insurance systems focused on risk and its estimation in financial form continue to evolve and adapt today *as if* they rest on shared perceptions that will gradually strengthen as well as on political understandings that will converge over time.

Many, perhaps most, individuals and groups implicated in those insurance systems still seem unaware of deepening metaphysical and epistemological doubts concerning the very ground underneath their societies. What arrives next in late modernity – in the midst of such doubts as well as repeated crises of confidence in the future – can be considered continuing social experiments. As it was in the eighteenth century, the key driver of change will be practical experience with failure.

Hacking ended his examination of the erosion of the scientific determinism that the Enlightenment had promised by highlighting and assessing the life work of Charles Peirce, the great philosophical proponent of pragmatism.[35] "I have aimed only at describing a man whose professional life as a measurer was immersed in the technologies of chance and probability, and who, in consequence of that daily experience, finally surrendered to the idea that there is absolute chance in the universe."[36]

Guided by the same insight, pragmatic students of the contemporary politics of global risk and uncertainty therefore begin their studies like the fabled two-handed economist. On the one hand, they know that chance remains ultimately untamed at a foundational level. On the other hand, they cannot help but observe that techniques of risk pooling, diversification, and transfer are spreading globally because they serve certain public interests. At the same time, those techniques tend to erode traditional forms of social and political community. Unless some ultimate

263–291; Amos Tversky, Paul Slovic, and Daniel Kahneman, eds., *Judgment under Uncertainty* (New York: Cambridge University Press, 1982); and Jonathan Mercer, "Prospect Theory and Political Science," *Annual Review of Political Science* 8, no. 1 (2005): 1–21.

34 Alexander Wendt, *Quantum Mind and Social Science* (Cambridge: Cambridge University Press, 2015).

35 Cheryl Misak, *Truth and the End of Inquiry: A Peircean Account of Truth* (Oxford: Oxford University Press, 1991/2004). Of relevance here is the effort by Rudra Sil and Peter J. Katzenstein to connect pragmatism to less deterministic approaches in international relations in cognate fields. See their *Beyond Paradigms: Analytic Eclecticism in the Study of World Politics* (Houndmills: Palgrave Macmillan, 2010).

36 Hacking, *The Taming of Chance*, 215.

force intervenes to replace them, they can only be reimagined. This must mean evaluating outcomes and placing different sets of values and plausible alternative systems of managing risks and coping with uncertainties into dialogue with one another.

Susan Strange, quoted in the epigraph to this chapter, was a practical and skeptical-minded mentor to generations of researchers in the fields of international relations and international political economy. She gave her students succinct advice on how to study risk-based political tradeoffs and social alternatives. "The dynamic character of the 'who-gets-what' of the international economy is more likely to be captured by looking not at the regime that emerges on the surface, but underneath, at the bargains on which it is based."[37] Of course international bargains now typically involve states, but not only states. Even in autocratic social and political systems, business firms, financial institutions, and an array of private interests, lawful or illicit, can be expected to be engaged in those bargains. Reimagining the next stage in the evolution of political structures capable of governing increasingly complex risks begins there.

RISK, UNCERTAINTY, AND POLITICAL AUTHORITY

The psychological and social utility of various forms of insurance sometimes succeeded in assuaging intrinsic fears of uncertainty.[38] By helping to carve out and manage risks, insurance instruments bolstered confidence in the future. They thus propelled the savings and investment proclivities that constitute modern capitalism. Promoted and supported by leading states now reliant on insurance practices, a new system of political economy eroded older hierarchies around the world. Not surprisingly, therefore, in his analysis of changing structures of political authority and social inequality Michel Foucault assigned prominence to insurance as an innovative technology of power and social discipline.

In the twentieth century, the growing evocation of risk and the broadening acceptance of the ideas and practices of insurance not only helped support a particular financial industry, but it also enabled the construction of novel instruments of governmental command. As Foucault

[37] Susan Strange, "Cave! Hic Dragones: A Critique of Regime Analysis," *International Organization* 36, no. 2 (1982): 497.

[38] On this point, see Menaka Philips, *The Liberalism Trap* (Oxford: Oxford University Press, 2023).

contended, citizens subject to regimes of risk control, surveillance, and discretionary protection could now, willingly or not, "live dangerously."[39] Along similar lines, Niklas Luhmann described new social manifestations of "governmentality" and its connected instruments of political reordering. He also opened a window to understanding how reordered societies were becoming ever more intricately bound with one another, both ideologically and practically, by the contractual construction, transfer, and management of risk.

Political economists speaking a slightly different language depicted that very same process as developing interdependent networks across the nation-states governing those societies. Todd Sandler, for example, set out to map specific policy arenas where various governments and other actors capable of exerting transboundary influence sought to build mutually beneficial economic and social linkages.[40] In doing so, he identified a vast array of risks that exposed the fragility of those linkages and their dependence on governments, but governments weakened by the essentially voluntary nature of their commitments to one another.

Given the complexity of the world we now live in, it is easy to be seduced by analytical frameworks promising crystal clarity and unambiguous guidelines for addressing the social and political tensions apparently hard-wired into our global risk-society. To resist them is to embrace ambiguity, which is actually the ground on which contemporary insurance and reinsurance systems exist. We must accept the irreducible condition of uncertainty that surrounds us, while building new kinds of collaborative institutions. This is tough going when it's so much easier simply to observe the global pull of risk sharing and resilience planning meeting persistent demands for local autonomy.[41]

"The instinct to insure," as Harold James put it more fully, "is linked to and derived from the instinct to organize, and to evolve more and more complex and interlinked structures of mutual support."[42] It should hardly be surprising that the process of building such structures requires

[39] François Ewald, "Insurance and Risk," in *The Foucault Effect: Studies in Governmentality*, edited by Graham Burchell, Colin Gordon, and Peter Miller (London: Harvester Wheatsheaf, 1991), 197–210.

[40] Todd Sandler, *Global Collective Action* (Cambridge: Cambridge University Press, 2004).

[41] Anthea Roberts usefully analyzes an array underlying social and legal relationships in "Risk, Reward, and Resilience Framework: Integrative Policy Making in a Complex World," *Journal of International Economic Law* 26 (2023): 233–265.

[42] James et al., *The Value of Risk*, 1.

coming to grips with basic conflicts of interest. Nor should it be surprising that only some of the challenges posed by the logic of cross-border risk sharing seem amenable to being carved out, concentrated, and governed jointly across private and public sectors.[43] The problem of crafting workable new instruments of mutual support is compounded by the persistent diversity of cultural values around the world as well as by the legacy of past conflicts.[44] Little wonder then that a still common response to the very idea of governing global risks is to imagine not deepening linkages but putting up walls.

Accepting such a natural human reaction when risk meets uncertainty is the first step toward understanding the promise of unbounded insurance and reinsurance experiments. They can seem apolitical, and they can manifest themselves in myriad public and private arrangements that deploy accessible technologies to isolate and transfer probable costs widely. Many of them aim to turn threats into opportunities by stretching boundaries around "risk pools that are large enough to ensure that expected losses are reasonably predictable and thus subject to governance."[45] In doing so, they engage indirectly in the construction of a contested but shared political economy. At its core are imperfect markets facing limits. Making those markets sustainable, pushing those limits outward, and transcending them when necessary then become practical tasks. The basic challenge is to adapt existing structures of political authority in a world reshaped both by new sources of uncertainty and more complex risks.

In liberal societies, where political priority gets assigned in principle to individuals' rights and responsibilities, any role assigned to insurance and reinsurance markets in determining the distribution of the costs and benefits of risk governance may be questioned. Indeed, it must be questioned if one is convinced that insurers through their modeling and business practices are the ones who essentially "establish what is to be considered uncertain."[46] The shrouding of boundaries between public

[43] Michael G. Faure and Ton Hartlief, *Insurance and Expanding Systemic Risks* (Paris: OECD, 2003).

[44] Christian Reus-Smit dissects this phenomenon in *On Cultural Diversity: International Theory in a World of Difference* (Cambridge: Cambridge University Press, 2018).

[45] Richard V. Ericson and Aaron Doyle, *Uncertain Business: Insurance and the Limits of Knowledge* (Toronto: University of Toronto Press, 2004), 5.

[46] Luis Lobo-Guerrero, "Insurance, Subjectivity, and Governance," *International Relations* 33, no. 4 (2019): 606. See also his path-breaking trilogy in the field of international political sociology, *Insuring War* (2012), *Insuring Security* (2011), and *Insuring Life* (2016), all published by Routledge.

and private sectors by governments, firms, or organized interest groups should not be assumed to be benign.[47] Nevertheless, policies informed by the logic of insurance long ago began to be seen as effective tools for managing difficult trade-offs in liberal societies. Maritime trade, for example, could be supported partly by private insurance contracts instead of wholly by public subsidies. Such policies also had the advantage of not forcing accountable governments to face alone the challenge of clearly differentiating controllable risks from uncontrollable sources of uncertainty.[48]

Risk control and *risk diversification* are commonly seen as governing techniques that have now spread across liberal as well as many illiberal societies. Control regimes, such as rules authorizing police forces to operate without warrant, aim to keep the prospect of future adversity at bay through the threat of coercion. But national and international histories are full of examples of such regimes actually delivering only the illusion of control. Diversification regimes, conversely, involve pooling risks, spreading costs, providing compensation, and stabilizing expectations.[49] In the real world of advanced industrial economies, both types of regime are often combined. Insurance and its justifying metaphors may sometimes readily encourage risk sharing and diversification. In the midst of emergencies, however, coercive control may emerge suddenly from the shadows, where even in liberal societies it resides.

At the international level, where unified government does not exist, notions of risk control and diversification are not so easy to separate.[50] In the absence of empire, hegemony, or a stable hierarchy or

[47] On the limits and inherent indeterminacy arising from the social nature of all knowledge claims, even the claim that we are inevitably locked in a world of risks surrounded by radical uncertainty, see Jacqueline Best, "Ambiguity, Uncertainty and Risk: Rethinking Indeterminacy," *International Political Sociology* 2, no. 4 (2008): 355–374.

[48] The debate is joined by economic geographers. See, for example, Ian Scoones and Andy Stirling, eds., *The Politics of Uncertainty: Challenges of Transformation* (London: Routledge, 2020), especially Chapter 3 by Leigh Johnson, "Sharing Risks or Proliferating Uncertainties?," 45–57.

[49] Of course, various forms of power are implicated in both categories, and a vibrant literature in political science is devoted to disentangling them. See, for example, Michael Barnett and Raymond Duvall, "Power in International Politics," *International Organization* 59, no. 1 (2005): 39–75; and Peter J. Katzenstein and Lucia Seybert, eds., *Protean Power: Exploring the Uncertain and Unexpected in World Politics* (Cambridge: Cambridge University Press, 2018).

[50] Robert O. Keohane, "The Demand for International Regimes," *International Organization* 36, no. 2 (1982): 351–354.

balance of power, the design and delivery of effective control regimes become difficult to imagine.[51] It's also problematic to construct reliable diversification regimes aimed at preventing disasters or sharing the losses that they would actually entail.[52] Allies who anticipate military conflict sometimes accept security regimes combining control and diversification. Similarly, common economic interests can encourage joint arrangements for risk diversification, but the probability of future disputes over fairness mean that considerations of control never entirely fade away. Efforts to achieve new societal equilibria between expectations of risk control and opportunities for risk diversification have sometimes stimulated dramatic political transformations. Again, the state form of governance itself at one time reflected such a transformation.[53] Profound changes in governing systems, however, have rarely been efficient, smooth, or fair. Power struggles are to be expected when vested interests in the status quo must be overcome. But whether such struggles must end in tragedy is highly debatable.[54]

The now-commonplace assertion that our world needs new, more efficient, and fairer risk-sharing regimes, at least in certain policy arenas, suggests that such struggles must be contemplated.[55] Whenever populist demagogues or extreme nationalists make it hard to imagine a peaceful resolution of such struggles, creative imaginations tend to shut down. Having lived through World War II, Susan Strange likely had that

[51] Robert Jervis, "Security Regimes," *International Organization* 36, no. 2 (1982): 357–378. Also see Steven Bernstein et al., "God Gave Physics the Easy Problems: Adapting Social Science to an Unpredictable World," *European Journal of International Relations* 6, no. 1 (2000): 43–76.

[52] Arthur Stein, "Coordination and Collaboration: Regimes in an Anarchic World," *International Organization* 36, no. 2 (1982): 299–324.

[53] Saptarishi Bandopadhyay offers a compelling argument concerning the role of signal disasters in accounting for the rise of the state. See *All Is Well: Catastrophe and the Making of the Normal State* (Oxford: Oxford University Press, 2022).

[54] Richard Ned Lebow, *The Tragic Vision of Politics* (Cambridge: Cambridge University Press, 2003); David A. Welch, *Security: A Philosophical Investigation* (Cambridge: Cambridge University Press, 2022).

[55] The work of applied sociologists has moved in a similar direction. See, for example, Ortwin Renn, *Risk Governance: Coping with Uncertainty in a Complex World* (Abingdon: Routledge, 2006). Later work coordinated by Renn helpfully provides an overview of conventional and systemic risks and an orienting framework for managing them. IRGC, *Introduction to the IRGC Governance Framework* (Lausanne: EPFL International Risk Governance Center, 2017). Also see the "Earthscan Risk in Society" Book Series, edited by Ragnar Lofstedt and published by Routledge.

problem in mind when she wrote the words in this chapter's epigraph.[56] It is worth considering the possibility that contemporary insurance and reinsurance experiments and the metaphors they inspire open a pathway toward feasible new political arrangements to govern complex transnational risks and to cope well enough with deepening systemic uncertainty.

Chapter 3 sets out a conceptual framework for carving discrete zones of global risk out of uncertain contexts and for differentiating the means by which they can feasibly be governed. On this basis, the rest of the book examines insurance and reinsurance practices evolving to cover specific risks, and, at their limit, related metaphors that might help rationalize the extension of collaborative public authority.

[56] John G. Ruggie was a pioneer in this cause. See his *Constructing the World Polity* (London: Routledge, 1998). Albert Hirschman had much earlier drawn analogous attention to the essential role of practical experience in enlightening paths forward. See, for example, *The Strategy of Economic Development* (New Haven, CT: Yale University Press, 1958/1969).

3

The Politics of Governing Risk

Insurance, like accounting, seems irreparably undramatic.

—Thomas Morawetz, "Insurance: How It Matters as Psychological Fact and Political Metaphor"

Rigorously estimating the probability of various harms and designing insurance systems to redistribute their costs were significant and relatively recent developments in human history. The most innovative instruments culminating in what we recognize today as insurance and reinsurance emerged not from government agencies, laboratories, or corporate research departments, but from practice – mundane and typically communal experience. The first insurance experiments in Europe only a few centuries ago were accommodated by changing moral and social codes permitting the rational estimation of loss probabilities and the expansion of burden-sharing communities. Modern capital markets accelerated and spread such changes around the world. In this chapter I sort through their contemporary political implications.

ECONOMIC DYNAMISM AND POLITICAL CHANGE

Insurance experiments in early market economies fragmented and redistributed the burden of losses imagined to arise in the wake of future catastrophes. If and when those losses were realized, their ultimate purpose was to render more resilient the lives of individuals and the societies in which they lived. The key was to get those individuals to pay for protection or for those societies collectively to subsidize such payments. People who were left out of these kinds of security arrangements when disasters struck remained where they had always been – dependent on self-reliance, neighborly assistance, or the magnanimity of overlords. While the similar idea of paying taxes in exchange for rulers' protection is more ancient, the success of early insurance experiments spawned a useful metaphor. Taxes could be defended as the price of public insurance.

As we saw in Chapter 2, the frontiers of risks to be managed via insurance arrangements pushed ever outward during the past five centuries. The process was central to the logic and global spread of capitalism. Risk pooling and portfolio diversification by specialized firms and a larger base of investors led to more comprehensive economic units. In this realm of human activity economy and society were, in practice, mutually constitutive. Governments constructed the necessary burden-sharing systems, including enforceable constraints on inevitable moral hazard – the idea that insurance contracts reduce incentives for insured parties to carefully manage risks and exercise prudence.[1] As experiments in risk diversification and risk control expanded, the role of governments expanded too.

I outline later (Figure 3.1) a basic two-by-two table, which will help to differentiate the myriad challenges posed for governments by risks that cross territorial boundaries. After sorting through the nature and variety of problems demanding authoritative solutions that are or could conceivably be delivered by way of insurance technologies, or plausibly justified with related metaphors, the table suggests four different ideal types. This provides analytical scaffolding for the rest of the book.

DIFFERENTIATING GLOBAL RISKS

The dramatic risks currently confronting all of humanity are commonly divided according to the underlying sources of change driving them: technological, environmental, military (including terrorism and insurgencies), epidemiological, and economic.[2] Of course, the prospect of natural disasters, even those affecting large regions, is hardly new. What changed with modernity, according to sociologists such as Beck, was the vast expansion of "self-generated" risks that cross established political boundaries. Distinguishing between self-generated risks and new sources of uncertainty, however, is no trivial exercise.

[1] David Rowell and Luke B. Connelly, "A History of the Term 'Moral Hazard'," *The Journal of Risk and Insurance* 79, no. 4 (2012): 1051–1075.

[2] Ulrich Beck, *World at Risk* (Cambridge: Polity Press, 2009).

Elite convention, exemplified for example at the annual meeting of the World Economic Forum in Davos, insists on using the word *risk* for a full range of cross-border problems.[3] It sees specific risks as varying by the global scope of their causes and consequences, by the degrees of uncertainty surrounding them, and by the precise distribution of the losses potentially generated by future disasters. Dealing with each discrete risk then commonly comes to mean confronting three kinds of challenges. The first is epistemological: The frontiers of current knowledge in specific risk arenas have to be acknowledged because beyond them lies not more risk but only uncertainty. The second is institutional: Governing arrangements have to be organized to permit experimentation with instruments for risk assessment, disaster prevention, and emergency management. The third is political: The perception of risks introduces new political conflicts, social cleavages, and various forms of responsive mobilization.

On this very basis, Beck himself conceived a rough typology. He called risks associated with nuclear power, genetic engineering, and artificial intelligence "technological" risks. Environmental risks included global warming, overpopulation, and biodiversity loss. Security risks included uncontrolled proliferation of weapons of mass destruction, not necessarily high tech in nature. Health risks encompassed food safety and the spread of pathogens. And finally, systemic economic risks were those connected with financial engineering and business interruption in tightly linked global value chains.

Among powerful states and across diverse societies today, leaders are being challenged to identify which of such risks are capable of actually being managed by plausible private or public efforts. After all, in modern societies people expect leaders to prevent imaginable catastrophes and prepare post hoc recovery and compensation schemes if prevention fails. Leaders around the world also face rising demands for new forms of preventive regulation, workable forms of assertive action if required, and necessary political settlements capable of sustaining effective risk governance. Even if such expectations cannot be met, they have already opened debates on the dynamic relationship between public and private sectors as well as on the degree of formality and transparency required to address looming threats. In rich countries, under any scenario fundamental political questions remain concerning the

[3] See, for example, World Economic Forum, *The Global Risks Report*, 18th edition (Geneva: World Economic Forum, 2023).

distribution of adjustment burdens both before and after conceivable disasters. Less well-resourced states face more intractable challenges since they are often incapable of taking preemptive measures to reduce risks or recover from disasters after they occur.

Skepticism regarding the willingness of states in either rich or poor countries to use their power wisely, and soon, in the cause of systemic stability and sustainability is now unexceptional. "Nations inclined by their nature to rivalry and mutual exclusion," Beck asserted in his last book, "seem to be part of the problem and not of the solution in the world risk society of the twenty-first century."[4] The claim recapitulates his earlier reflections on the dialectics of anti-modernity and the counter-productivity of nationalism. But, again, the nation-state is a fact of life, and the system built by and around nation-states is unlikely to collapse any time soon. Wishful thinking threatens to induce paralysis in the face of challenges to that very system, and so too does stubborn denial.

By leaping to the supranational or cosmopolitan "moment," Beck underestimated the promise of deeper forms of interstate collaboration in the near term.[5] He was clear, however, about the circumstances that the governments of states must overcome. These circumstances involve four kinds of complexity: causal complexity (trying to establish clear links between relevant variables); organizational complexity (identifying the actors and organizations necessarily engaged in addressing specific and interrelated risks); instrumental complexity (conceiving feasible policy instruments to cope with demands for prevention and/or compensation); and institutional complexity (designing durable and legitimate structures to carry through with promising policies).

Imagining functional systems made up of many interacting and cross-cutting variables has long been a challenging exercise across the social sciences. Constructing models to extrapolate from past experiences has become more sophisticated over time. But when datasets are sparse, and uncertainty and complexity correlate as they often do, modeling becomes more difficult. Whether, like the economist Herbert Simon, we expect to observe tendencies toward hierarchy as complex systems adapt and uncertainty deepens, it's becoming ever more difficult to forecast and

[4] Ulrich Beck, *The Metamorphosis of the World* (Cambridge: Polity Press, 2016), 183. (The manuscript was completed by Elisabeth Beck-Gernsheim.)

[5] Immanuel Kant's *Perpetual Peace* (1795) arguably inspired the perspective undergirding such a dream. However, the term had many meanings even in the eighteenth century. See Pauline Kleingeld, "Six Varieties of Cosmopolitanism in Late Eighteenth-Century Germany," *Journal of the History of Ideas* 60, no. 3 (1999): 505–524.

plan.[6] Since Simon's day, thinking about decision making in uncertain circumstances has in fact become a field of study in its own right.[7] Thus far, it has helped design innovative tools to enable some forecasting even when uncertainty overwhelms conventional modeling. For example, scenario generation – the specification and rigorous comparison of situational vulnerabilities – has already become routine, not least within the strategic planning units of insurance and reinsurance firms. But insurers and the states licensing them know that actual adaptation within complex systems, if it occurs at all, will follow much trial and error.[8]

Against just such a conceptual backdrop, we can also think about the construction of, and resistance to, practical mechanisms for governing global risks as profoundly shaped by adaptive interaction between the characteristics of particular risks and the time horizons available for confronting them. For example, on one hand, uncertainty surrounding a lethal virus that poses the risk of pandemic might spur panicked responses from leaders facing terrified constituents. But even rough understandings of specific viruses combined with pre-established norms of cooperative behavior, on the other hand, can sometimes give decision-makers the confidence and time they need to craft more effective responses. Degrees of uncertainty might still exist, but the context for decision is what analysts call "bounded rationality."

Where risks are fairly straightforward and reasonably well understood, and where time horizons are short, organized groups can sometimes agree to binding preventive arrangements in anticipation of crises. An example here would be member-states granting a requisite degree of authority for the management of specific sovereign debt restructuring operations to the International Monetary Fund. Conversely, when risks are complex and surrounded by uncertainty and the time horizon for disaster to manifest itself is perceived to be long, we might see a diversity of uncoordinated experiments in risk reduction. In such cases – as in policy arenas implicated by climate change after it became rationally

[6] Herbert Simon, "The Architecture of Complexity," *Proceedings of the American Philosophical Society* 106, no. 6 (1962): 467–482.

[7] For a comprehensive overview, see Vincent A.W.J Marchau et al., eds, *Decision-Making under Deep Uncertainty* (Cham, CH: Springer, 2019). Also see the website of the DMDU Society: www.deepuncertainty.org/.

[8] In decentralized policy settings, this insight also informs the theory and practice of democratic experimentalism. See Michael C. Dorf and Charles F. Sabel, "A Constitution of Democratic Experimentalism," *Columbia Law Review* 98, no. 2 (1998): 267–473; and Charles F. Sabel and Jonathan Zeitlin, *Experimentalist Governance in the European Union* (Oxford: Oxford University Press, 2010).

Degree of complexity→ *Time horizon for action↓*	*Low*	*High*
Short	**Chapter 4**. Cases of probable and limited harms: property (natural disasters), accidents, health. Private insurers and reinsurers play key roles. International understandings and standards readily emerge; markets backed by explicit or implicit official support. Insurance-as-governance helps resolve distributive and redistributive conflicts. Supervisory roles of firms and governments are complementary.	**Chapter 6**. Cases where much uncertainty surrounds possible systemic collapse, as in cascading financial crises. Private and public reinsurance systems become entwined. Burden sharing is improvised. Imminent prospect of catastrophe evokes assertive decision-making. Complex leader–follower dynamics play out. Fragmented responses promise failure. Collaborative supervision follows to manage unavoidable moral hazards.
Long	**Chapter 5**. Cases involving shared objectives, mutual vulnerability and potentially extreme harms. Prominent example is nuclear power generation for civilian purposes. Innovative private/public risk-transfer mechanisms can evolve. Collaborative public reinsurance is vital to limit private liability. Private and public monitoring can work together to reduce risks.	**Chapter 7**. Cases of gradually evolving global catastrophe, such as climate change. Diverse perceptions and interests encourage adaptive behavior. Demands for collective action meet obfuscation. Postponement of difficult decisions may be ill-advised but is possible. Limited role exists for private insurance and reinsurance, but price signaling can be important. Intense collaboration among public authorities is essential.

FIGURE 3.1 Insuring global risks: time, complexity, and politics

untenable to deny the phenomenon – the need for better coordination may only become clearer over time.

Many complex risks cross national boundaries today, and they somehow have to be managed. The basic principles of insurance systems – risk pooling and diversification – provide a common-sense beginning to the consideration of politically feasible collaboration across diverse but unavoidably integrating societies. Of course, when the prospect of disaster is imminent and undeniable, the idea of insurance becomes irrelevant. Strictly speaking, certainty eliminates risk, and so too does radical uncertainty. When it becomes impossible to estimate probabilities, all that is left is blind speculation or the assertion of some other set of ordering principles. Think here of the rationale for Hobbes's *Leviathan*, where raw and centralized coercion becomes the only method conceivable for halting the war of all against all and the ultimate barrier to nasty, brutish, and short lives. In such a fearful context, the selective allocation of values, or distribution of losses, takes place through brute force. We can glimpse it in practice whenever an army is authorized immediately after a natural catastrophe to step in to restore order, prevent looting, and redistribute adjustment burdens without serious recourse. We can perhaps glimpse something even worse if no army steps in and local losses and the costs of recovery simply fall where they may. For real-world examples, look no further than any poor countries hit by catastrophic floods or earthquakes and forced to manage the consequences on their own.

In the shadow of such thought experiments, considerations of the diversity of global risks as well as of practical instruments informed by the logic of insurance become clearer. Required is a willingness to resist Hobbesian fantasies and think anew about feasible ways to anticipate, prevent, and manage the consequences of imaginable disasters. Along this line, Figure 3.1 shows the range of possible collective responses to risks that vary in their complexity as well as in the time frames relevant to managing them. The chapters that follow explore cases from each quadrant.

INSURANCE AS GLOBAL GOVERNANCE

The essence of risk assessment involves estimating the probability of future harm from one or another contingency.[9] Despite the human proclivity for folly, such assessments – whether made by individuals, firms,

[9] Richard V. Ericson and Aaron Doyle, *Uncertain Business: Insurance and the Limits of Knowledge* (Toronto: University of Toronto Press, 2004).

or governments – lead logically to contemplating feasible measures to reduce or eliminate that probability. Prudence then calls for putting effective instruments in place for managing any moral hazards such measures may imply and for managing the effects of harms that nevertheless might occur.

Ever since the discovery of risk, such principles have applied to any individual, any group or firm, or any government capable of foreseeing likely future dangers. Risk assessment, crisis prevention, and emergency management – have long been basic elements in the life of functioning, persisting communities. In such communities, individual and collective interests both shape and are shaped by a fundamental sense of common threats. Political contestation – the struggle over the distribution of the costs and benefits of decision or indecision within any discrete community – brings underlying interests to the fore. Setting priorities among diverse interests depends on the existence of an organized capacity to do so.[10]

Because people inside any society have many and different interests, conflict is to be expected when risks must be faced. The role of governments is to manage such conflicts. The task becomes more complicated when spillovers occur across different policy arenas. Firms as well as individuals may like the risk mitigation provided by stable exchange rates, for example, but they also want to be able to move their money freely in and out of their country. The price of their currency relative to others may thus become volatile, which may hurt some more than others and generate tensions. At its root, the capacity to resolve such tensions durably, and especially without depending directly upon coercive force, depends upon societal perceptions of governmental legitimacy. Governing capacity endowed with legitimacy, in short, reflects a sense of shared fate and a willingness to acquiesce when hard decisions are made.[11] The fundamental challenge in building such a capacity is the same in local as well as global society. Under conditions set by open economies, which allow people, goods, services, money, and ideas to flow more readily across national and regional boundaries, it does not

[10] Michael Zürn, Martin Binder, and Matthias Ecker-Ehrhardt, "International Authority and Its Politicization," *International Theory* 4, no. 1 (2012): 69–106.

[11] The concept can be grasped intuitively, but there is a large and expanding literature in political theory on the basic idea. For an essential overview, see Melissa Williams, "Citizenship as Agency within Communities of Shared Fate," in *Unsettled Legitimacy: Political Community, Power, and Authority in a Global Era*, edited by Steven Bernstein and William D. Coleman (Vancouver: UBC Press, 2009), 53–73.

take much imagination to see such a global society emerging. Conflicts within it, generated, for example, by the dumping of waste into shared oceans, may then come to be viewed as internal to that society. The need for an adequate degree of governing capacity at world level becomes a logical necessity.

We return to the inherent complexity of the challenge of building just such a capacity in the following chapters. For now, I want to simply underline that if we're in the realm of risk, we're in the realm of probability and calculation, even if an irreducible degree of uncertainty remains in the background. If we then conceive of ultimate risk management as resting on some kind of governing authority, we can imagine it developing in three steps: building capacity (or power as it is commonly understood), effectively deploying that capacity (or solving problems that spill over conventional boundaries), and then legitimizing that deployment (or garnering wide-enough social acceptance to render sustainable the agencies charged with implementing collaborative decisions). Especially when successful risk management crosses conventional political boundaries, we may have to reject the common view that legitimation always needs to come first.[12] Collaborative risk assessment may well develop into an effective capacity for binding action even when the legitimation process lags.[13]

[12] "While it is conceivable in theory that political authority should be created in response to an antecedent demand for legitimacy, I believe this is unlikely to happen in practice. What is more likely is the increase and deployment of power in the interests of those who hold it, followed by a gradual growth of pressure to make its exercise more just, and to free its organization from the historical legacy of the balance of forces that went into its creation ... I believe the most likely path toward some version of global justice is through the creation of patently unjust and illegitimate global structures of power that are tolerable to the interests of the most powerful current nation-states. Only in that way will institutions come into being that are worth taking over in the service of more democratic purposes, and only in that way will there be something concrete for the demand for legitimacy to go to work on." Thomas Nagel, "The Promise of Global Justice," *Philosophy and Public Affairs* 33, no. 2 (March 2005): 147.

[13] See Thomas Franck, *The Power of Legitimacy Among Nations* (New York: Oxford University Press, 1990); Ian Hurd, "Legitimacy and Authority in International Politics," *International Organization* 53, no. 2 (1999): 379–408; Ian Clark, *Legitimacy in International Society* (Oxford: Oxford University Press, 2005; Allen Buchanan and Robert Keohane, "The Legitimacy of Global Governance Institutions," *Ethics and International Affairs* 20 no. 4 (2006): 405–437; Bernstein and Coleman, eds., *Unsettled Legitimacy*; Steven Bernstein, "Legitimacy in Intergovernmental and Non-State Global Governance," *Review of International Political Economy* 18 no. 1 (2011): 17–51; and Jonas Tallberg and Michael Zürn, "The Legitimacy and Legitimation of International Organizations," *Discussion Paper Series* (Berlin: Wissenschaftszentrum für Sozialforschung, January 2014).

Remember here that it's often close to impossible to make absolutely clear distinctions between risks and uncertainties.[14] Full and reliable data sets for straightforward statistical calculations are not always available. But educated guesses based on experience, available data, constructive debate, and appropriate analogies can often be made. Shared perceptions in a zone between readily calculable risks and rising sources of uncertainty are the starting point for pragmatic decision-making. An awareness of such psychological temptations as excessive pessimism, overoptimism, and groupthink can assist in the process of getting to that point.[15] But whether we are considering individuals, firms, or governments, converging in that zone is never easy, especially across cultural and political frontiers. This is where insurance practices evolving in one context can provide useful metaphors for shaping risk governance in another.

In Chapter 4, we'll see how such metaphors find fertile ground as private insurance and reinsurance markets naturally evolve and present opportunities as well as practical challenges for established political authorities. In Chapter 5, we'll observe unavoidable liability risks associated with the commercial production of nuclear energy encouraging creative responses that don't require the transformation of existing governmental structures. They do, however, entail the profound need for reliable forms of collaboration across territorial boundaries.

In Chapter 6, we'll examine pressures for immediate responses in cascading systemic crises that can't be delivered by private markets or formal intergovernmental organizations as they currently exist. In the aftermath of such crises, debates over preventing future repetitions raise the prospect of either deep political transformation or economic fragmentation. As we shall see, the history and logic of insurance and reinsurance can clarify and help resolve such debates. Finally, in Chapter 7, we encounter serious global threats that are complex along various dimensions as well as gradually increasing in their depth and breadth. The notion of insurability here comes into play as a useful tool for measuring the limits of both markets and existing forms of political collaboration.

The problem of designing more ambitious governing instruments, especially in cases outlined in Chapter 7, is formidable – or, as some close observers say, "super-wicked" – but it is not insuperable.[16]

[14] Stephen C. Nelson and Peter J. Katzenstein, "Uncertainty, Risk, and the Financial Crisis of 2008," *International Organization* 68, no. 2 (2014): 361–392.

[15] Paul Slovic, ed., *The Perception of Risk* (London: Earthscan, 2000).

[16] Kelly Levin, Ben Cashore, Steven Bernstein, and Graham Auld, "Overcoming the Tragedy of Super Wicked Problems," *Policy Sciences* 45, no. 2 (2012): 123–152.

Imagining future political conflicts unleashed by that problem, the analytical mind leaps to measures that would render existing cross-border systems either more resilient or less tightly linked.[17] But the scale and interconnectedness of everyone implicated in the most complex global risks confronting us continue to expand and deepen by the day. In that intrinsically challenging context, Chapter 8 draws out how feasible governing transformations may be inspired by lived experience with insurance practices and metaphors.

GLOBAL RISK GOVERNANCE IN PRACTICE

To prevent the disasters that the risks examined in the following chapters portend, and to manage emergencies that might occur despite everyone's best efforts to forestall them, solid social and political structures are required. Two ancient ideas typically define such structures: solidarity among those implicated - unity in a common cause; and subsidiarity – the lodging of effective and legitimate governing capacities wherever they can best address the sources of danger. The sovereign, territorially bounded nation-state I discussed earlier developed as a locus of authority for governing risks that could not reliably be addressed by villages, cities, and discrete regions. When a single state later proved inadequate to more complicated tasks, say in preventing financial instability or chlorofluorocarbon damage to the ozone layer of the Earth's atmosphere, voluntary intergovernmental arrangements among cooperating states could sometimes succeed. If such arrangements turn out in the future to be inadequate for other governing tasks, however, resistance to more ambitious efforts is to be expected.

Prominent political sociologists have studied processes through which this kind of resistance to change can be overcome. Applying what they call differentiation theory to international relations, some of them see

[17] Nicholas Taleb, *The Black Swan: The Impact of the Highly Improbable* (New York: Random House, 2007). Charles Perrow has made the case for de-linkage. *Normal Accidents: Living with High-Risk Technologies* (Princeton: Princeton University Press, 1999). But note the counterargument by others related to the prospect of developing high-reliability organizational responses. Todd La Porte, "High Reliability Organizations: Unlikely, Demanding, and at Risk," *Journal of Contingencies and Crisis Management* 63, no. 4 (2006); Todd R. La Porte and Paula Consolini, "Working in Practice but Not in Theory: Theoretical Challenges of High-Reliability Organizations," *Journal of Public Administration Research and Theory* 1 (1991): 19–47; and Todd R. La Porte and Gene Rochlin, "A Rejoinder to Perrow," *Journal of Contingencies and Crisis Management* 2, no. 4 (1994).

deepening conflict among segmented and still-stratified political systems as a functional requirement for the development of new governing structures capable of generating new policies at the appropriate level.[18] During the 1990s, the term "global governance" became a popular way to refer to just this kind of change. It encompassed, for example, the establishment of innovative procedures for dispute settlement within extant international organizations, or informal regulatory understandings inside clubs of like-minded countries. This kind of response to new challenges, however, was understood to be dynamic and open-ended. As James Rosenau asserted in this vein:

> There is no single organizing principle on which global governance rests, no emergent order around which communities and nations are likely to converge. Global governance is the sum of a myriad mechanisms seeking if never quite reaching a degree of control equivalent to what the successful nation-state has achieved with its territorial boundaries. And now, even as that "success" is increasingly undermined by global pressures, global governance itself is driven around the world by different histories, goals, structures, and processes.[19]

But the Janus face of increasingly complex global risks, which signifies opportunities to grasp as well as dangers to avoid, may well prompt a deeper process of political transformation. Repeated crises, continuing failures to prevent them, and shared perceptions of future disasters indicate the need for more profound institutional innovation.

Whether such a process can actually transform authoritative relationships poses key analytical and political questions. Scholars have identified, described, and analyzed many nascent forms of what might plausibly be depicted as transnational authority – power formally or informally accepted as legitimate and operating across widely acknowledged social and political boundaries. Such forms can range from regional arrangements to formal and informal international organizations, to regime complexes, formal and customary legal structures, and robust networks that mix public and private institutions and norms.[20]

[18] Mathias Albert, Barry Buzan, and Michael Zürn, eds., *Bringing Sociology to International Relations* (Cambridge: Cambridge University Press, 2013). On the difficulties inherent in the contemporary insurance industry that make movement toward cross-border cooperation difficult, see David Singer, *Regulating Capital* (Ithaca, NY: Cornell University Press, 2007).

[19] James Rosenau, 'Governance in the Twenty-first Century', 16. Philip Cerny and colleagues call the resulting order "heterarchy." See Cerny, ed., *Heterarchy in World Politics* (Basingstoke: Routledge, 2022).

[20] An entire field of study, conventionally falling under the banner "international organization," focuses on the such structures and processes, now broadly including

This kind of research is directly relevant to the myriad questions surrounding problems of global risk governance confronted in the following chapters. Much of that research, in fact, recalls and puts new flesh around the bones of earlier approaches to the study of problems that cross conventional boundaries.

In 1956, for example, the respected scholar-diplomat Phillip Jessup described the realm of "transnational law." He offered the following definition: "All law which regulates actions or events that transcend national frontiers. Both public and private international law are included, as are other rules which do not wholly fit into such standard categories."[21] Immediately confronting realist critics who expected him to note that law can't exist unless it is first promulgated by a sovereign authority, Jessup went on to argue:

> Perhaps it is some innate instinct for orderliness which leads the human mind endlessly to establish and to discuss classifications and definitions and to evolve theories to justify them ... The intellectual process is essential, but it involves dangers. The more wedded we become to a particular classification or definition, the more our thinking tends to become frozen and thus to have a rigidity which hampers progress toward the ever-needed new solutions of problems whether old or new. Conflicts and laws are made by man. So are the theories which pronounce, for example, that international law cannot confer rights or impose duties directly on an individual because, says Theory, the individual is not a subject but an object of international law.[22]

Jessup was building here on earlier insights. In 1921, Benjamin Cardozo asserted, "Law and obedience to law are facts confirmed every day to us all in our experience of life. If the result of a definition is to make them seem to be illusions, so much the worse for the definition; we must enlarge it till it is broad enough to answer to realities."[23]

nongovernmental institutions and other hybrid forms verging on traditional understandings of political authority. No single source can do it justice, but for good overviews, see Jacob Katz Cogan, Ian Hurd, and Ian Johnstone, *The Oxford Handbook of International Organizations* (Oxford: Oxford University Press, 2016) and Liesbet Hooghe, Tobias Lenz, and Gary Marks, *A Theory of International Organization* (Oxford: Oxford University Press, 2019). On the "authority" theme, see Mathias Albert, *A Theory of World Politics* (Cambridge: Cambridge University Press, 2016); Michael Zürn, *A Theory of Global Governance* (Oxford: Oxford University Press, 2018); and Emanuel Adler, *World Ordering* (Cambridge: Cambridge University Press, 2019).

[21] Philip Jessup *Transnational Law* (New Haven, CT: Yale University Press, 1956).

[22] Ibid., p. 4. Also see Peer Zumbansen, ed., *The Many Lives of Transnational Law* (Cambridge: Cambridge University Press, 2020).

[23] Benjamin N. Cardozo, *The Nature of the Judicial Process* (New Haven, CT: Yale University Press, 1921), 127.

That same kind of pragmatic thinking rightly frames our exploration of the contemporary world of global risk governance in the next chapters. Whether specific practices in each case should be considered authoritative or not is an open-ended question. What they indicate when taken together, however, is that the search is on for functional and durable instruments to accurately assess global risks against an inevitable background of uncertainty, to successfully reduce the likelihood of the disasters they portend, and to sustainably manage and distribute with finality the burdens they bring at both the stage of anticipating emergencies and the stage of recovery. In short, across various arenas of policy focused on diverse kinds of risks that can't be successfully addressed inside established political boundaries, we will be examining dynamic searches for effective, legitimate, and durable governing instruments.

In just such a context, the history of insurance and reinsurance practices and the potential utility of related metaphors suggest feasible and pragmatic steps forward. In essence, insurance systems involve measuring and pooling risks *ex ante*, reducing those risks to the extent possible, transferring and sharing associated burdens, and providing compensation *ex post*. In practice, such systems and metaphors inspired by their operations have shaped vital instruments that capitalist democracies use to govern themselves. Social security programs provide a key case in point.

The implications of transposing such systems to the global level through market-led mechanisms have long been subject to debate.[24] The following chapters highlight the efforts of contemporary nation-states to take that debate seriously as they experiment with programs that take on risks directly, mandate risk pooling, or subsidize and backstop private firms and their clients.[25] As we shall see, the incompleteness and unintended consequences of such experiments drive a dynamic process forward. But the key empirical question is whether the existing structure of the global political economy describes an absolute limit on joint capacities to measure, assess, and manage more expansive risks and to cope with new sources of uncertainty.

As we probe that question, it is worth keeping in mind a comment made by Geoffrey Hinton, the Nobel Prize-winning pioneer in the field

[24] See, for example, Brad Evans and Julian Reid, *Resilient Life* (Cambridge: Polity Press, 2014).

[25] See Michael G. Faure and Ton Hartlief, *Insurance and Expanding Systemic Risks* (Paris: OECD, 2003).

of artificial intelligence (AI). When he was once asked whether generative AI was so risky that its development should simply be stopped, he replied: "We might have been better off without fossil fuels [because of climate change]. We'd have been far more primitive, but it may not have been worth the risk."[26] Although human beings have rarely if ever self-consciously chosen such a path, what Hinton targets here is a point of encounter experienced throughout the history of our species – the point where, shrouded in uncertainty, diverse perceptions of risk meet aspirations aimed at transcending them. In hindsight, here is where the evolution of private and public insurance begins.

[26] Joshua Rothman, "Why the Godfather of AI Fears What He's Built," *New Yorker*, November 13, 2023.

4

The International Evolution of Private Insurance and Reinsurance

> The history of insurance and reinsurance over the past several centuries reveals an inexorable trend towards global economic integration and social solidarity. Even though, in the twentieth century, that momentum would periodically be stalled by protectionism, revolution, and war, the long-term trajectory is unmistakable and follows the larger cultural pattern of insurance steadily working its way into the centre of modern economic, social, and political life.
>
> —Geoffrey Clark, "The Cultural Context of Insurance in the West"

Insurance systems rest on the foundation of human psychology. As discussed in Chapter 2, they began their historic evolution where instinct met new technologies. In the private sector today, we can still see this as the point where relatively simple risks meet relatively short time horizons (i.e., the situation in the upper-left quadrant of Figure 3.1 in Chapter 3). Over the last several centuries – the blink of an eye in the sweep of human history – many kinds of risk in this quadrant were mastered by the technologies of insurance. All of them were gradually carved out of the uncertain terrain upon which our species evolved. Long before the discovery of risk and the invention of insurance, the primordial challenge of coping with uncertainty was at least partially met with another social invention, which we call government. This chapter examines the intersection of insurance and government, the division of responsibilities for risk management between them, and the territorial limits around the practice of insurance as a source of social protection, resilience, and integration. Along the way, we will begin to see how metaphors drawn from that experience came to be intimately linked with the fundamental purposes of modern government.

INSURANCE AS GOVERNANCE

Michel Foucault evocatively described insurance as a technology for imagining and dealing with the future. His student, François Ewald, put the matter more specifically: "[Insurance] is the practice of a certain type of rationality: one formalized by the calculus of probabilities."[1] As we saw in Chapter 2, certain societies and their governments were pioneers in harnessing that practice. Very soon thereafter, the decisions (and intentional nondecisions) of many governments encouraged not only the development of insurance and eventually reinsurance markets but also their cross-border integration. Guided by the rationality Ewald described, they created ever-larger opportunities for pooling risks and diversifying the portfolios of investors willing to cover them. In the modern era, liberal-democratic governments also began to share the burdens of public risk management with capital markets more generally as they accelerated the expansion of those markets and, reluctantly but inevitably, took responsibility for their stability.[2]

Conceived as a set of practices to manage risks and share the burden of recovery after accidents and disasters, insurance indeed provides an apt metaphor for core functions of modern government as they have evolved over time. For example, we might imagine that, in exchange for payment of the insurance premiums commonly called taxes, governments began providing given populations the degree of certainty required to instill confidence in the future. The resulting social stability then rested on how reliable "protection" was in the perceived context of unavoidably shared risks and readily imaginable disasters.[3] The scale of resources in fact available to cover those risks, once again, is another way to describe the extent to which the modern state can tax its citizens or borrow from domestic or foreign capital-holders. Struggles over the use of those fiscal resources after a disaster occurs, together with

1 François Ewald, "Insurance and Risk," in *The Foucault Effect: Studies in Governmentality*, edited by Graham Burchell, Colin Gordon, and Peter Miller (London: Harvester Wheatsheaf, 1991), 199.

2 Focusing on life insurance and pension systems in contemporary Great Britain, Arjen van der Heide explicates this process in *Dealing in Uncertainty: Insurance in the Age of Finance* (Bristol: Bristol University Press, 2023). The instrumental innovations actually accelerating the movement of risks back to life insurance policyholders are well explained by Vicki Zhang in *Uncalculated Risks: The Transformation of Insurance, the Erosion of Regulation, and the Economic and Social Consequences* (Toronto: Canadian Scholars' Press, 2015).

3 Again, for sound conceptual as well as empirical reasons, Charles Tilly, evoking Thomas Hobbes, put protection schemes at the center of his work discussed in Chapter 2.

debates about responsibility, obligation, and accountability, would then define the very essence of domestic politics.[4] This is clearest in contract-based liberal-democratic states, but surely something like such struggles and debates may also be expected in autocracies that are wary of the prospect of revolution.

The idea of insurance-as-governance provides more than a provocative metaphor. Prices set in private insurance markets send signals to society that can encourage necessary behavioral adjustments without the deployment of coercive force. Public insurance schemes, for their part, can render acceptable a redistribution of resources that might otherwise be difficult to justify. In fact, such schemes date back to the beginnings of modern government in capitalist economic systems, just as they came to define the meaning of socialism elsewhere.

I once worked inside the building in Berlin that had housed the administrative offices of the *Reichsversicherung*, the imperial social security system initiated by Otto von Bismarck. Although Bismarck's plan came at a time when not many people lived into old age, it provided modest supplements to payments made to the poor and to pensions for the disabled and elderly. It essentially adapted insurance programs already developing in Saxony and Prussia to pacify a working class disrupted by rapid economic transformation and to counter pressures for migration overseas. Historians have thus long appreciated the irony in how the "cradle to grave" welfare state was born not in a liberal democracy but in a conservative autocracy. Be that as it may, the evolving practices of social insurance thereafter obviously crossed boundaries between public and private sectors and reverberated around the world.

In the United States during the Great Depression, debates on government "relief" payments to the indigent, unemployed, disabled, and elderly partially resolved themselves in the construction of a social insurance system filled with tensions and contradictions. Initially it was conceived as a mostly "pay-as-you-go" or self-funded retirement system, so conservatives could emphasize its insurance-like elements and insist that official fiscal accounts were unimpaired. Progressives, on the other hand, were able to use those elements to protect a system that did ultimately rely on payroll taxes as well as periodic fiscal engineering and policy reform to prevent shortfalls. In future battles over the scale and scope of government intervention in a "free market" economy, employed or unemployed

[4] Rachel Friedman, *Probable Justice: Risk, Insurance, and the Welfare State* (Chicago: University of Chicago Press, 2020).

workers could argue that they required no "relief" – no unearned welfare payments – for they had paid premiums *ex ante* for insurance to cover various risks and that changing the terms of such insurance *ex post* would be illegitimate.

Under the conditions of advanced capitalism, governments also allocate resources indirectly by playing the role of private-insurance promoter and regulator. These days that role typically has two main faces: enforcing standards for fair market conduct to protect consumers while fostering healthy competition among insurance providers; and providing prudential oversight in the cause of systemic stability.[5] In some countries, these functions are separated across different agencies; in others, they are distributed across different levels of government; and in distinct settings such as Europe, they are subject to considerable regional pressures toward common policies and routines. In all cases, the principal domain of government regulators remains national. They are tied to the constitutional structures and political conventions of still-distinct states, and their attention remains primarily focused on state-licensed insurance and reinsurance providers and local circumstances.

Where conventional insurance schemes have reached their geographical limits, the governments of states have sometimes proven successful in expanding the boundaries of risk.[6] From Bismarck's day to our own, governments have sometimes innovated *ex ante* through mandatory risk pooling and public subsidy or by encouraging the practice of reinsurance, and sometimes *ex post* by covering losses actually incurred by constituents. After 9/11, for example, the risk directly associated with global terrorism was taken out of many insurance and reinsurance policies. When subsequent incidents occurred, decisions to cover any or all losses were made by particular governments, all of which could be expected to look first, and perhaps only, after their own citizens and residents. In some cases, governments were subsequently able to restart private markets for terrorism-related insurance by providing public guarantees or backstops.[7] As ever, the limit to

[5] In *The Power of Standards: Hybrid Authority and the Globalisation of Services.* (Cambridge: Cambridge University Press, 2019), Jean-Christophe Graz clearly demonstrates how in insurance and reinsurance markets the exercise of both roles has evolved mainly to the benefit of the owners of mobile capital.

[6] See Michael G. Faure and Ton Hartlief, *Insurance and Expanding Systemic Risks* (Paris: OECD, 2003).

[7] Other obvious examples include disaster relief and public insurance provided by US state and federal authorities in the aftermath of hurricanes.

such initiatives has been defined by a state's fiscal capacity, but the technology of insurance has proven itself to be flexible.

Now what about "global" risks that are shrouded by unique sources of uncertainty but might be understood to extend beyond the jurisdiction and established capacities of particular states and civil societies? The scale of the dangers both threatened and perceived means that above a certain threshold such risks can begin to overstretch the conventions of insurance. There exists no private firm or public agency authorized or able on its own to create big enough risk pools to manage them. When the disasters they estimate actually occur, the losses simply fall where they may, typically most harshly on those with the least ability to protect themselves. And yet the conceptual categories of risk and insurance might still be useful.

It is necessary here to emphasize again that at the heart of all insurance systems are methods of burden sharing. Only communities reliably sustain human life. Over time, real communities expand the bonds of solidarity to "cover" larger and larger group risks. Where fires once wiped out whole cities and left bankruptcy in the ashes, insurance and reinsurance firms now spread the risks of catastrophic fire far beyond city limits. And when those firms lose their bets that a fire will not occur, they also spread the costs and provide resources for recovery. True, they sometimes go bankrupt and don't pay out. But most developed insurance markets today are typically effective, broad, and deep. It is also true that access to them remains uneven throughout the world and that none are primed to provide adequate compensation for now readily conceivable global catastrophes.

That said, national boundaries have certainly been breached through private innovations, such as by the expansion of insurance providers' subsidiaries abroad on the basis of reinsurance treaties that spread liabilities widely, and by various kinds of intergovernmental arrangement.[8] We will explore more fully in Chapter 8 the nature of the limit such instruments face when it comes to "governing" global risks that lie in

[8] Charles Goodhart and Dirk Schoenmaker, "Burden Sharing in a Banking Crisis in Europe," *Sveriges Riksbank Economic Review* 2 (2006): 34–57; Dirk Schoenmaker, *Governance of International Banking: The Financial Trilemma* (Oxford: Oxford University Press, 2013); and Dirk Schoenmaker, "Is Burden Sharing Needed for International Financial Stability," in *The Changing Fortunes of Central Banking*, edited by Philipp Hartmann, Haizhou Huang, and Dirk Schoenmaker (Cambridge: Cambridge University Press, 2018): 203–226. Chapters 5 and 6 were inspired by connections first made on this theme by Goodhart and Schoenmaker.

between the psychological zones of radical uncertainty and plausible calculation. If the future is entirely unknown and unknowable, then past experience provides no guidance. But can "educated guesses" still rationalize insurance-like instruments when it comes, for example, to addressing threats posed by climate change?

The difficulty of imagining adequate coverage for such all-encompassing risks need not be an analytical endpoint. Even as we begin to cross borders and zones of uncertainty, the language of insurance can still be helpful as a clarifying tool. It can be even more than that if actual holders of capital sometimes prove willing to provide cover for risks they do not fully understand. If "insurers gamble, trying to manage any fallout through a variety of pricing, claims control, financial risk redistribution, and investment strategies," then we may reasonably ask whether apparent political constraints surrounding such activities are malleable as well.[9]

Such a worldview today frames the strategies of leading firms in the insurance industry, especially the world's top reinsurers such as Munich Re and Swiss Re. The industry is growing more rapidly as firms compete to provide more coverage – "capacity" they call it – for clients who face rising risks within and across conventional territorial boundaries. Business opportunities abound because much of the world remains underinsured. When disasters occur in such contexts, the costs incurred that might have been widely dispersed through insurance contracts fall narrowly on the most exposed victims. Increasing capacity basically means attracting new capital willing *ex ante* to share in those costs in the hope that *ex post* the profits generated from insurance premiums and new risk-mitigation strategies will exceed the actual payments for losses. The overall effect is to enhance social resilience – the ability to bounce back after catastrophes.[10]

Reinsurance firms increase aggregate underwriting capacity by insuring primary insurance providers, whether in the life, property and casualty, health, or other sectors. When primary providers purchase their own policies from reinsurers to cover some of their possible futures losses, they essentially free up capital. This enables them to underwrite more risks.

Reinsurance developed relatively recently in economic history. Very recent related innovations, such as selling insurance-linked securities to

9 Richard V. Ericson, Aaron Doyle, and Dean Barry, *Insurance as Governance* (Toronto: University of Toronto Press, 2003), 9.

10 Nassim Nicholas Taleb takes the idea further and makes the case for systems that become less fragile over time, despite episodes of volatility and disorder. See *Antifragile* (New York: Random House, 2012).

investors in deeper national and international capital markets, aim to achieve the same objective. They provide new capital and increase the capacity of insurance systems overall. Indeed, the "inexorable trend" referred to in this chapter's epigraph depends upon deepening pools of clients who are willing and able to pay for protection from risks they face as well as pools of providers willing and able to accept such risks in the expectation that the long-run returns on the capital they ultimately deploy will meet or exceed alternative uses of that capital. To the extent widespread growth on both sides of insurance contracts portends "greater global economic integration and social solidarity," a large-scale process is underway involving the widening and deepening of insurance markets. Observers refer to the ultimate outcome as a cross-border risk network, an expanding liberal risk regime, or a global safety net crafted by converging epistemic cultures. As anyone close to the industry knows, however, such optimistic images have another side.

> The speed with which disasters now spread and the potential scale of risks we do not yet understand or know means that private insurers must try to limit the scope of any cover provided. Such risks are then left to states as insurers or reinsurers of last resort—or they simply remain uncovered.[11]

To skeptics of the proposition that private insurance faces a limitless frontier, the inherent complexity of global risks seems to correlate with a rapidly expanding gap between what needs to be insured and what actually can be. Peter Borscheid again calls attention to Beck's misgivings as well as to the distinction between risk and uncertainty.

> Seeing uncertainties as not only increasing but uncontrollable, Beck speaks of modern society in its dealings with risks as "an unsecured society, one in which the protection afforded by insurance decreases as the size of the peril increases." In an age in which the economy's demand for security increases as a consequence of globalization, deregulation, and changes in global politics, the world is evidently becoming less secure at the same time as the insurance industry is expanding.[12]

The story I tell here is framed by the debate between those who see great promise in enlisting the private sector to help manage and mitigate

[11] Peter Borscheid, "Introduction," in *World Insurance: The Evolution of a Global Risk Network*, edited by Peter Borscheid and Niels Viggo Haueter (Oxford: Oxford University Press, 2012), 31.

[12] Ibid. "When it comes to natural disasters, for example, uninsured economic losses have in fact increased much faster than insured losses. Between 1985 and 1995, over 42% of losses of this sort were insured. That figure fell to 28% by 2008 and to 25% by the summer of 2011."

global risks and those who are more skeptical. Within an emergent global society, private insurance cover in any of its forms reaches the level required only if capital is raised, distributed, and regulated at the level required by the nature of specific risks. To cover some of these risks, private insurers have to be able to distinguish uncertainty and risk, even if only roughly, and then to scale up their operations transnationally.

A more nuanced view accepts the nationalist underpinnings of contemporary economic life. Insurers cross borders when they are permitted or encouraged by the states that license, regulate, or host them. Because they possess ultimate fiscal authority, those same states can and sometimes do provide backstops for interdependent markets exposed to global risks. Their ability to do so can only increase when they cooperate voluntarily with one another.

In any event, debates over the future of such cooperation itself highlight the need to examine both the real-world practices of private insurance providers and the authorization of those practices from their point of inception. The ultimate question is whether existing forms of political authority and the modalities of voluntary intergovernmentalism define an ultimate limit. The history of insurance and reinsurance shines a light on the search for an answer.

THE INSURANCE INDUSTRY OVER TIME

As noted in Chapter 2, historical research points to the nearly simultaneous evolution of innovations in maritime shipping, modern trading networks, and manufacturing techniques. Together, they stimulated the expansion of European empires. The decisive invention of risk as we now conventionally understand it coincided with the earliest phase in a chain of related developments. What soon followed was the construction of contemporary insurance providers' precursors. Of course, in ancient history, the earliest human beings took collective steps to protect themselves from dangers. Notions of reciprocity, partnership, and burden sharing were reflected in our species' earliest social organization.

Archeological evidence from ancient Babylon and China suggests that such ideas were embedded long ago in transport practices that allowed trade to develop beyond kinship groups and across great distances.[13] What we now call risks were deconcentrated by distributing goods across seagoing fleets, and lenders facilitating trade soon began to take

[13] Niels Viggo Haueter, *A History of Insurance* (Zurich: Swiss Re, 2013/2017).

the prospect of some losses into account in their ledgers. Evidence also exists that people in ancient Egypt, Greece, and Rome made agreements in advance of troop deployments that mutual aid societies would properly bury deceased soldiers and care for their families. In short, it is not hard to find the antecedents of property and casualty, life, and health insurance in human history long before the modern era. It is also not hard to locate the philosophical, theological, and psychological impediments – including measures deeply ingrained in societies from Christian Europe to the Islamic Middle East – that discouraged gambling, all of which had to be overcome before an inherently speculative industry could flourish.

The urge to seek collective protection from the vagaries of life eventually met the more systematic collection of data. Uncertainty was never banished, but probabilistic reasoning could now work on relatively more certain ground. Written risk-transferring contracts recognizable as marine insurance existed as early as 1370 in Genoa, Italy.[14] What would soon become an insurance industry at scale emerged in Europe in tandem with the growth of financial markets supporting international trade, the creation of far-flung colonies, and the building of the infrastructure that would underpin emergent industrialization. By the end of the fifteenth century, enough experience and information existed to justify the first known legal treatise on the subject: *Tractactus Perutilis et Quotidianus de Assecurationibus et Sponsionibus Mercatorum* (On Insurance and Merchants' Bets) by Pedro de Santarém. A systematic study of the evolving practice of marine insurance, it contained specific references to the relationship between risk and premium.[15]

In the late seventeenth century, Edward Lloyd's coffee house in London provided a meeting place for financiers wanting to place bets on cargo ships safely reaching their destinations and returning. Like the rational homeowner who buys insurance cover today, shippers won by coming out on the losing side of the bets they placed with people willing to write their signatures and exposure limits on the bottom of bills of lading setting out a ship's cargo. The price of insurance cover provided by "underwriters" then became part of the cost of doing business over great distances. Similarly, the Great Fire of London in 1666, which incinerated

[14] David Holland, "A Brief History of Reinsurance," *Reinsurance News* (February 2009), 10.

[15] The treatise was written in 1488 and published in 1552. See https://museuvirtualdoseguro.pt/en/pedro-de-santarem-petrus-santerna-lusitanus-2/ (Lisbon, Virtual Museum of Insurance), accessed March 1, 2022.

nearly a square mile and 13,000 buildings at the core of the burgeoning city at the cost of one-quarter of Great Britain's annual national income, stimulated both the interest in pooling risks with tangible economic effects and the willingness of increasingly prosperous investors to buy shares in such risk pools.

By 1681, Nicholas Barbon and eleven colleagues had established an "Insurance Office for Houses," which provided cover for 5,000 new homes. Other companies soon followed and added other kinds of insurance to their offerings. In 1696, for example, the Hand in Hand Fire and Life Insurance Society was founded at Tom's Coffee House, not far from Mr. Lloyd's. The rise of Phoenix Assurance followed. The dominant position it soon achieved can be partly explained by demand for fire insurance coming from dangerous sugar refineries at the heart of the rapidly expanding transatlantic economy. A period of accelerating financial speculation associated most notoriously with the South Sea Company led in the 1720s to most early insurance firms being banned from taking the joint stock form as limited liability was then coming into vogue. In an effort to stabilize markets after the bubble burst, the Crown granted formal insurance monopolies to Royal Exchange Assurance and London Assurance Company. In addition, because the government of the day was concerned that some early forms of reinsurance involved mere speculation and no constructive transfer of risk, much of this activity was banned in 1746. More subtle "underwriting" practices nevertheless continued to evolve informally in the coffee houses.

The world's first specialist fire insurance company, much like Barbon's facility but with public backing from its inception, was established by the city of Hamburg in 1676. The General-Feuer-Cassa emerged as a collective solution to inadequacies evident in a myriad of mainly rural mutual-aid arrangements known as fire guilds that had arisen as early as the fifteenth century. In environments where fire was a constant hazard, neighboring farmers had banded together to jointly cover damage and rebuild afterwards. In 1591, beer brewers in Hamburg adopted the same idea. They entered into a formal agreement to compensate for fire damage up to a certain amount as long as rebuilding occurred within a year. Other groups soon emulated them.[16]

[16] Greg Bankoff, Uwe Lübken, and Jordan Sand, eds., *Flammable Cities: Urban Conflagration and the Making of the Modern World* (Madison: University of Wisconsin, 2012).

The Feuer-Cassa was designed to broaden coverage, to link fire guilds in a common system, and to promote prudence by clarifying local responsibilities for firefighting. (Those responsibilities were not shifted fully to an official fire department until 1872.) After 1817, most Hamburg residents were required to participate, and supplementary insurance policies were negotiated with certain Prussian as well as British insurers. When much of the old city of Hamburg burned in the Great Fire of 1842, the damage far exceeded the capital resources available to what was now called the Hamburger Feuerkasse. The city-state itself was forced to float a bond to raise the funds necessary to rebuild its core, a collective debt that took forty years to repay. That same necessity to attract capital at larger scale finally overcame any residual moral doubts about risk-taking and speculation and led in 1846 to the establishment of the world's first reinsurance company Kölnische Rückversicherungs-Gesellschaft. Cologne Re (later Gen Re), as it was referred to in the English-speaking world, was designed to provide insurance to the original underwriters of fire risks. Its investors essentially provided callable backup capital to the Feuerkasse and soon to its public and private analogues elsewhere.

THE GLOBAL EXPANSION OF INSURANCE AND REINSURANCE

The first reinsurance treaty between direct insurers ceding and Cologne Re accepting underwritten risks under specific conditions and at agreed prices dates from 1852. The Feuerkasse as well as Cologne Re later developed insurance lines to cover weather-related and other disasters. Other insurers and reinsurers were soon established throughout Germany, some of which cooperated with one another in co-insurance arrangements. Many failed before the century's end. The big exception was Münchener Rückversicherungs-Gesellschaft (Munich Re), a joint venture among banking and insurance interests in Bavaria dating from 1880. Two years later, the firm spawned Allianz Versicherungs-Gesellschaft, which opened its first office in Berlin. In a successful bid to retain local control, allow the building of capital pools that were large enough to cover peak risks, and also to avoid excessive reliance on foreign investors in their controlling equity, the agreement issued to one another special voting stock and facilitated interlocking shareholding arrangements. These initiatives turned out to be important elements in Germany's modern social-economic evolution as well as in its deliberate national effort to catch up with Great Britain and other early industrializers.[17]

As I noted in the introduction, a similar history unfolded in Switzerland after 1861, when the town of Glarus went up in flames. Two years later, the Helvetia Versicherungen in St. Gallen (Helvetia General Insurance Company), the Schweizerische Kreditanstalt in Zurich (later Credit Suisse), and the Basler Handelsbank (later UBS AG) jointly established the Schweizerische Rückversicherungs-Gesellschaft of Zurich (Swiss Re). Their association agreement was approved by the government of the canton of Zurich and the founders subscribed jointly to an initial capital fund.

In Britain's American colonies, similar fire insurance initiatives in both private and mutual forms took off between 1732 in South Carolina and 1752 in Philadelphia. As in both Britain and Germany, one of their implications was to hasten the development of effective municipal authorities capable of providing such collective services as fire departments. Around the time of the American Revolution, it had become clear that something new was afoot in world economic history.

What was truly novel at the turn of the eighteenth century in major capitals on both sides of the Atlantic, and especially in London, was the scale of wealth now available to harness and exploit the insuring instinct through legal markets in a range of risk-management products. As Clive Trebilcock puts it, "No promising seed-bed was provided by the traditional pattern of peasant subsistence, where tiny shares of national wealth were thinly spread across a myriad of squatter agriculturalists, or the equally hallowed patterns of princely or lordly domination, where autocratic power provided its own security for massive accumulations of worldly goods."[18] Instead, merchant societies and commercial empires emerged on the basis of lucrative, long-distance shipping, including the transport of slaves to burgeoning sugar and cotton plantations across the Atlantic, the complementary aggregation of rural wealth through land enclosures and new agricultural techniques, and radical innovations in power generation and manufacturing funded by surplus capital. At the same time, traditional understandings of self-sufficiency eroded under the pressure of such events as the great Lisbon earthquake of 1755 and the great fires noted earlier.

[17] Michael Menhart et al., "Product Innovation and Population Dynamics in the German Insurance Market," *Zeitschrift für die gesamte Versicherungs-Wissenschaft* 93, no. 3 (2004): 477–519.

[18] Clive Trebilcock, *Phoenix Assurance and the Development of British Insurance*, vol. 1 (Cambridge: Cambridge University Press, 1985), 1.

A philosophical revolution coincided with a modernizing countryside, expanding factories, and densely concentrated and territorially voracious cities. The result was more housing, more physical capital, and more personal wealth to protect combined with a dawning ideology involving notions of individual rights and personal responsibility, albeit with deliberate carve-outs along lines of gender, race, class, and power. In short, "The bustle of eighteenth economic life was not just a suitable context for innovation in insurance; rather it formed the exact marketplace for innovation in insurance."[19] As Nacol explains,

> Although "risk" emerged as part of a specialized professional vocabulary, it ultimately created space for a new philosophical orientation to the future and a new sense of how human beings might think and act with it in mind. Prudential reasoning, understood as care for the future, began to claim pride of place in politics and commerce. But more importantly, probabilistic thought – the philosophical and eventually statistical basis of assessing risk – became a commonplace approach to negotiating an uncertain future and determining how to respond to it in terms of both action and feeling.[20]

The interest in financial protection for new wealth as well as the ability to provide it motivated the first major company to put life insurance at the core of its operations. In 1693, Edmund Halley developed an innovative mortality table. By 1706, the idea of life insurance had attracted some 2,000 initial subscribers to the Amicable Society for a Perpetual Assurance Office in London. Each subscriber paid an annual premium based on their age and number of shares. At the end of the year, portions were paid to the widows and children of any deceased members.

In 1769, "New Lloyd's" became a more formal marketplace where underwriting syndicates began to organize themselves to provide cover, again mainly for transoceanic shipping. Mounting experience with overseas trade – in spices, opium, tobacco, and eventually slaves and cotton – brought with it enough data to diffuse risks and make bets on something other than a purely speculative basis. Lloyd's remains today a market for insurance and reinsurance run by underwriters and brokers, not a single corporation. Its syndicates are independent, subject to unlimited liability, but now joined together by certain standards of conduct and collaborative funds to guarantee the settlement of claims.

[19] Ibid., 3.

[20] Emily C. Nacol, "Insurance and the Language of Risk in Early Modern Political Thought," in *The Routledge Companion to Media and Risk*, edited by Bishnupriya Ghosh and Bhaskar Sarkar (Routledge, 2020), 80. Also see Lorraine Daston, *Classical Probability in the Enlightenment* (Princeton: Princeton University Press, 1988).

With a similar focus on data generated by experience with fires, by the time Phoenix Assurance was established in 1783, some seven firms in Great Britain had successfully built a market for fire and property insurance. Two of those firms were mutual societies started by merchant collectives or unincorporated partnerships, while others were chartered by the Crown and granted limited liability. "Both types were basically speculative enterprises, preserves of the wealthy and influential ... moved less by the fire-threat to small capitals than by the potential for investment they saw in large capitals accruing from fire premiums."[21] Because of advances in what were becoming the actuarial sciences, that potential could be forecast over time. The business of life insurance also soon expanded in both mutual and chartered forms in Great Britain, the Netherlands, France, and eventually the United States.[22]

From the outset in rapidly industrializing Great Britain, a key distinction between the entrepreneurial capitalist and the insurance provider soon became apparent. As business historian Clive Trebilcock puts it:

> Essentially, all insurance companies are collective organizations. Almost by definition, insurance is a poor province for the dynamic individual capitalist ... It is a communal matter, opposing the resources of the group to the risks encountered by the individual. Its central purpose is scarcely suitable for the classical entrepreneurial adventurer, the risk-taker *par excellence*; for its central purpose is specifically the minimization of risk. There is something mutual about all insurance companies whether or not they are formally titled that way ... Here, the cautious spreading of risks, the precise calibration of premiums and the juggling of legal niceties which successful underwriting required—matters of precise calculation and well-informed patience—often combined to frustrate the cut-and-thrust of the compulsive adventurer.[23]

Although a culture of calculation, probity, and caution has indeed characterized the modern insurance industry from the start, excessive speculation and the threat of insolvency have always plagued it as well. Many of the early firms offering innovative insurance policies in London and on the continent ultimately failed. Indeed, cycles of boom and bust have marked the development of the industry from the start. The fact is that "compulsive adventurers" have never shunned the industry, despite

[21] Geoffrey Clark, *Betting on Lives* (Manchester: Manchester University Press, 1999), 7.

[22] Historians have long pointed out that this occurred despite wider cultural misgivings resulting in a taboo against betting on human lives, a taboo that first and most clearly broke down in Britain. Ibid.

[23] Clive Trebilcock, *Phoenix Assurance and the Development of British Insurance*, vol. 1 (Cambridge: Cambridge University Press, 1985), 7.

high rates of failure and ever-looming threats of large payouts. From its inception, the keys to success have included picking from the array of risks facing human communities those that are relatively simple in character and then staying focused on relatively short-term assessments.

THE PUBLIC AND PRIVATE FOUNDATIONS OF INDUSTRIAL ECONOMIES

Speculation was quite obvious during the great period of industrial expansion in the middle of the nineteenth century, when railway construction advanced rapidly on both sides of the Atlantic. Since accidental deaths and injuries also occurred in tandem, a new market came into being. Insurance providers, such as the Railway Passengers Assurance Company established in London in 1848, began to offer accident insurance to railway passengers, with premiums scaled to the risks associated with different compartments and classes of tickets. The proliferation and specialization of insurance companies on particular kinds of risks reached a peak in the years just after 1849, when royal monopolies were withdrawn from Royal Exchange and London Assurance. After 1870, which business historians commonly see as a hinge point in the evolution of finance capitalism, consolidation following episodes of economic depression and industrial bankruptcies would become the theme. Insurers grew quickly and went bust just as fast.

In the midst of growing public perceptions in the late nineteenth century that insurance had itself become a source of economic instability, the industry began to be more tightly supervised in Great Britain, on the continent, and in the United States. Opportunities for amalgamation, risk pooling, and diversification under single capital structures abounded, but now they were under government supervision. Cautious retrenchment and innovations in financial speculation at larger scale nevertheless occurred simultaneously. Syndicates at Lloyd's, for example, began to underwrite contracts for automobile insurance and property theft in the 1880s. Trebilcock concludes his magnificent study of Phoenix Assurance, one of the industry's leaders in this era, by drawing out the following lesson (in gendered language common at the time):

> Efficient practice for insurers involves the difficult skill of judging when not to learn from experience. Naturally, this is a requirement facing decision-takers in many fields of endeavour, but ... for merchants in disaster, it is particularly insistent ... For the insurer, disaster is not only the biggest threat to his livelihood but also his stock-in-trade ... His relationship with catastrophe requires impeccable

calibration. If he courts too much business, he accumulates too much hazard. But if he allows unpleasant experience to provoke an exaggerated fear of hazard, the aversion will distance him from the most central activities of his business.[24]

By the opening of the twentieth century, the industry had matured after essentially expanding outward from a European base. Two distinctive business cultures had developed within it, one British and one continental. The British approach was linked tightly to the trade and migration flows that constituted empire. It relied on in-depth local knowledge in trusted networks. In Asia, its hub was Hong Kong, while in Canada, South Africa, Australia, and New Zealand, its agents relied on innovations in communication technologies to connect back to London as they adapted now-traditional underwriting practices to new environments. Underwriting practices centered on data-driven, legal, and arm's-length relationships between insurer and insured shaped that culture. British elites brought them to the colonies and adjusted them as local conditions required.

Hannah Farber has convincingly argued that maritime insurance practices in particular played a critical role in the earliest days of America's founding.[25] Although the United States shared many aspects of British culture, its decentralized legal systems gave a federal character to those practices as insurers began to penetrate an inwardly focused economy. Similarly, in China, India, and Japan during the late nineteenth century, agents and former employees of long-established insurers (*compradores*) brought British customs with them. With the major exception of Hong Kong, their legacies would be attenuated after the forces of decolonization gathered. Economic nationalism would eventually reshape all financial markets, including insurance markets. Most of those with British heritage, however, would remain characterized by obvious commitments to the actuarial sciences and to maintaining as strong a wall as possible between the realms of law and politics. Even so, in the twentieth century, distinctive national champions would emerge in former British colonies. They would lead in the race for market share across Asia and the rest of the developing world.

Another insurance culture gradually spread outward from late-industrializing continental Europe. Cooperative-based insurance structures in southern Europe and regionally concentrated systems for fire

[24] Ibid., 757.

[25] Hannah Farber, *Underwriters of the United States: How Insurance Shaped the American Founding* (Chapel Hill: University of North Carolina Press, 2021).

and property insurance in northern Europe reached their limits in the mid-nineteenth century. As local economies deepened, stakeholders in risk portfolios needed to diversify if they were to remain solvent. Primary insurers developed relationships with reinsurance companies. The logic of risk pooling and diversification took hold as smaller countries sought protection from trusted institutions nearby. Early leaders of Swiss Re and Munich Re nurtured that trust through operationalizing innovations in actuarial science, carefully collecting and assessing data from experience, and broadly diversifying across specific risks and across economies with differing business cycles. They also took into account unique political and social dynamics as well as distinct demographic profiles across the markets that interested them. "In the second half of the nineteenth century professional reinsurers established business dealings with as many domestic and foreign primary insurers as possible in a bid to achieve more comprehensive risk distribution on a cross-regional basis," notes Peter Borscheid. "For the first time they formed a truly international safety net in the place of what had previously been merely isolated alliances between primary insurers, most of them geared to London."[26] The biggest and fastest-growing reinsurers simultaneously took equity stakes in some primary insurers themselves.

Insurance companies and the authoritative institutions of the state evolved together during what some historians have come to call the first great globalization phase of modern capitalism, while others describe their interaction simply as elements of complex and competing imperial systems emanating mainly from Europe. Political economists highlight the particular role of private markets in enforcing a London-centered network of power. In a path-breaking study, Virginia Haufler contends, "The institutions of the insurance industry evolved in tandem with the centralization of political authority in the state; both could be seen as newly developing institutions of protection, with insurance essentially supplementing the still incomplete power of the state and vice versa."[27]

[26] Peter Borscheid, "Introduction," in *World Insurance: The Evolution of a Global Risk Network*, edited by Peter Borscheid and Niels Viggo Haueter (Oxford: Oxford University Press, 2012), 9.

[27] Virginia Haufler, *Dangerous Commerce* (Ithaca, NY: Cornell University Press, 1997). Much work followed on both the concept and the practice of private–public interaction in the reconstitution of authority. See, for example, Claire Cutler, Virginia Haufler, and Tony Porter, eds. *Private Authority and International Affairs* (Albany, NY: SUNY Press, 1999); Rodney Bruce Hall and Thomas Biersteker, eds., *The Emergence of Private Authority in Global Governance* (Cambridge: Cambridge University Press, 2002);

That the state would dominate became clear in the wake of economic crises and the political and military contests coinciding with them. By the turn of the twentieth century, the idea that protection from life's many vagaries could reliably be provided for the many and not just for the few by unregulated markets had been proven a chimera. Those few who refused to recognize what Haufler called the increasingly complicated socialization of risk went into hibernation in the summer of 1914.

In the decades before World War I, insurance markets grew ever more clearly segmented along national lines. London led in underwriting risks arising from trade and international investment, while continental reinsurers developed considerable expertise in covering peak risks around the world. Munich Re's payouts and survival after the San Francisco earthquake of 1906, when many others were failing and disappearing, is noteworthy here. But throughout this era, protectionist responses to the opportunities and risks of industrialization came inexorably to the fore.

Foreign insurers and reinsurers could set up operations in many promising markets, for example, in the United States after 1871, but the industry overall exhibited a clear home-country bias. Competition with London-based insurers during the next decades accelerated in Europe as well as in North America and Japan. At the same time, the political logic of public insurance programs at the national level was gaining appeal. For example, policies that are today linked to the progressive left attracted considerable support in the 1880s from both industry and the reactionary right in a unifying Germany. They combined ambitious industrial policies to catch up with Anglo-American competitors with specific national initiatives providing basic accident and health insurance, as well as old-age pensions.

For three decades, Great Britain tried to resist similar pressures, on the one hand leaving life, accident, and property insurance to the private sector and on the other hand trying to maintain open trading policies conducive to the Empire's stability. A decisive national election finally changed things. In 1911, the new Liberal government passed the National Insurance Act, which combined public and private contributions to support insurance systems for unemployment, illness, and maternity. In their early years, benefits calculated with actuarial principles in mind mainly targeted particular cyclical and seasonal

Stefan Renckens, *Private Governance and Public Authority: Regulating Sustainability in a Global Economy* (Cambridge: Cambridge University Press, 2020).

industries. The foundation was nevertheless established for the kinds of future expansion that world wars would eventually stimulate.

In the United States, the Social Security Act of 1935 accomplished something similar. It modeled the idea that a governmental program of redistribution could be compatible with "free" markets by adopting the actuarial principles of insurance, by calling individual contributions "premium payments" and not taxes, and by acknowledging loose but popular solvency tests for future governmental stewards of the people's "social security funds." At the same time, with actual payments from those funds limited in scale and scope, plenty of room remained for private insurers to play a supplemental role. Accelerating economic growth would eventually provide increasing opportunities for insurers to develop new product lines in the health, accident, property, casualty, and other sectors. Reinsurance specialists also began putting down deep roots in national markets during the interwar period.

The first US-based reinsurer grew out of the 1921 merger of two Norwegian firms' local affiliates. General Casualty and Surety Reinsurance Corporation, renamed General Reinsurance Corporation in 1923 when American investors came fully into control, soon took a leading position in a national market that was, until then, mainly served by agencies of European firms. During the "roaring" twenties and depressed thirties, the firm pioneered in the design of reinsurance treaties – arrangements with primary insurers especially in the fire and casualty sectors that covered a fixed proportion of their liabilities. Such treaties left the main risk-management responsibilities for individual policies with the primary insurer, but they often came to signify deep and durable relationships with particular reinsurers. The company also began to offer "facultative reinsurance." More transactional in nature, these agreements allow primary insurers to seek cover for particular types of risk carried on their books. The risk was typically large and well understood, and the agreements permitted the reinsurer to pick and choose among individual clients and charge tailored premiums.

General Reinsurance's shares were acquired in 1928 by a new holding company, the General Alliance Corporation, which jointly with the estimable Royal Exchange also controlled the United British Insurance Company. In practice, this allowed the two firms as a group to create and co-reinsure large-scale casualty and surety (guarantees of contractual performance) pools, a significant innovation at the time. After dedicating itself solely to providing reinsurance both domestically and internationally, the group survived the Depression and war years. What followed its merger with a Mellon group affiliate after the war was a long period of remarkable growth. Its holding company became a public corporation in 1980. Fourteen years later, it moved into a formal alliance structure with Cologne Re. In 1998 General Reinsurance was acquired by Warren Buffett's Berkshire Hathaway, and in 2009 Gen Re secured a controlling interest in the historic Cologne Re.

With the backing of France's government, Société Commerciale de Réassurance – now SCOR SE – entered the reinsurance market in 1970. Specializing in property and casualty as well as life reinsurance, the company absorbed the US reinsurance business of Allstate in 1996 and others around the world a few years later. China's national champion originated in the People's Insurance Company of China, which was founded in 1949. In 1996, the ministry of finance and the Central Huijin Investment Company established China Re as a state-owned reinsurance company with interests across a full range of sectors. By 2020, consolidation and expansion thus resulted in a few large firms dominating national and international markets.

All things considered, the need for scale and risk-portfolio diversification, as well as the search for new sources of investment income in the short, medium, and long runs, drove the rapid development and concentration of the insurance and reinsurance industries ever since the nineteenth century. As we have seen, British firms held the early leadership position. The growth of large survivors from periods of strong competition and market turbulence was mainly a function of their homeland's position in international trading and shipping networks. Great Britain early on became the main exporter and importer of capital in this sector. While its insurance markets certainly went through dramatic boom and bust cycles, they adapted well because trade always recovered. Even though most reinsurance activities remained banned until 1864, co-insurance arrangements deepened among the many British underwriters. On the continent, conversely, reinsurance of necessity became a primary vehicle for raising capital, building scale, and diversifying risk and investment pools.

In the context of late industrialization and weak capital accumulation in central Europe during the late nineteenth century, Harold James noted that reinsurance served "as a substitute for capital imports."[28] The same claim could be made for Japan after 1890, when firms that

[28] Harold James, "The Insuring Instinct," in *The Value of Risk: Swiss Re and the History of Reinsurance*, edited by James et al. (Oxford: Oxford University Press, 2013), 9.

would become national champions began buying reinsurance cover in London, and for China after 1949.[29] Although strategies of national control would never disappear and markets would close during war years, in both cases reinsurance became a vital instrument for risk transfer and capital-market deepening. It also provided an enriched metaphor that was useful for governments seeking both to rationalize their basic purposes and to set limits on their financial responsibilities.

THE CONTEMPORARY PRACTICE OF PRIVATE INSURANCE AND REINSURANCE AT WORLD SCALE

By any measure, aggregate private insurance markets worldwide grew rapidly after 2000. Estimates of gross premiums collected by insurers showed a nearly threefold increase over the next two decades. From a base of USD 2.5 trillion in 2000, insurers worldwide were generating USD 6.78 trillion by 2022. Even more noteworthy is the fact that life insurance began to decline in relative terms. Life insurance accounted for 55 to 60 percent of gross premiums for many decades up until the early twentieth century. After 2010, however, non-life premiums started accounting for over 50 percent of the total business of primary insurers.[30] Fairly stable over time, nevertheless, was the amount of overall primary insurance business ceded to reinsurers – approximately 5 percent of gross premiums.

The United States has long been home to many of the world's biggest insurers, which is no surprise given the size of its domestic markets and given the unusually large role that its healthcare system assigns to the private sector. UnitedHealth Group, with over USD 200 billion in net annual premium revenue, is almost double the size of the world's next largest insurer, Ping An Insurance Company of China. Although seven of the top fourteen insurance firms in the world are based in the United States, the Chinese market for life and nonlife insurance is rapidly growing. Indeed, the rating agency A.M. Best in the early 2020s listed three Chinese firms among the world's top fourteen. Rounding out the list were one French, one Italian firm, and two German firms.

On the other hand, European firms have long held dominant positions in reinsurance markets. In historical terms, US-based Berkshire

[29] Swiss Re, *A History of Insurance in Japan* (Zurich: Swiss Re, 2013/17), 24.

[30] www.statista.com/statistics/273156/gross-premiums-generated-by-the-insurance-industry-worldwide-since-2006/, accessed April 11, 2025.

Hathaway was a late entrant with an interest less in traditional underwriting than in harnessing reliable long-term cash flows to support its investment portfolios. In terms of net premiums written, Munich Re, Swiss Re, and Hannover Re typically account for as much in net premiums written (over USD 100 billion in total) as the seven next largest reinsurers in the world. Among those, China Re appeared in the top league tables in the early 2020s, already accounting for the same level of annual business as Lloyd's.[31]

As demand for insurance began to rise sharply across the industrial and industrializing world, basically after the 1970s, the desire to transfer peak risks to others grew as well. Reinsurance firms came into their own early in the twentieth century, and especially after the 1914–1945 era began to fade from memory. With economic growth in the postwar period came physical concentrations of expensive properties, business operations, and prosperous populations. Peak risks multiplied, as did demand for reinsurance cover. The largest payouts experienced over the four decades since 1970 were linked to geographically limited natural disasters. Topping the list was nearly USD 85 billion in the wake of Hurricane Katrina in 2005. The next highest payout came in over USD 38 billion after the 2011 earthquake and tsunami in Japan. Eight other hurricanes ranked among the top fifteen most costly disasters for insurers. The only non-weather related event in that group was the 2001 terror attacks in New York and Washington; that total payout exceeded USD 25 billion.

Reinsurance and Innovation in International Capital Markets

Very recently in historical terms, the idea of tapping into broader capital markets for reinsurance purposes has taken off. Alternative risk transfer products began emerging late in the twentieth century. They grew rapidly and have mainly taken the form of insurance-linked securities, such as industry loss warranties and catastrophe bonds. In short, hedge funds, wealth managers, and other intermediaries brought some of their clients' resources into new markets that effectively supplemented the capital available to underwriters of peak risks. The market for catastrophe (CAT) bonds, which led the way, traces its roots to the early 1990s.[32]

[31] www.reinsurancene.ws/top-50-reinsurance-groups/, accessed April 11, 2025.

[32] Korey Pasch, "Developing Disaster," *Journal of Natural Resources Policy Research* 8, nos. 1–2 (2018): 131–153.

In the wake of Hurricane Andrew in 1992, the idea of novel risk-transfer instruments moved from university seminar rooms to Wall Street. Those instruments enabled sophisticated investors to take on some of the risks that insurers had traditionally transferred to reinsurance companies. The CAT bond was a security with a face value, a time to maturity typically less than three years, and a fixed interest rate coupon. Purchasers made a simple bet. If a basket of natural catastrophe risks covered by the insurer crystallized, the CAT bondholder would "indemnify" the insurer and lose his/her investment. If, on the other hand, no relevant disaster occurred, a typically quite handsome return on that investment was the result. Later experiments and market opportunities led to new forms of CAT bonds that paid out based on prespecified triggers. With these bonds, called index or parametric bonds, investors either lost the principal they invested or earned their return and recovered their investment if a particular event occurred within a set time and in a certain location – such as a likely to be disastrous 150 mph wind in Miami Beach. Roughly two-thirds of insurance-linked securities (ILS) now take the indemnity form, and one-third are parametric.

Given their riskiness (the bonds are typically rated in the B range, far below supposedly risk-free benchmarks such as US Treasury bills), the payout on CAT bonds is typically high, but also typically lower than the cost of traditional reinsurance. Importantly, it is also typically uncorrelated with returns generally available in related markets. Both of these factors made CAT bonds increasingly attractive to large investors looking to diversify the risks in their portfolios and smooth out their long-term returns – investors such as hedge funds, pension funds, and university endowments. They became especially attractive during periods of low interest rates, when such investors more aggressively "searched for yield."

Early issuers of CAT bonds, which included direct insurers, saw them as providing competition for reinsurance firms. Reinsurers, facing new pressures on their profitability, initially saw them that way too. Over time, though, insurers and reinsurers alike came to view them as useful instruments to manage volatility on their own balance sheets. For example, they enabled reinsurers to securitize bundles of risks, transfer them to national and international capital markets, and use the capital thereby released to purchase more risks from insurance providers. "Retrocession" – that is, spreading a risk underwritten by passing some of it on to other reinsurers for a fee – had long ago become common practice. In the cause of portfolio diversification, a new tool to accomplish the same thing had been invented. During the period of loose monetary policies and low interest rates following the global financial crisis of 2008, many other kinds of investors looking for yield and diversification were attracted to growing markets for CAT bonds and other kinds of insurance-linked securities, such as securitized bundles of automobile insurance policies. Although new issues fell in volume as interest rates rose after 2021, the total outstanding volume of such securities rose from under USD 10 billion in 2006 to USD 100 billion at the start of 2024.[33]

Frequent issuers of CAT bonds now include agencies such as the World Bank. But they are mainly used by the world's leading insurers and reinsurers to transfer some of their own risks to "third parties," thus enabling them in principle to take on more commitments. The need for this, as well as the increasing opportunity for profit, is revealed whenever a disaster hits a highly insured location in an advanced economy. If existing property and casualty policies, for example, are priced on the basis of historical real estate values but actual real estate markets are inflating rapidly and are suddenly severely damaged by a hurricane, vast losses can mount quickly. The price of insurance and reinsurance after such an event then rapidly adjusts upwards, and opportunities arise for insurance-linked securities to become more profitable.

This is exactly what happened after 2000, thus driving predictable cycles of insurance contraction, adaptation, and expansion. The capital actually available to provide global reinsurance cover has grown modestly over time and has lately been supplemented by the development of ILS markets. In 2024, for example, of the nearly USD 600 billion in private reinsurance capital available to cover potential losses, about 15 percent came from those "alternative" capital markets.[34] Almost two-thirds of that capital was targeted at risks to property in the United States. The perils are well known and geographically concentrated, properties are developed, and their owners are wealthy enough to purchase private insurance. Early innovations in insurance-linked securities have therefore been concentrated in US capital markets, including their close offshoot in Bermuda.

The alternative capital now available as markets around the world become more receptive to insurance-linked securities still pales in comparison to capital provided in conventional ways by reinsurers. But ILS

[33] www.artemis.bm/deal-directory/, accessed May 29, 2024.
[34] Ibid.

markets are growing. As they develop, expand, and become more interconnected, they provide sites for innovation. Traditional reinsurance firms, for example, have found them increasingly attractive, as they seek to reduce their exposures to business interruption claims generated by rising cybersecurity failures.

Some economic sociologists and scholars of business strategy nevertheless foresee unreliability and warn that ILS markets pose growing challenges to the kind of long-term relationships that traditionally provide depth and stability to reinsurance systems.[35] Like other examples of financial innovation and engineering I discuss in Chapter 6, however, even contracts grounded in those traditional relationships are increasingly becoming tradable financial commodities. Overall, markets for private reinsurance are becoming both more volatile and more competitive.

The risks covered by traditional as well as alternative reinsurance providers still mainly fall into the upper left-hand box of Figure 3.1. Their degree of complexity is relatively low, while the time horizon between premium payment and potential insurance payout is relatively short. Experience with each risk produces new data, which can be used formally or informally to build better predictive models that might gradually extend time horizons. As ever, the point at which prudent investment slides into unreasonable speculation remains opaque and uncertain. But until "pure" speculators walk away, confidence in the future is generated among those whose risks are covered. Investment instruments whose performance, even if speculative, is again not typically correlated with trends in other financial markets also tend to develop. Such instruments then expand options for portfolio diversification more widely. It is true, though, that they themselves entail a new kind of risk. They can "abstract from underlying risks, make mathematical assumptions about the correlation of these risks, and remove judgment from the hands of the professionals who understand them."[36]

Financial wizardry can disrupt long-standing relationships among insurers, reinsurers, and their clients. But it can also summon adaptive behavior from the most sophisticated players. Just as retrocession arrangements allow reinsurers to lay off some of the risks they have

[35] The outstanding work along this line is Paula Jarzabkowski, Rebecca Bednarek, and Paul Spee, *Making a Market for Acts of God: The Practice of Risk-trading in the Global Reinsurance Industry* (Oxford: Oxford University Press, 2015).

[36] Ibid, p. 179.

taken on and diversify their potential liabilities, the largest and most sophisticated reinsurers are experimenting with ILS-like instruments to expand both sides of their balance sheets to enhance profitability in hardening markets. In 2022 and 2023, for example, Swiss Re secured over USD 1 billion in alternative capital protection for severe underwriting losses through collateralized stop-loss arrangements using one of its own "captive" reinsurance subsidiaries backed by a loan from J.P. Morgan's investment banking arm.[37] (A captive subsidiary is designed to consolidate certain risk portfolios and take advantage of specialized regulatory regimes in places such as Bermuda, which also either do not tax insurance and reinsurance profits or otherwise give favorable treatment to such profits.) For our purposes, I want to underline here how such "innovations" in contemporary capital markets can blur the boundary between risks that the private sector in-principle manages on its own and risks that are covered by private insurers implicitly or explicitly relying on some form of support from the public sector. We return to that theme in Chapter 6.

In any case, the contemporary history of insurance and reinsurance demonstrates that private-sector burden sharing on an increasingly global basis has become well established when it comes to natural disasters and many other kinds of risks. The key is that they are limited in scale and maturity, even if some speculative room remains around their edges. The ability of private markets to engage in constructive risk transfer, whether directly through reinsurance underwriting or indirectly through more open and more innovative capital markets, rests for the foreseeable future on discrete and converging interests between those who can afford to buy cover and those who can provide it. Winners today may lose tomorrow, but the traditional reinsurance game is iterative. Well-capitalized reinsurers hit by unexpected losses from multiple disasters in one year can make up for them with firmer pricing in the "hard" markets that follow. Clients as well as their insurers often seek more coverage after such periods, and relationships of mutual dependency thus deepen over time. Financialization, on the other hand, brings more impersonal interactions and also more opportunities for risk diversification. It promises new sources of capital and the benefits of more competition in an increasingly intricate and inherently global reinsurance industry, but it also exposes new layers of political contingency.

[37] www.artemis.bm, March 8, 2023, accessed April 11, 2025. Swiss Re's "special purpose vehicle" registered in Bermuda is Matterhorn Re.

Emergent and ever more complex risks might be expected to push conventional private insurance and reinsurance providers to their limits. Risks associated with climate change, for example, have in some places forced providers of property and casualty insurance to raise premiums dramatically or withdraw entirely from certain markets. Similar retreats are occurring in domains of cyber-risk, especially where unpredictable and potentially massive business-interruption losses can be caused by hacker-terrorists or antagonistic governments. Industry insiders today worry out loud about vulnerable business and governmental infrastructures and the chaos associated with operations undertaken stealthily by hostile states or by super-empowered individuals or groups. Insurance and reinsurance policies routinely covering business interruption might be overwhelmed in the near future, especially if standard exemptions for "war damage" prove inadequate or irrelevant. Likewise, becoming imaginable are new threats posed by advances in generative artificial intelligence (AI). The most sophisticated modeling and the simplest exercises in thinking about worst-case scenarios meet here at the edges of known and unknown risks.[38]

In fact, the emergence of technologies in the borderlands surrounding generative AI bring both opportunities and challenges. On the one hand, new tools are evolving to enhance the risk assessment and risk mitigation capacities of insurers and reinsurers. On the other hand, they raise cautionary flags for underwriters, especially those without access to significant capital resources. In many national contexts, regulations also limit the potential future roles of established markets on such uncertain terrain. In Chapter 7, I explore other areas where existing private insurance and reinsurance practices push against these and other kinds of limits. But for now, note two old questions that are taking on fresh meaning. If they cannot confidently protect clients or themselves in an expanding realm that exists between risk and uncertainty, who insures the reinsurers? And what happens if the answer is *no one*?

INSURABILITY AND THE PROTECTION GAP

Profitability in insurance and reinsurance firms boils down to related but separable calculations on the two sides of their balance sheets. On the liability side, operating losses over time must fall below net premium revenues. That is, the so-called combined ratio between the two volumes

[38] See Dennis Noordhoek, *Regulation of Artificial Intelligence in Insurance* (Zurich: Geneva Association, 2023).

should be less than 100 percent. Liquid liabilities and capital reserves provide the buffer for difficult periods, but the basic principles of insurance underwriting still apply in the long run. Underwritten risks must be random, potential losses must be reasonably calculable, and capital must be available to cover them. On the other side of transactions, meanwhile, clients need to be aware of the underlying risks they face, be willing to transfer some or all of those risks, and have adequate capital levels of their own to pay premiums.

On the asset side of insurer and reinsurer balance sheets, investments across the short- and long-term spectrum must be structured to anticipate amounts and timing of payouts as well as to continue providing expected returns to shareholders. Skilled underwriting and investment income earned along the way thus become insurers' and reinsurers' main sources of profitability. Something similar is true for investors in insurance-linked securities. Rates of return on every security purchased do not have to be positive – that is, some investments may need to be written off. Over time, however, earnings across an entire investment portfolio must exceed losses. They must also exceed the opportunity costs of not having made other investments with similar risk profiles. Insurers and reinsurers conventionally label these kinds of balancing efforts "risk management." But they are really all putting their capital to work mindful of relative degrees of uncertainty. In principle, the most reliable ways to deal with that reality are to limit the kinds of disasters to which they are exposed, to share such exposures with others, to diversify across different sectors and regions, and to build scale in order to be better able to absorb losses as well as to squeeze out profits when competition builds.

As we noted in Chapter 2, the historically well-supported idea behind these strategies is that the provision of insurance remains, at root, an exercise in disciplined speculation. "Uncertainty is where the money is," a senior reinsurance executive once told me. "By the time statistical probabilities are clear, serious profit is squeezed out of the business. In a competitive environment, the challenge is to make as informed a bet as possible on emerging risks still shrouded in uncertainty. Rough estimates and potentially lucrative contracts are not precluded by a dearth of quantitative data."[39] In other words, over time insurance contracts become commodities, and it is easy for others – whether insurance firms or investors in capital markets – to get into the game and constrain profitability.

[39] Interview with reinsurance executive, Munich, November 25, 2013.

While big insurers and reinsurers can wring "bread-and-butter" profits from advance sales, billing, claims-processing, and other managerial systems after commodification, they can seek bigger gains elsewhere. In competitive environments and before risk calculations are firm, the challenge is to make as informed a bet as possible on matters still blanketed in uncertainty. Doing so just before competitors make the same bet, but not too far ahead, also plays a role. That is where innovation occurs, and innovation takes organization, knowledge, and risk capital – funds that can be lost without taking down an entire enterprise. This calls for the kind of scale and capital required to hire top analysts in many fields – from meteorology to volcanology to computer science to organizational behavior. Better knowledge allows for better underwriting contracts, which can include clauses letting insurers hold clients to risk-mitigation standards that the insurers define and inspect. Gradually, experience with actual accidents and disasters yields clearer risk calculations and more finely tuned pricing. Such calculations then make it easier to fold new transactions into standard operating systems and normal practices of pooling, diversification, and capital allocation.

Large reinsurers estimate that at least 10 percent of future revenues (and likely more) will be generated inside risk arenas where limited or no data sets currently exist. Natural disasters related to changing climates, for example, represent such arenas in many parts of the world. Over time, new experiences stretch the capacities of underwriters. To the extent that some have the capital to speculate a bit as experience builds new foundations for probability calculations and others are forced to compete with them, the borders of insurability are pushed outward. Michael Power explained the phenomenon like this: "Uncertainty is therefore transformed into risk when it becomes an object of management, regardless of the extent of information about probability ... When uncertainty is organized it becomes a 'risk' to be managed."[40] The organization of imperfect knowledge before specific disasters strike then sets the stage for more detailed and more accurate risk assessment afterwards. A shortage of quantitative data does not necessarily preclude rough estimates and potentially lucrative contracts. Instead, analytical capacity combines with experience-based

40 Michael Power, *Organized Uncertainty: Designing a World of Risk Management* (Oxford: Oxford University Press, 2007), 6. As Emily Nacol explained in private correspondence, such an account is capacious enough to suggest an organic linkage between systematic probabilistic reasoning and earlier forms of speculation in ancient and medieval history.

intuition as well as reputation to define the cutting edge of the private insurance and reinsurance industries.[41]

Michael Power suggests another way of thinking about that capacity. Both foresight and hindsight establish the organizational prerequisites for the "logic of auditability" to be successfully operationalized inside insurers and reinsurers over the long haul. In the absence of subsidies or backup resources from governments, perfecting and deploying that logic is the essence of the private insurance industry. Of course, nothing can prevent dramatic surprises, sometimes disastrous ones – such as the asbestos legal-claims shock of 1988 to 1992 that fundamentally compromised the old syndicate insurance model of Lloyd's of London and entailed many bankruptcies. Something similar followed spikes in business interruption claims caused by the unexpected COVID-19 pandemic thirty years later. But the organization of a systematic auditing function supported by capital adequate enough to absorb unexpected losses institutionalizes a capacity to learn and remember lessons even from such surprises.

At the beginning of Chapter 2, I cited John Kay and Mervyn King, whose own analysis moves along this very line. In their chapter on insurance, they contrast the classic and often caricatured approach of traditional specialized Lloyd's underwriters, who based their pricing decisions on narratives reflecting past experiences rather than on more encompassing statistical datasets, and the continental reinsurers, who marshaled every quantitative and qualitative resource available in order to determine reasonable premiums. Both kinds of insurance cultures aimed to manage uncertainty by the essential insurance act: mutualizing both revenues and losses at scale, albeit always in the knowledge that perfect foresight is impossible. But the continental model proved more successful in the long run. More information is better than less. At the most basic level, however, as Kay and King shrewdly point out, insurance is necessary as well as possible only "when databases are good, but not too good ... when ignorance is considerable, and that ignorance is common to both insurer and insured." A life insurance policy precisely crafted to fit an individual who knows precisely when they will die would either be a waste of money or completely unaffordable. "When risks become certainties, they cease to be insurable."[42]

41 The basic point is well explored in Richard V. Ericson and Aaron Doyle, *Uncertain Business: Insurance and the Limits of Knowledge* (Toronto: University of Toronto Press, 2004).

42 John Kay and Mervyn King, *Radical Uncertainty: Decision-Making Beyond the Numbers* (New York: W.W. Norton, 2021), Chapter 18.

Such a conclusion again raises the questions on the limits of insurability that Beck asked when he drew our attention to the idea of uninsurable global risks. Given a high degree of uncertainty and vast distributive complexities in such cases, risk premiums would be incalculable, or necessary insurance premiums would have to be so high that no purchaser could be attracted. Kay and King describe the relevance of uncertainty at the other end of the spectrum, where risks become certainties and are impossible to cover. In this light, risks insurable by the private sector exist on the middle ground. And that is where psychological and commercial calculations meet the vagaries of politics.

Generations of private insurance professionals have been trained to think about that middle ground with the following factors in mind.[43] Risks may be considered insurable if: (1) anticipated loss occurrences are random; (2) maximum possible losses are financially bearable; (3) average losses upon occurrence and the average time between loss occurrences may be reliably estimated; (4) a feasibly payable and reasonably profitable premium can be calculated; (5) moral hazards can be reduced to the level that encourages prudence by the insured party; (6) public policy and legal restrictions don't undercut the rationale for private insurance or its net profitability; and (7) individual insurance providers may impose cover limits.[44] As long as the first factor is present, that is, as long as future disasters can plausibly be viewed as occurring randomly, all of the other factors are open ended and malleable in the context of relationships of trust between private insurers and governments. In short, limits on insurability in private markets remain in principle, but they can expand somewhat in practice. Only governments can expand them more aggressively and more comprehensively.

Another term, widely used in insurance/reinsurance circles, helps us explore what is historically continuous and might now be changing at the shifting point where risks and uncertainties meet: "the protection gap." Rather imprecisely, the term suggests the often increasing distance between the kind of insurance coverage that might conventionally be considered desirable and feasible on the demand side and the coverage that is actually available on the supply side. With regard to basic insurance provided by private firms, it describes uninsured losses that could have been insured before they were incurred. For reinsurance

[43] Baruch Berliner, "Large Risks and Limits of Insurability," *The Geneva Papers on Risk and Insurance* 10, no. 37 (1985): 313–329.

[44] Ibid., p. 325.

companies and ILS markets, it connotes the shortfall in external capital available to supplement insurers' own resources. At the extreme points of the insurability spectrum, we might imagine the protection gap is zero at one end, where no private insurance or reinsurance is available or feasible, and infinite at the other, where demand impossibly exceeds supply. Again, the concept becomes most useful and illuminating on the middle ground, where private insurance or reinsurance cover would seem to be affordable and available. That ground exists mainly in relatively rich countries, but it is now opening in emerging markets and many developing economies.

In the public arena, the idea of protection gap can be adapted to refer to the internal and external sources and uses of a country's fiscal capacity. In addition to taxing and spending parameters, it might be enhanced or reduced by the availability and costs associated with any support provided by markets, other countries, or international agencies. Across both private and public arenas, then, the protection gap is a function of the risks confronted as well as of a range of variables affecting economic strength, technological change, social innovation, and political motivation. According to reinsurers' conventional estimates, in the early years of the twenty-first century less than half of potentially insurable economic losses from natural as well as man-made catastrophes were insured. That proportion, moreover, seemed to be dropping over time. Simultaneously, uninsurable losses – that is, losses that private insurers would not consider covering at all or with premiums markets would not bear – were widely perceived to be increasing rapidly.

Large reinsurers have occasionally tried to estimate the size of the protection gap for life, health, and property risks as a percentage of global gross domestic product (GDP). In 2015, for example, a study by Swiss Re noted that between 1975 and 1984 insured losses from all sources amounted to 0.2 percent of global GDP, while potentially insurable but actually uninsured losses totaled 0.08 percent. Three decades later (for the ten years between 2005 and 2014), the comparable figures were 0.08 percent insured and 0.19 percent uninsured.[45] The vast majority of both insured and uninsured losses over this entire era reflect developments in US and Japanese markets. The subsequent opening and liberalization of other national markets since around 2010 has made such global estimates difficult and less meaningful.

[45] Swiss Re, *Sigma Magazine* 1 (2015).

Industry insiders, however, remain convinced that uninsurable losses were growing very rapidly, while markets for potentially insurable losses were expanding slowly because of pricing pressures. For the same reason, even in and among relatively prosperous advanced and emerging-market economies, reasonable expert assessments indicate a clear problem of distribution.

While the concept of a "protection gap" may mainly be used as a marketing tool, it has opened up serious policy discussions. In rich countries, economic recovery after disasters tends to be much faster when high volumes of private insurance cover exist. In emerging-market economies, moreover, a similar logic brings out a potential linkage between available coverage and the pace of overall development, particularly after natural catastrophes. When the CEO of Swiss Re was asked to comment on old risks well understood as well as new risks associated with new technologies, he claimed that "the protection gap exists everywhere," including in well-understood arenas such as healthcare and personal accidents. He insisted that there is no shortage of affordable insurance products in both old and new arenas of risk but that sometimes, especially in rich countries, the main problem is to get people to buy them.[46] Thinking through opportunities that are increasingly complex and long term is difficult for most people most of the time.

EMERGING MARKETS AND NEW TECHNOLOGIES

Across markets in many emerging market economies, demand already exists for more affordable insurance. Insurers and reinsurers expect that experience and market deepening will begin to generate the kind of data they need to develop new products to cover natural catastrophes. Whether innovation in digital technologies can accelerate this process is already the focus of much debate and planning. In large markets such as India's, the direct person-to-person sale of insurance products already looks inadequate to the task.

The shorthand name for the indirect and digital alternative to direct marketing is InsurTech, which basically entails targeting new technologies at every step in the insurance–reinsurance value-chain to enhance efficiency, automate routine processes, and generally harness

[46] L. S. Howard, "Insurance Protection Gap Is a Growing Global Problem," *Insurance Journal* (January 17, 2018).

new sources of profit. AI, sensors, online advertising, blockchain ledgers, machine learning, and big data analytics are already being deployed, even as each in its own way brings new kinds of risk to be managed. But the speed of adjustment is now changing. New technologies are introducing new opportunities but also great uncertainties into the operations of insurance and reinsurance firms themselves. Thinking about the probability of unintended consequences from technological change is hardly new for their executives and directors, but the sense that change is happening too fast is palpable. For their part, clients and regulators are not taking long to register rising concerns about data privacy and security, market concentration, and the erosion of national controls.[47]

Anticipating technological disruption, leading insurers and reinsurers today commonly contend that governments must lay the foundations for new risk markets, even as they assert that the same risky technologies can also help to close protection gaps, prevent fraud, and attract more private capital. According to one industry study:

> In developing and emerging markets in particular, technology offers the potential to increase insurance penetration by addressing obstacles in the areas of distribution and claims settlement which, for example, hinder the wider uptake of microinsurance. In mature insurance markets, on the other hand, perceived product complexity and opacity at the customer end impede an expansion of the reach of insurance products. Technological advancements could effectively address this issue, for example, by enabling customers to put together products the way they really want to.[48]

Policy debates in this sector tend initially to concentrate on deep but hardly new trade-offs involved in replacing older forms of social solidarity with the individual opportunities, inequalities, and novel disciplines that liberal markets always introduce. When such implications are then accepted as given, the search is on for new policy frameworks that lean against extreme liberalism to preserve the social utility of insurance by encouraging adequate risk pooling, open and competitive markets, fair pricing, and sound financial and prudential management at the national level. But rapidly developing technologies

[47] Tony Porter provides a balanced review and accessible assessment of the opportunities and challenges associated with InsurTech in "At the Frontiers of Digitization and the Financialization of Risk: The Global Politics of InsurTech," *Finance and Security* 11, no. 2 (2025): 1–20.

[48] Kai-Uwe Schanz and Fabian Sommerrock, *Harnessing Technology to Narrow the Insurance Protection Gap* (Zurich: The Geneva Association, 2016).

profoundly compromise efforts to realize ambitious national dreams. Global insurance and reinsurance markets retain their attraction for transferring risks and more broadly sharing the burdens of adjustment.

Contrary to those who accuse them of risk aversion either in problematic rich country contexts or in new emerging market environments, insurance executives insist that accepting and managing risks and closing protection gaps is their very *raison d'être*. Even if new technologies both open opportunities and complicate basic activities, their firms live out their *raison d'être* in repeated cycles. When the costs of insured disasters or of new technical infrastructure fade in memory, too many competitors often wind up chasing falling premiums. Immediately after disasters, losses can overwhelm weaker players, reinsurers scrutinize their exposures, and market sentiment allows for a hardening in the prices of policies. A period of under-insurance or a rise in protection gaps typically follow.

Doris Höpke, a prominent member of Munich Re's management board, summarizes the overall situation in the realm of insurable risks, even as they expand later in risk cycles, in the following terms:

> This is how I see the future role of insurance: We want to be the central partner for comprehensive risk management, to be a resilience provider, if you will. The basis for insurance, and for risk management of any type, is to monitor and understand risks, and to subsequently develop forward-thinking solutions that can strengthen society in the long term. And of course we want to help reduce the considerable gaps in insurance that can still be found in many industrialised countries, like insurance for flood losses in Germany. Otherwise, many people will have no way to cover their losses, or will have to hope they receive state support, even though these losses could have been insured in exchange for a suitable premium.[49]

The aspiration is laudable, and the opportunities for private insurers and reinsurers to play a bigger role in the world are obviously abundant. Unless no protection is to be available at all, or unless people are rich enough to self-insure, the only serious alternative means for enhancing a society's resilience across many arenas of contemporary risk is for governments to pick up the tab and, one way or another, raise taxes or take on debt. This, for example, is the implication of the perennial debate in Florida over the price of property insurance along the state's risky coastlines. Private insurers complain about caps that make their products unprofitable, while some property owners effectively benefit

[49] www.artemis.bm, October 18, 2021, accessed October 27, 2021.

from implicit or explicit governmental subsidies. Public insurance or subsidized private insurance are often complicated when two or more levels of government are involved.[50] After a disaster, public assistance for rebuilding may or may not be provided, quickly or slowly. And repeated or statistically probable disasters in the same place can be expected to persuade private insurers to exit the field. More difficult public policy questions then arise. Should private-insurance rates be allowed to rise to much higher levels? Is it wise for societies to ignore such signals, or for governments to counter them with public subsidies? Precisely who will benefit from such decisions, and who will pay – in both the short run and the long run?

For most of the world's people, and most of the world's potentially insurable property, private insurance is unavailable. For the poor, the protection gap has always been huge. In many former colonies and relatively new states, the public purse is also typically inadequate. Of course, initiatives to fill this general protection gap for well-understood local disaster risks that someday may be privately "insurable" are not entirely absent. Indeed, the World Bank and other agencies, in line with aspirations articulated at UN climate meetings since 2017 and now routinely supported by G20, V20, and G7 commitments, continue pushing the boundaries between development assistance and public/private insurance provision.[51] But a whole new set of challenges arise when such risks and the disasters they portend cross borders and approach global scale.

At first glance, the role of the private sector might be imagined as quite limited. As we will see, however, this doesn't have to be the case. Insurance and reinsurance markets can deepen in the wake of large loss events in line with governmental signals.[52] They lie at the core of an evolving chapter in the not very long history of global capitalism. The private sector contributes new concepts that may well shape the next chapter in that history. If we are lucky, that chapter will turn on the successful management of global risks that are becoming more

50 Diana Radu, "Disaster Risk Financing: Main Concepts and Evidence," *Discussion Paper 150*, European Commission, October 2021.

51 Institute for Environment and Human Security, "Disaster Risk and Readiness for Insurance Solutions in Small Island Developing States," *Report No. 26* (New York: UN University, December 2020). A range of related initiatives mainly related to climate change are developing under the rubrics InsuRisk and InsuResilience.

52 Kenneth S. Abraham and Tom Baker, "What History Can Tell Us About the Future of Insurance and Litigation after COVID-19," *DePaul Law Review* 71 (2022): 169–208.

obvious and more measurable by the day. What we know now is that they will necessarily be framed by uncertainty.

Along the invisible frontier between risk and uncertainty at the global level, we are witnessing once again a process of innovation. Here the insuring instinct meets the requirement for sound judgment. Here speculation flirts with danger and sets the stage for consolidation *and* diversification. In the terms of Figure 3.1, private agencies begin seeking opportunities in arenas of risk that are somewhat more complex while pushing out their time horizons for adequate returns. At the same time, their intimate relationship with public authorities, even if ambiguous ever since the late nineteenth century, comes more fully into view.

I will examine that relationship in Chapter 6, where we look more closely at the risks assessed, managed, and perhaps mitigated by financial intermediaries such as banks and securities firms. But for now, I want to flag the arguments that insurers and reinsurers make concerning their very limited role in propagating the kinds of systemic risks that become visible during international financial crisis. On the traditional balance sheet of the classic insurance firm, assets and liabilities are expected to be reasonably well matched in terms of their maturities. The annual scale of underwriting losses can occasionally be surprising, but shouldn't be so over a number of years. Liquid assets should be available to cover expected losses, and prudent capital buffers as well as backup reinsurance lines should be available. In general, the balance sheets of insurers and reinsurers should not be highly leveraged, which should permit the taking on of exceptional debt during periods of unanticipated losses.

When insurers and reinsurers nevertheless go bust – and they sometimes do – clients suffer. But classic financial runs in this sector don't routinely occur. Regulatory authorities around the world tend to focus on the overall solvency of insurers – their ability to pay claims efficiently as they come due. They also supervise the quality of management, operating systems, and market competition before they issue licenses or approve mergers. Of course, calculating the ability to pay ultimately comes down to questions of capital adequacy, but insurers are generally not as leveraged as banks are, nor are they usually involved in transforming short-term liabilities into long-term assets.

When it comes to issues of systemic risk and overall financial stability, regulators therefore typically differentiate significantly between firms mainly engaged in insurance and those in the business of banking and the marketing of securities. The details quickly become quite technical, but the contrasting supervisory approaches can easily be discerned by comparing, say, the lengthy Solvency I and Solvency II insurance exercises inside the European Union with the Basel Process for banks I discuss in Chapter 6. That differentiation can become more complicated when insurers sell cover for traded financial instruments, such as credit-default swaps and other kinds of derivatives, or when they own or insure entities engaged in such trade. This is what happened when a speculative arm of the American Insurance Group (AIG) found itself caught up in the cascading global crisis of 2008–2009. In the wake of that crisis, insurance regulators around the world began working toward more common understandings of capital adequacy. One of their key objectives was a comprehensive agreement on an international capital standard for internationally active insurance groups.[53] Among other items on their common agenda was the related issue of the effects of mergers between insurers, reinsurers, and private equity firms. While additional capital may be attracted, underlying risks are only transferred, not extinguished. For good reason, supervisory authorities would begin to worry about where those risks were migrating and what the implications were for the system as a whole.

PUSHING BEYOND LIMITS

The insuring instinct joins the risk-facing client and the risk manager. Insurance providers sell guarantees of compensation when prespecified perils crystallize. Clients' willingness to buy such guarantees is a function of calculations of probable loss, their level of risk aversion, and the cost. The capacity of firms to provide such guarantees – to accept potential future liabilities – depends only partially on probabilistic calculations. Uncertainty is the fundamental target. The successful ability to manage it rests on adequate capital reserves, advanced technologies of knowledge production, and sophisticated practices of pooling, diversifying, and transferring risks. Leading reinsurance providers carefully conserve

[53] See the website of the Basel-based International Association of Insurance Supervisors (IAIS), www.iaisweb.org/activities-topics/standard-setting/insurance-capital-standard/, accessed April 11, 2025. Final outcomes were complicated by a long-standing difference between European and American approaches to measuring liquidity, solvency, and capital adequacy across groups and by the challenge of implementing any general standard in the United States in an industry mainly regulated at the state level. Thus, the focused task of the IAIS was to foster convergence between a new insurance capital standard and US-based capital "aggregation" measurements. The ultimate objective is "equivalent" standards among like insurers and reinsurers, wherever they are based.

these tangible and intangible resources. Over time, the boundaries around risks that are insurable by private-sector insurers and reinsurers alone have expanded outward because they have succeeded in deploying those resources. For example, the range and scale of natural disasters covered by the private sector have also grown as nontraditional players began complementing traditional sources of reinsurance with insurance-linked securities that are increasingly attractive to investors around the world.

Nevertheless, the process, economic classes covered, and the types of risks managed by traditional and innovative insurers have their limits. In the main, those risks are still characterized by relatively low degrees of complexity and relatively short time horizons. The private sector can bear losses, but not for long. If losses cannot soon be recouped and net profits cannot be booked over a discrete business cycle, private insurers and reinsurers will exit. If gains aren't realistically expected in given markets, or if some external sources of adequate subsidy aren't available, firms have no choice but to leave. Prominent examples now exist in property markets in Florida and California, where the prospect of flood and fire disasters became ever more certain in the wake of climate change, a subject I return to later. As we shall clearly see in Chapter 5, the key factor in lengthening strategic time horizons for private firms to expand their engagement with more complex risks and with the prospect of more certain losses threatening to cross political borders is explicit or implicit backup support from governments.

When it comes to the residual risks that insurance providers bear, compensation dynamics naturally beget systematic surveillance aimed at loss prevention. The struggle is always against moral hazard – the chance that insured clients will let down their guard because they have insurance. At base, mutually beneficial risk sharing depends on a sense of trust – that the insurer will pay out when and if necessary and the insured will take reasonable care to reduce the probability of such a payout. But trust is delicate and sometimes fleeting, especially when the norms meant to bolster it spread across different jurisdictions with potentially diverse underlying interests and legal cultures.

Profitable underwriting depends on crafting exquisite balances between the prudent acceptance of risk and the quality of people's efforts to mitigate that risk. Risks shrouded in uncertainty and posing significant threats of loss, even within a medium-term time horizon, can easily tip the balance toward limiting the underwriter's exposure. This hardly helps the system as a whole bring the private sector into coherent, fair, or effective burden-sharing arrangements.[54] Nevertheless, the invention of reinsurance and its evolution over time have shifted the cost-benefit calculus from a systemic point of view and expanded the terrain upon which private insurance providers may play a constructive role. That role can be viewed as replacing, supplementing, or complementing the traditional protective roles of government. Disciplined speculation informed by as much data as possible and advanced modeling techniques, backed by an adequate amount of capital that's able to be lost, form key elements in the package of resources private insurers and reinsurers bring to an increasingly unbounded world.

Geoffrey Clark, quoted at the outset of this chapter, elaborated on this theme. "Indeed, the global growth of reinsurance services from the early nineteenth century to the present day may be seen as the culmination of a prolonged process by which age-old forms of mutual aid and locally provided compensation have gradually been supplanted by impersonal indemnifying institutions operating according to rules-based protocols that take no heed of community identity, ethnicity, or religion."[55] Alas, complex risks involving extended time horizons can stretch even expansive protocols guiding the search for profit past the capacities of private markets. What they do not obviate, however, is the mutualization imperative historians have long seen such markets as signaling.

To the extent we can imagine those expanding markets operating on their own, they rest on a basic truth: Those who can pay the premium will reap the benefit of protection. But what about those who can't pay? As the history I recounted makes clear, they try on their own to avoid or absorb their losses if they can't reliably turn to their ultimate reinsurer: their governments. For private insurers and reinsurers contemplating complex or "emerging" risks, the same logic applies. Their linkages back to the political authorities licensing them and regulating them never lie far beneath the surface of their decision-making. That category now includes risks related to climate change, biodiversity, cyber technology, generative AI, life science innovations, geopolitical transition, and

[54] See Matthew Paterson, "Risky Business: Insurance Companies in Global Warming Politics," *Global Environmental Politics* 1, no. 4 (2001): 18–42.

[55] Geoffrey Clark, "The Cultural Context of Insurance in the West," in *Managing Risk in Reinsurance*, edited by Niels Viggo Haueter and Geoffrey Jones (Oxford: Oxford University Press, 2017), 68. This might be understood as the terrain in between algorithms that guide and laws that govern as creatively explored by Lorraine Daston in *Rules: A Short History of What We Live By* (Princeton: Princeton University Press, 2022).

much more. As the threats behind such risks become more certain, any role of the private sector comes increasingly to depend on governmental support. At that point, insurance-as-governance becomes more than a metaphor.[56]

As Figure 3.1 set out in Chapter 3, for relatively straightforward cross-border risks involving short time horizons, say in the health, life, property, and casualty sectors, private firms readily become masters in the arenas of risk assessment, compensation and prevention, and emergency management. Their fundamental social roles are to provide protection, bolster social resilience, and inspire confidence in the future. For liberal states, the expanding operations of such firms effectively extend authoritative governing functions.

When potentially insurable cross-border risks become more complex or begin to stretch out the time horizons for action, however, risk transfers through private markets become increasingly difficult and, in turn, risk conflicts become less amenable to private mediation and private legal arbitration. Private markets might strengthen official efforts to govern and reduce some risks, but multi-jurisdictional standardization and negotiation become necessary to advance the causes of accurate risk assessment, serious disaster prevention, and the enforceable sharing of associated burdens and opportunities. Indeed, when the line between risk and uncertainty blurs the mutual extension of public authority becomes essential if the limits of insurability are going to be pushed outward. As we have seen throughout this chapter, the political task has always been difficult but not impossible to master. Even in a world of sovereign states, some seemingly locked into geopolitical rivalry, promising collaborative insurance experiments linking private interests and public authorities continue to be launched. Chapter 5 presents a fascinating case in point.

[56] Yet another example came in late 2023, when private insurers and reinsurers reached an agreement with the government of Ukraine to enable it to continue exporting grain despite wartime conditions. See "Ukraine Reaches Deal with Insurers for Grain Shipments," *Financial Times*, November 15, 2023.

5

Insuring Cross-Border Risks in Commercial Nuclear Energy Production

> The United States knows that peaceful power from atomic energy is no dream of the future. That capability is here – now – today ... [It pledges] to devote its entire heart and mind to find the way by which the miraculous inventiveness of man shall not be dedicated to his death, but consecrated to his life.
>
> —Dwight David Eisenhower, Address delivered to the General Assembly of the United Nations, December 8, 1953

In the history of modern insurance and reinsurance, innovations in risk management have mainly occurred through processes of trial and error, not grand design. Political innovations permitting the private sector's expansion of risk management, often accompanied by insurance metaphors that rationalize them, are key elements in the modern art of coping with uncertainty. In this chapter, I focus on the evolution of a specific insurance regime that has enabled the commercial development of nuclear energy. The multifaceted risks involved are reasonably clear, but they are long term in nature. The time horizon for a viable insurance scheme is also therefore long. The case thus fits into the lower left-hand box of Figure 3.1 in Chapter 3. While in principle one might imagine that only governments are able to cover the third-party liabilities potentially arising from accidents in nuclear power plants, it turns out that private insurance providers play a central and vital role in much of the world.

INSURANCE AND THE GENERATION OF CIVILIAN NUCLEAR ENERGY

Adapting nuclear power for peaceful purposes was never going to be easy or unproblematic. Once it was harnessed to address one problem of global collective action – that of generating electricity without reliance on fossil fuels – nuclear power introduced other problems. The countries that first mastered the technology had to immediately answer two big questions. Who would pay to build the power plants, when governments had other priorities and cheaper options? And if private resources were to be tapped, who would cover the potentially exorbitant costs of possible accidents?

The story of how those questions were answered turns on mixing private and public instruments for risk management, national industrial policies, interstate competition as well as collaboration, and legal innovations prompted by subtle corporate and financial interests. The story complicates a common view even inside the insurance industry – that private insurers constrained by the need to diversify their portfolios cannot help to manage systemic and global risks. Although it has not yet reached its conclusion, the story so far turns on the effective stretching of the actual capacities of private insurers and reinsurers and the boundaries of cooperative intergovernmentalism. That stretching never completely closes the protection gap opened by commercial nuclear energy production, nor does it necessarily portend the emergence of a legitimate world reinsurer and regulator of last resort. But it has succeeded in facilitating the expansion of a global industry on the basis of collaborative insurance and reinsurance practices. To the extent they bind governments together, these practices suggest much more than integrated industrial policies. Mutual acknowledgment of commitments to share burdens implies recognition of a shared capacity to live up to them.[1]

MANAGING RISKS IN THE COMMERCIAL PRODUCTION OF NUCLEAR ENERGY

Radioactive debris from the 2011 Fukushima Daiichi disaster could not be contained after it entered the Pacific Ocean, nor could irradiated water from the plant's cooling tanks over a decade later. Likewise, in 1986, the wind carried radioactive fallout from the Chernobyl meltdown right across the northern hemisphere; in 2016, the toxic remains of the Ukrainian reactor were encased in a massive concrete bunker engineered by an international team and financed by the European Bank for Reconstruction and Development and a consortium of donor

[1] Michael Zürn, "Four Models of a Global Order with Cosmopolitan Intent: An Empirical Assessment," *Journal of Political Philosophy* 24, no. 1 (2016): 88–119.

governments including Russia, Ukraine, and most Organization for Economic Cooperation and Development (OECD) countries. The long-term dangers involved in the commercial generation of nuclear energy, at every stage of production, remain substantial and obvious. Liability concerns have long provided key stumbling blocks to the development of the industry.

Despite signal catastrophes and an array of smaller, less well-known accidents, the industry has never died. It persists, and lately even promises to grow significantly as a climate-stressed world moves toward the end of the fossil fuel era. Although the all-in cost of a kilowatt hour of nuclear energy still far exceeds comparable costs from energy generation from coal, oil, gas, or renewables, in 2024 ninety-three commercial nuclear reactors were operating at fifty-four nuclear power plants in twenty-eight US states.[2] They generated nearly 20 percent of the country's electricity. Around the same time across thirty-two countries in the world, 440 reactors met 10 percent of total electricity demand. Among industrial countries, France comes in at the high end, with nuclear energy accounting for over three-quarters of its electricity generation. During the past two decades, slightly more than 100 reactors have been taken offline around the world, while slightly fewer than 100 have commenced operation. Even with all the understandable concerns associated with the words Three Mile Island, Chernobyl, and Fukushima Daiichi, early in the second decade of the twenty-first century some sixty reactors were on order or under construction around the world, and 110 more were in various stages of planning. While some established firms from advanced industrial states are pulling out of the business, national champions from South Korea, China, and India are accelerating their plans to build more plants. In fact, despite obvious risks and the profound problems connected with the disposal of radioactive waste, signs of revival are emerging around the world.

Perhaps some of the special risks of nuclear energy will one day be reduced through innovative technologies, such as plants that can reliably consume all of their fuel and leave little waste for disposal. In the absence of such innovations, extreme predictions for the industry remain commonplace. Not all that long ago, for example, one prominent study undertaken for the US Council on Foreign Relations made the case that because of costs and a hardening regulatory environment, no nuclear

[2] US Energy Information Administration (EIA), www.eia.gov/nuclear/reactors/reactorcapacity.php, accessed October 22, 2024.

generation would take place on American soil after 2056.[3] Even so, conventional plant designs are currently being adapted around the world in line with diverse national regulations. Innovative plans for small or "modular" plants are also moving ahead. With demand for power rapidly increasing, especially to meet the needs of many high-technology industries dependent on artificial intelligence, other ideas are coming to the fore in the United States – including restarting refurbished nuclear facilities at Three Mile Island.[4]

The center of the action in this sector, though, lies in Asia. International negotiations on climate change have raised the prospect of significantly more nuclear power generation in developing countries there and elsewhere over the next couple of decades.[5] As was the case at the dawn of the nuclear age, much of that activity will depend upon the involvement of private markets, and therefore on insurance. Especially important are liability insurance arrangements for third parties – the innocent potential victims of accidents at nuclear generating stations or in the transport of radioactive fuel to or from those stations. Without such arrangements, private firms simply would not take on the risks of building and operating nuclear generators. The readily imaginable losses from accidents are so extravagant and the timeline for dealing with them so potentially long even risk-tolerant investors can easily find other more attractive options for their portfolios.

The risks of nuclear power generation are undeniably long term, national, and potentially transnational. The consequent question is straightforward. How did a private nuclear industry backstopped by plausible liability insurance arrangements arise? History reveals an answer that may well be relevant in similar arenas of risk and uncertainty.

THE EVOLUTION OF AMERICAN PRACTICES

The impulses of political economy and national security overlap in the nuclear energy policy arena. Hiroshima and Nagasaki still burned vividly in public imagination when President Dwight Eisenhower gave his famous "Atoms for Peace" speech at the United Nations in December

[3] Charles D. Ferguson, *Nuclear Energy: Balancing Benefits and Risks*, CSR no. 28 (New York: Council on Foreign Relations, 2007).

[4] Casey Crownhart, "Why Microsoft Made a Deal to Restart Three Mile Island," The Spark, Newsletter of the MIT Technology Review, September 26, 2024.

[5] World Nuclear Association website, www.world-nuclear.org/, accessed December 12, 2023.

1953. The United States was then pursuing a delicate Cold War strategy of deterring potential Soviet incursions in Western Europe by simultaneously drawing down conventional forces and building up the operational capacity of its nuclear technologies.

In fact, the development of those technologies had deep European roots. The key scientific discoveries all happened in Europe. The pioneering work of Otto Hahn, Lise Meitner, Rudolf Peierls, Niels Bohr, and many others took place there. German scientists played key roles, especially after some sought asylum in the United Kingdom. Scientists in France were trying to catch up when the German invasion in 1940 forced many to move across the Channel. The British government, moreover, was much quicker than the United States in taking the initial steps toward the application of atomic fission in its weapons' programs. It made the crucial decision to share its knowledge and innovations with the United States. Together, the allies then began to take seriously the threat that Germany might develop and deploy a fission-based weapon first. The United States soon began pouring vast resources into the Manhattan Project, within which British, Canadian, and other European nationals played significant roles.[6]

After the war, Eisenhower and his advisers had only a basic view of the manifold risks involved when they latched onto the idea that military and civilian purposes could simultaneously be served by the further development of nuclear technologies. They just had to convince risk-averse and fiscally exhausted citizens to see nuclear energy as helping to meet the rising need for electricity as national economies recovered from years of depression and conflict.

American and allied governments could have retained direct control over the infrastructure for both weapon systems and nuclear-energy-generating stations. They could have borne the full responsibility for any liability for accidents, including to third parties, such as people living downwind from a nuclear generating station. But the potential cost was too much for governments to bear. By the early 1950s, US politics had pivoted back to its traditional ideological preference for relatively small central government, notwithstanding the continuing reality of a defense budget swollen by the Cold War.

[6] This helps explain the fact that by the early 1950s civilian nuclear energy infrastructures were about as advanced in the United Kingdom, France, and Canada as they were in the United States. See John Baylis, "Exchanging Nuclear Secrets: Laying the Foundations of the Anglo-American Nuclear Relationship," *Diplomatic History* 25, no. 1 (2001): 33–61. I thank Dani Nedal for this reference.

Even in the wake of the Marshall Plan, the US-led strategy for expanding the American economy and rebuilding a prosperous and peaceful world therefore came to rest on the assumption that private markets would provide the vast bulk of the financing required for civilian nuclear energy production. Following naturally from such an assumption, leading national nuclear agencies and laboratories in the United States and the United Kingdom began collaborating on the adaptation of nuclear fission technologies for peaceful purposes with engineering and equipment manufacturing firms such as Westinghouse and CA Parsons. (Parsons was eventually merged into Rolls-Royce and is today part of Germany's Siemens AG.)

In 1942, the world's first self-sustaining nuclear reaction had been harnessed at the University of Chicago. The Manhattan Project subsequently used that fundamental technology to create the first atomic weapons. A year after the end of the war, the US Congress established the Atomic Energy Commission (AEC) with a view to adapting the technology for generating electrical energy for civilian use. The AEC underwrote the construction of an experimental breeder reactor that promised to create more fissionable material than it would initially use at a secure site in Idaho. Although the reactor began producing electricity in December 1951, commercial application of the technology soon became bogged down in tense debates on governmental control, global security, the risks of radioactivity, and role of insurance.

Although private equipment suppliers had been involved in the top secret American production and deployment of fissile material during and after the war years, their potential liabilities were effectively indemnified by governmental guarantees. The same was true in the United Kingdom after the war ended. From then on, however, those firms faced not only the prospect of broader foreign competition but also increasing reluctance from public authorities to continue bearing the full burden of financing and insuring the construction of new power plants. Security interests and economic opportunities had to be rebalanced.

Firms were partially unleashed by governments looking to private markets for support in feeding nuclear power into national electricity grids. They also discerned future prospects for the export of associated technologies. In both the United States and the United Kingdom, however, one problem came immediately to the fore: how to provide essential insurance for private-sector investment in an industry on the one hand promising seemingly endless supplies of energy and on the other posing potentially massive environmental and health risks. If the public sector bore all of those risks, what would justify private-sector profits? But if the private sector was going to bear the risk of losses associated with a low-probability but incalculably high-cost disaster, no rational investor would ever be likely to take the plunge. And what rational private insurer would ever offer to cover such risks?

From the beginning, discussions among government officials and the leaders of universities, utilities, and concerned citizens focused directly on the issue of third-party liability, that is, payments-in-principle to those harmed by accidents at nuclear plants they neither owned nor controlled, the fallout from which could not necessarily even be contained within national or state borders. In the United States, national, state, and local governments as well as public and private universities could claim immunity. Private corporations in Anglo-American legal systems, however, typically enjoyed limited liability, which in practice meant that any payouts in the wake of nuclear accidents would be capped by available equity. Beyond that limit was corporate bankruptcy and the erasure of claims for compensation. For potential private investors in a nascent industry, both declarations of sovereign immunity and the established convention of corporate bankruptcy were show-stoppers.

That remained the case when in 1953 the AEC invited Westinghouse and Duquesne Light Company to adapt a naval propulsion reactor and build a demonstration generating station. At the time, there was no substitute for government ownership of the facility, a situation that did not immediately change when the Atomic Energy Act was passed by the US Congress in 1954. The act allowed the AEC to grant other licenses for the private construction of nuclear power plants but set no formal limit on the liability of the owner or lessee. It also insisted that licensees "hold government harmless from any damage resulting from the use or possession of special nuclear material."[7] Not surprisingly, private investors remained unmoved.

In 1956, the first commercial nuclear energy reactor opened not in the United States but at Calder Hall in the United Kingdom. The Soviet Union also opened a state-owned and controlled nuclear generating station that same year. An editorial in the *New York Times* said this about the resulting zeitgeist.

[7] Atomic Energy Act, Section 55(e)(8). Cited in "Memorandum on Nuclear Risk Insurance" OECD Insurance Sub-Committee of the Joint Trade and Intra-European Payments Committee, June 19, 1956 (OECD/NUC-RC/01/002; Folder ID 201 498 344, OECD Archives, Paris.).

What we need is a liberalization of the Atomic Energy Act of 1954 ... There is no mystery about designing and constructing a power reactor, but there are still restrictions that hamper the development of nuclear power. Secrecy always hampers scientific and technological progress ... That seventeen years after the discovery of fission we should not have a single large commercial plant in operation [in the United Sates] speaks for itself.[8]

By 1957, both economic and ideological competition helped untangle the puzzle spurred by Ike's appeal to the "miraculous inventiveness of man." Tentative moves by insurance companies provided the Shippingport generating station with some basic cover for public and property liability through the creation of a national pool that shared risks across joint stock and mutual insurance companies (Nuclear Energy Property Insurance Association and Nuclear Energy Liability Insurance Association). The pool was backed by reinsurance contracts negotiated in the London market and among continental European reinsurers. However, such an arrangement provided only limited cover (USD 50 to 70 million in the third-party liability category). The quiet if reluctant implication remained that government would pick up the tab for any excess losses. As a result, future growth in the new industry hardly looked promising. With the economic interests of US industrial and insurance firms now engaged and strategic spurs provided by both the United Kingdom and the Soviet Union, further political responses were required.

Various bills were soon taken up by Congressional committees. One early proposal required the AEC to indemnify reactor owners incurring third-party liability for any amounts they might have to pay in the event of an accident over and above the cover provided by private insurance companies. Others anticipated allowing the AEC to issue bonds to provide additional cover following a disaster. No one knew, however, what amounts would be sufficient to compensate future victims. With government unwilling to formally accept unlimited liability and thus to provide an implicit subsidy to reactor operators, with local utility companies unable to accept a high liability, and with the owner of a single reactor capable of covering a liability only equivalent to its net equity, the essential problem remained obvious.

The solution was embedded in the Price-Anderson bill, which was eventually passed by both houses of Congress and signed into law by President Eisenhower on September 2, 1957. It basically pinned all liability-in-principle on the owner of a nuclear facility on a no-fault basis

[8] Editorial page, *New York Times*, September 19, 1956.

for any accident involving radioactive fallout. It limited the actual liability to the maximum private insurance cover then available. That maximum was pegged at USD 60 million per insurable risk.[9] The federal government then pledged to commit a further USD 500 million on top of that to cover excess claims.

The Price-Anderson Nuclear Industries Indemnity Act was not intended to exist in perpetuity. Its framers had hoped that it would provide an initial incentive over a ten-year period. They expected a safe and responsible nuclear energy industry to soon be able to expand its insurance coverage at manageable rates on its own, that is, without the subsidy implied by governmental backup facilities. They also hoped that a sunset clause in the act would encourage insurance firms to cooperate in establishing adequate private insurance pools. American Nuclear Insurers (ANI), a pool of nearly sixty property and casualty firms, was actually in place as soon as the new Price-Anderson Act came into effect. What then emerged was a tiered system of insurance cover, the first tiers provided by way of private policies held by individual plant operators and by the ANI, and a back-up tier provided by an unfunded and capped pledge from the AEC. In practice, this left the provision of any additional cover beyond that cap to the discretion of a future Congress.

The American nuclear industry took off. As it did, a new tier of insurance – a burden-sharing collective made up of reactor owner and lessees themselves – became a key element in an evolving insurance system. From the late 1950s until the March 1979 accident at Three Mile Island in Pennsylvania, nuclear energy generation expanded across the country. The Price-Anderson Act was adjusted and renewed in 1967, and the cover it provided increased to keep pace. The Three Mile Island experience certainly slowed things down, but it also underscored the impracticality of government ever stepping back entirely.

The Price-Anderson Act was renewed again in 2005 for an additional twenty years. Currently, the governmental role is implemented by the United States Nuclear Regulatory Commission, which operates inside the Department of Energy. Owners and lessees of private nuclear facilities

[9] Actually, three pools came into existence in 1956. The Nuclear Energy Liability Insurance Association for third-party liability insurance; the Nuclear Energy Property Insurance Association for property insurance; and the Mutual Atomic Energy Reinsurance Pool for mutual companies handling both kinds of insurance. The initial cover available was USD 60 million for each risk, thus USD 120 million in total per site. At the time, this was seen as a massive achievement for insurers facing limited data and a high degree of uncertainty. Richard D. McClure, "A Review of Nuclear Energy Insurance," *Casualty Actuarial Society Review* 55 (1968): 255–294.

were to pay an annual premium of about USD 400,000 per reactor site for USD 450 million in cover for third-party liability. Unlike in other countries, as discussed more fully later, this referred to economic liability, not strictly legal liability. With jurisdiction in this field divided between federal and state governments, the basic principles of American-style federalism complicated matters. The renewed Price-Anderson Act therefore continued to allow the economic channeling of responsibility for any accident to the specific plant operator, but did not preclude the possibility that other entities may be found at fault by local authorities and therefore held legally responsible in some measure.

That first tier of insurance coverage was to be provided by the ANI pool, with about half of its capacity coming from international reinsurance companies and syndicates. If the actual cost of damage from an accident exceeded that amount, a second tier was in place. That secondary financial protection program was a mutual pooling arrangement made up of all US-based reactor operators. If necessary, additional funds would be paid into the pool retrospectively. After an accident occurred and liability payments significantly in excess of the primary cover had to be made, each participant agreed to eventually pay USD 121 million per reactor per accident, with annual instalments of USD 19 million.[10] In principle, this promised to yield a total of approximately USD 14 billion paid by utility companies throughout the United States.

Although amounts were expected to be adjusted over time, that remains the regime inside the United States. In short, the secondary coverage originally pledged by the US Treasury in the late 1950s has been dramatically expanded through mandated risk sharing, or mutualization. The government continues to provide additional annual financing as well, since the Department of Energy spends about USD 10 billion a year on its civil nuclear-related activities. Beyond primary and secondary commitments, Congress retains its discretionary reinsurer of last resort role if the cost of a major accident exceeds all formally pledged coverage.[11]

[10] In addition, there exists a nuclear operators' mutual arrangement to provide property and business-interruption insurance for actual plants. Established in 1980, Nuclear Electric Insurance Limited maintains a USD 5 billion cash fund, which it coordinates with the ANI pool. "Liability for Nuclear Damage," World Nuclear Association, https://world-nuclear.org/information-library/safety-and-security/safety-of-plants/liability-for-nuclear-damage#us-framework, accessed April 2025.

[11] About USD 150 million has been paid in claims and associated costs since 1957, all of it by the insurance pools. Half resulted from the Three Mile Island accident. "Liability for Nuclear Damage," World Nuclear Association website, June 2017.

Imaginable if unlikely nuclear accidents could cause damage readily valued in hundreds of billions or even trillions of dollars over many years. The essential purpose of primary and secondary insurance commitments in the United States, as well as the perceived existence of an ultimate reinsurance facility limited only by the fiscal capacity of the US government, remains consistent with the purpose of its precursors during the Eisenhower administration. While the country has never abandoned the nuclear power industry (despite its obvious travails), the firms at its core were hardly constrained by national boundaries.

American power generators naturally sought to export their technologies. Competitors naturally emerged in their target markets, often with the encouragement of local governments. Like other American policy initiatives in the postwar years, the Price-Anderson Act assumed the emergence of a global market. Leading firms and their insurers agreed. They needed a global regime capable of coping with the reparations and compensation necessary in the event of accidents, but only regional solutions at that point seemed practicable. International legal change over the past fifty years followed political pressures to permit their growth. The development of the global nuclear industry was facilitated by remarkable innovations in cross-national burden sharing.

PRAGMATIC COLLABORATION IN EUROPE

In August 1955, the International Conference on the Peaceful Uses of Atomic Energy convened in Geneva, Switzerland, under the auspices of the United Nations. Earlier that same year, the United States initiated discussions on its practical implications inside the Paris-based Organization for European Economic Co-operation (OEEC), the agency first associated with the Marshall Plan that later evolved into the OECD. Its Special Committee for Nuclear Energy began meeting in 1956, coordinating its activities with the insurance subcommittee of the Organization's Committee on Intra-European Costs and Payments.[12]

From the start, the basic aim of the subcommittee was to assist the world's leading industrial countries in coming to common legislative and regulatory understandings on matters of mutual concern. The six countries at the heart of the European Coal and Steel Community also

[12] See Julia Schwartz, "The Nuclear Law Committee – A Historical Perspective," *50th Anniversary of the Nuclear Law Committee Colloquium* (NEA/SEN/NLC(2007)2) (Paris: Nuclear Energy Agency), February 6, 2007.

took a distinct interest in the development of nuclear energy in Europe. In March 1957, they formally established the European Atomic Energy Community (Euratom) with a view to create a Europe-wide market for surplus nuclear energy generated by individual members. Over time, Euratom grew to include all European Union member countries plus Switzerland, while its mandate expanded to cover the full range of cross-border issues connected with nuclear energy. It remains closely affiliated with other EU institutions, but it is legally independent and not under the jurisdiction of the European Parliament.

The same strategic and industrial interests behind the Price-Anderson Act in the United States and its equivalent in the United Kingdom encouraged the OEEC to establish its Special Committee for Nuclear Energy to explore the full range of issues needing to be addressed before industrial development could accelerate in and across European political borders. In fact, an initial nudge came from the New York-based Atomic Industrial Forum, Inc., which had sponsored a study on that theme in November 1955 by professors at Columbia University "in the interests of the manufacturers and electric utility companies, the insurance industry, and the public."[13] The study was expected to follow up on a preliminary report completed in June 1955 by the Insurance Study Group for the AEC. That group consisted of leading executives from ten US insurance companies, including such household names as Aetna, Travelers, Hartford, and Liberty Mutual. They had already concluded that "the most difficult problems in connection with the insurance of atomic energy installations lie in the field of third-party liability insurance."[14]

As it was inside the pioneering states, one of the first issues needing serious analysis concerned liability for accidents both in individual power plants and in the cross-border transportation of nuclear materials. In March 1956, the Special Committee "instructed the Secretary-General [of the OEEC] to examine with the Chairman of the Insurance Sub-Committee of the [standing] Joint Trade and Payments Committee, the conditions in which the Sub-Committee might begin immediately a study of the legislative problems which arise as regards nuclear risk insurance."[15] The subcommittee, in turn, set up a working party to

[13] Letter dated April 25, 1956, copied in OEEC TFD/PC/992 Addendum, Paris, June 11, 1956. OECD Archives, Box NUC-RC /01/001 Folder 201 498 343.

[14] Ibid.

[15] OEEC TFD/PC/992 Addendum, Paris, June 11, 1956. OECD Archives, Box NUC-RC /01/001 Folder 201 498 343.

undertake the required foundational research for Europe, where members expected conflicts of national laws to arise. Their work was undertaken in tandem with discussions then beginning inside Euratom.

The working party began by commissioning a preliminary report from a Swiss insurance executive (W. E. Belser) who completed it on a personal basis under the auspices of his own Centre for the Study of Atomic Risks. The report began by noting that accidents had already occurred at an experimental Canadian reactor at Chalk River, Ontario, in 1952. This was followed by another accident at the same site as well as at the AEC's Idaho reactor in 1955. All were kept secret at the time, and they involved no loss of life. But when they were eventually reported, they highlighted the long-term risks involved in the production of nuclear energy.[16]

> Although the experts are generally of the opinion that the possibility of an explosion such as occurs in the case of an atomic missile can be excluded, an explosion of a chemical type, comparable with that of a boiler, is possible ... The result might be a disaster, the extent of which would depend upon the type of reactor, its location in relation to housing, and upon the meteorological and hydrological conditions at the time. In addition to the direct effects, there would be the indirect consequences caused by clouds of radioactive dust or mist settling on crops or pasture. Drinking water might be contaminated and the milk of cows which had grazed on the radioactive grass might endanger human life, and this would also apply to fish that had been in contaminated water. Costs of decontamination might be very high ... There is also a potential risk in connection with reactors in the form of the residues which have a radioactivity of extreme intensity. Like plutonium 239 and uranium 233, with which they are mixed, such residues are highly toxic. They give rise to the most difficult problems with which the scientists, technical personnel, and the authorities are faced.[17]

The harmonization of national legislation with regard to such risks might be an ideal objective but it was still not feasible. Most of the relevant countries were just then beginning the process of establishing their own national legislative and regulatory frameworks for the development of nuclear energy. Although direct insurance cover for the property and staff of nuclear energy producers was generally seen as manageable, Belser was quick to point out here the basic dilemma facing private insurers for indirect liabilities to third parties that conceivable disasters could cause.

[16] OEEC, Report on Nuclear Risk Insurance (Belser Report), Paris, May 11, 1956. OECD/NUC-RC/-1/001 Folder 201 498 343. (p. 7).

[17] Ibid., 7–8.

The interest of the insurers in the face of this new form of energy is clearly to play their traditionally important role in the economic development of the country or even the continent by paying compensation for losses or damages sustained by the insured. For this purpose, the insurers must have knowledge of the risks involved so as to be able to assess them and fix the appropriate premiums. It is past experience that enables them to provide security for the future. In the absence of any statistics, the insurance companies will be left to assess the risks on the basis of other factors, amongst which the legislative position is of especial importance. With few exceptions, such legislation is non-existent in all countries. And in addition to this serious deficiency, there are other difficulties: the lack of any definition of the substance to be insured, or of the possible extent of the damage; the varying degrees of risk inherent in radiation … [This] will of necessity mean that changes will have to be made in the traditional terms and even the fundamental concepts of certain branches of insurance.

Belser continued: "In adopting a positive attitude toward these still unknown risks, the insurers expect the other interested parties to refrain from making any demands that would be contrary to the rules of business that has been conducted successfully on sound lines and in accordance with long established practice."[18] This implied that at most what could be expected on a national basis would be governments accepting insurers' pooled capacities, particularly to cover indirect liabilities, up to a maximum limit. Since those liabilities could easily spill over national borders, especially in Europe, it might therefore be necessary "to envisage re-organising the international market in the form of a pool, and, if this proved insufficient, to arrange for reciprocal reinsurance through a series of national pools." "[National] markets are in a position to provide substantial cover providing the risk is properly spread over all the companies. Consequently, it might well be possible to meet the demand if each company, in addition to the business retained for its own account, drew on its entire sources of reinsurance and retrocession. However, this solution … would probably result in an enormous volume of business accumulating with the reinsurers, which might jeopardise their position."[19] Beyond this, Belser concluded with a key observation.

[If claims were exorbitant,] only the State would be in a position to meet them, [but] taking this argument to its logical conclusion, we would point out that should experience prove that the risks were on such a scale as to jeopardise even public finances, then the whole question of whether nuclear energy should

[18] Ibid., 11–12.
[19] Ibid., 17.

be exploited would arise ... It is therefore in this respect that harmonization of [national] legislation is necessary ... The entire European market [should therefore be considered, along with] possible co-operation with markets outside Europe, more especially the United States.[20]

The Belser Report thus set the stage both for legislative and regulatory debates just getting underway in most national capitals, as well as for preliminary discussions at the transnational level between the OEEC and the European Insurance Committee, the umbrella organization for major European insurers and reinsurers.

In February 1957, British insurers convened a conference attended by delegates from European insurers and by the general managers of the main European reinsurance companies, including Swiss Re and Munich Re. By the middle of 1957, Germany and Switzerland had drafted relevant national legislation, and national nuclear insurance pools had already become operational in the United Kingdom and Sweden. Denmark, France, and Germany had by then put basic organizational structures for national pools in place, while Belgium, Italy, the Netherlands, and Switzerland soon followed. Although the idea of a pan-European pool would have to wait, an emerging consensus aligned with the Belser Report's implications was not difficult to discern. Most important from the reinsurers' point of view was the idea of an aggregate limitation of their ultimate responsibilities.

As a June 1957 report of the OEEC Insurance Sub-Committee put it: "National and international reinsurers will participate in the pools as direct insurers. There was unanimous agreement that all insurance should be dealt with on a net line basis. In other words, each company participating in a pool would undertake that its acceptance would be for its own account and not for reinsurance, so that reinsurance will be relieved of a great deal of anxiety over the accumulation of risks." It was also agreed that national pools would disclose their internal constitutions to one another and otherwise remain transparent with one another on the nature and extent of the risks they agreed to cover. Moreover, "reciprocal insurance between pools will be based either on the principle of participation by quota or on that of joint reinsurance." Private insurers and reinsurers also recommended that "pools granting cover to other pools by way of reinsurance should be able to constitute guarantee deposits or provide guarantees with the minimum of restrictions, and that technical reserves deposited should not be subject to

20 Ibid., 21–22.

taxation or other fiscal measures."[21] Finally, their early advice to the OEEC was that any coverage they would provide for third-party liability needed to be "absolute," which meant strict limitations on the amounts and timing of claims.

In this regard, the draft German law had already set a limit of DM 15 million per incident and installation, while debate on the length of time for any submission of claims continued.

> Whilst for social reasons, a long period of prescription is doubtless desirable (since symptoms associated with exposure to radiation may not appear immediately), a shorter period is necessary from the point of view of insurance ... It is important to underline the relation between the length of prescription and the amount of premium: the longer the prescription, the higher would premium necessarily be ... [In addition,] where the State intervenes above the total amount fixed, in order to respect the principle of limiting the operator's absolute liability, the State ought not to have recourse against the operator except in cases where the latter has been guilty of serious negligence, for otherwise insurers would be faced with insurmountable difficulties.[22]

All of this implies that nuclear plant operators would consolidate all risks associated with equipment manufacturers and other suppliers through contractual arrangements, and that a single forum, ideally in the jurisdiction of the state where an accident occurs, would be the place to decide final settlement of any disputes or conflicts.

What followed inside the OEEC as well as in European member-states were three years of intense study and debate on a common legal definition of nuclear accidents entailing third-party liability, the cost and time limits needed to accommodate insurers and reinsurers, the precise role of the state, the adequacy of national courts in adjudicating claims, and the wisdom of establishing international machinery for arbitrating settlements when insurance interests crossed national borders. The insurance subcommittee commissioned specific analyses of such issues from scientific experts and compared and contrasted evolving national laws and practices. In the meantime, they were realizing that market mechanisms alone would not be likely to succeed in promoting the nuclear energy industry. As one key study put it:

> In a free economy no one can force financiers to invest their money in a particular industry ... The ratio of return on capital to the risks (in installations generating

[21] Draft Report of the Insurance Sub-Committee, Paris, June 24, 1957. OECD NUC-RC /01/002 Folder 201 498 344, pp. 4–5.

[22] Ibid., 9–10.

electricity from nuclear sources as opposed to conventional fossil fuels) is not very favourable ... The fear of such risks is a psychological fact which legislators must take into account. What matters most of all is not the real gravity of the risk—which in any case is difficult to determine—but the importance attached to it by financial interests.

It went on to say that "If the liability of the nuclear industry must be limited in order to help it develop, the injured parties must be given some recompense in the form of State responsibility."[23]

One of the clearest studies again came from W. E. Belser.

The insurers argue as follows: since we cannot in any case cover all claims arising from a major accident, our cover must be limited so that we can meet the claims arising from a serious accident, in the usual meaning of the term when we cover industrial risks, and it seems to us that a cover equivalent to Swiss Francs 20 million for each installation is, despite the fact that the dangers of nuclear energy are new to us, a fairly substantial indemnity, taking into account the resources of the various European insurance markets, without excluding the possibility of higher cover if new legislation calls for it. It would be useless to try to define a major accident, particularly from the international point of view, for it depends on too many different factors, psychological, social, economic, and financial. We must therefore be prepared to fix the limit on an empirical basis. It is clear that the limitation of liability has no practical value to the operator of a nuclear undertaking unless the insurer can cover the whole of the limited liability.[24]

Since it would likely be necessary for national pools to augment their own capacities with recourse to international reinsurers, Belser raised two additional concerns. Since circumstances could be imagined whereby international reinsurers might be precluded by law, by inflation in monetary aggregates, by the unanticipated scale of an accident, or by the length of time involved in specific claims from fulfilling their obligations, national pools might in the end be required to fall back on their own capacities. Again, he asserted, this made it necessary to place limits on both individual claims and on ultimate total liabilities per incident that private insurers would have to bear.

[23] "The State and Liability for Personal Injury or Damage Caused by Nuclear Installations, by O.K. Kaufmann." A Study for the OEEC Steering Committee for Nuclear Energy, Group of Experts on Third-Party Liability, Paris, March 4, 1958. OECD NUC/01/006 Folder 201 498 348, p. 5. The study noted the exception that had evolved over time in maritime law that limited liability to a shipowner for losses caused, for example, by shipwrecks.

[24] "Limitation of Liability in Time and Amount from the Insurance Point of View, by W.E. Belser." A Study for the OEEC Steering Committee for Nuclear Energy, Group of Experts on Third-Party Liability, Paris, March 10, 1958. OECD NUC/01/006 Folder 201 498 348, p. 4.

By 1959, the industry had achieved enough clarity on all of these issues to enable the drafting of an OEEC Convention on Third Party Liability in the Field of Nuclear Energy. Disputes and differences of opinion remained, for example, on the definition of a "nuclear incident" and whether it required radioactive contamination, the strictness of channeling legal responsibility to the operator of an installation, and the limitation of liability to be covered by private insurance providers. As debate among national delegations to the OEEC – including the United States, European electricity generators, European insurers, and OEEC officials – continued throughout the year, Euratom was working up its own ideas for a similar agreement among its six members. At the same time, the International Atomic Energy Agency (IAEA) accelerated its own efforts to draft a convention on third-party liability for nuclear accidents among its own members.

Dwight Eisenhower's "Atoms for Peace" speech initiated the process of establishing the IAEA, which formally commenced operations from its Vienna base in July 1957. Eighty-one member-states of the United Nations ratified its founding document, confirming its status as an independent but affiliated agency of the UN with a dual mandate of discouraging the proliferation of nuclear weapons and harnessing the potential of nuclear energy for peaceful purposes.[25] Sterling Cole, formerly a Republican Congressman from upstate New York, was elected as its first director general. Despite Cole's displeasure that the OEEC and the European Nuclear Energy Agency (ENEA) had already begun working on the issue of the insurance of risks and restricted its scope to Western Europe, IAEA officials began closely tracking the evolving draft convention in 1958. With its much bigger membership, including many developing countries as well as countries on both sides of the Cold War, the issues that the IAEA faced were much more complicated than those confronting the OEEC. Below the leadership level, specialist officials initiated an intense dialogue on both common interests and differences.

A comment from an IAEA official's October 1958 letter to the OEEC's legal counsel provides a sense of the contrasting positions involved.

> I do not see how we can depart very far from the draft [Convention of the OEEC on Third-Party Liability] ... [T]he provision of the OEEC draft would of course have quite a different practical meaning if applied to an under-developed country ... But, in view of the OEEC precedent and of the sensitiveness about sovereignty of new countries, how can we even propose departures from the

[25] David Fischer, *History of the International Atomic Energy Agency* (Vienna: IAEA, 1997).

local jurisdiction rule? Similarly, how can we demand a genuine financial security which would put atomic energy quite beyond the reach of under-developed countries, and therefore would be politically impossible? We cannot do much by means of a convention, I think—however ingeniously we draft it—to remedy the severe factual limitation of liability inherent in economic under-development and political stability. In these circumstances there may be debate about whether it is wise for us to follow the OEEC model and encourage abolition of whatever liability suppliers may have under existing laws. Yet if we do not do that, supplier countries will not be interested in our convention, and we might as well abandon the project ... At the present time, as far as I can see, the least inept thing we can do is stick closely to the OEEC draft, with only enough elegant variations of wording to save us from the charge of plagiarism.[26]

A single global convention would remain an unrealistic goal for many years. However, the original IAEA initiative did at least raise the idea that member-states were in principle subject to international law in this field and that those who developed nuclear energy programs bore "international responsibilities." That principle remained in the background of continuing multilateral discussions on third-party liability.[27]

In the OEEC, those discussions accelerated late in 1959. Member-states persistently disagreed on five main issues: the precise definition of an insurable incident, the amount of coverage to be provided by private insurers – somewhere between 5 and 10 million EMA (European Units of Account, the precursor to the euro), whether and how accidents occurring during the transport of nuclear materials should be handled, the channeling of all claims after an accident solely to the operator of the nuclear installation, the absolute limit for which private insurance would be responsible, and a specified commitment for any excess coverage by member-states. In that regard, the six members of Euratom were just then discussing a limit of 100 million EMA in their own separate draft treaty.[28] (After the Special Drawing Right (SDR), a new international reserve asset, was created by the International Monetary Fund in 1969, the OEEC decided to use it instead of US dollars or other established or synthetic currencies, as the numéraire.[29])

[26] Letter from Gurdon Wattles, IAEA to Jerry Weinstein, OEEC-ENEA, October 24, 1958. OECD/NUC-RC/03/009. Folder 201 498 359.

[27] OEEC-ENEA memo by J. L. Weinstein, Paris, 17 March 1959. OEEC-ENEA, October 24, 1958. OECD/NUC-RC/03/009. Folder 201 498 359.

[28] EMA was used to indicate an evolving continental European currency between 1975 and 1979. It was replaced by the European Currency Unit (ECU) and then by the euro in 1999.

[29] A numéraire, or base value, provides a benchmark against which the value of similar goods, services, or financial instruments may be compared.

As the OEEC Convention was in the final stage of drafting, a few potential signatories insisted on reservations with respect to various articles. Austria and Germany had difficulty with the idea of channeling all third-party liability to the operator of an installation and, because of moral hazard concerns, the principle that such liability could be limited. To be sure, the idea assumed that an exception to generally accepted tort law would be necessary if the nuclear industry was to develop. Channeling regardless of fault implied that efficiency trumped justice. In short, it rested on the notion that risks associated with this particular industry needed to be broadly distributed, and that retribution against someone who might someday really be at fault would not be permitted.

Partly ameliorating this accommodation was the assumption that installation operators would insist that suppliers have their own insurance against which could in principle make claims. Germany and Austria nevertheless sought to add the following rider: "National law may, however, continue to provide that persons other than the operator may be liable besides him on condition that these persons will be discharged by insurance or other financial security from this liability, including defence against unjustified actions." Other countries vigorously opposed this addition, for they insisted that channeling was "a central feature of the Convention."[30]

Following further consultations with experts and a series of compromises among the principal contracting member-states, the draft Convention on Third Party Liability in the Field of Nuclear Energy (hereafter called the Paris Convention) was submitted to the Council of the OEEC on 8 January 1960. The convention made installation operators exclusively liable for damage caused by accidents as well as during the transport of nuclear materials to or from specific sites. The term "installations" was intended to cover reactors; factories manufacturing, processing, reprocessing or enriching nuclear substances; and facilities for storing such substances. Where common international legal practice conditioned similar liability on negligence or fault, the convention focused on radioactive contamination and labelled such liability as "strict," whether or not fault could be determined. It then limited that liability to a minimum of what would later amount to SDR 5 million and a maximum of SDR 15 million. Each nuclear installation in a contracting member-state was expected to cover this potential liability with adequate financial security, most commonly to be provided by private insurance and reinsurance

[30] OECD/NUC-RC/01/009 Folder 201 498 351.

arrangements. Claims made by injured parties were bound to be submitted within ten years of any accident; no right to compensation would be considered valid after that time. Moreover, no discrimination in terms of nationality, residence, or domicile was to be permitted. Finally, the convention specified that the courts of the country where an accident occurs would adjudicate all compensation claims. On the basis of reciprocity, the terms of the convention were to apply across the territorial borders of all signatories, including territorial seas.

A period of detailed debate and clarification ensued. One interesting question was whether facilities mainly devoted to the production of nuclear materials for military purposes were covered.[31] Since it was often impossible to make clear distinctions in this regard, the consensus view was that they were included. Insurers also raised a number of other specific issues, including queries on the criteria used to determine whether an "accident" was caused by intentional safety measures that could result in the release of radioactive materials. In general, the consensus again was to err on the side of inclusion. In short, what insurers mainly received by virtue of the convention's terms was certainty about the ultimate amount of their potential liabilities on a per installation basis.

Even as the ratification process for the Paris Convention was underway, the signatories began negotiating the Brussels Supplementary Convention of 1963 and an additional protocol.[32] With the expectation that the maximum liability amount per incident would be SDR 150 million, an adequate number of signatories had ratified the entire package by January 1964. Under the auspices of the OECD's ENEA, the Paris and Brussels Conventions as well as the protocol came into effect on January 28.[33] The two conventions operate jointly; a state may not join the Brussels Convention without having already signed the Paris Convention.

Henceforth, every nuclear installation in the signatory countries must have registered financial security equivalent to the required amount.

[31] Correspondence between Minister Haunschild of Germany and Jerry Weinstein (OEEC), March to April 1961. OECD/NUC-RC/5/001, Folder 201498565.

[32] In September 1961, the OEEC was reconstituted at the Organization for Economic Cooperation and Development (OECD), with eighteen European member-states plus the United States and Canada.

[33] Formally established on February 1, 1958 with the name European Nuclear Energy Agency, with the United States participating as an associate member, the name was changed on April 20, 1972 to the Nuclear Energy Agency of the OECD after Japan became a member.

That is, each installation had to demonstrate its ability to provide compensation to that level for injury to or loss of life of any person, and for damage to or loss of any property caused by a nuclear accident, including during the transport of nuclear substances to and from their physical site. Any damage to a nuclear installation itself was specifically not covered. Facilities that did not involve high levels of radioactivity, such as those for uranium mining and milling or for the production of radioisotopes, were exempted from the convention and were expected to be covered by general tort law in force within the signatory countries themselves. The convention also applied to nuclear substances in transport from one nuclear operator to another, with liability imposed on the operator sending the nuclear substances since it was normally considered to be responsible for its packing and containment.

In the case of transport to or from operators in states that were not party to the convention, special provisions ensured that an operator the convention regime applied to would be held liable. In 1968, the NEA Steering Committee recommended that the convention cover nuclear incidents occurring or nuclear damage suffered on the high seas, and in 1971 it recommended that the convention apply to damage suffered in a Paris Convention state even if the nuclear incident occurred in a state not party to the convention. Most of the signatories soon adopted those recommendations. For its part, the United States continued to accept concomitant obligations, but only as affirmed under its preexisting Price-Anderson regime. The main point of agreement remained that nuclear operators outside the United States would bear sole responsibility for the financial consequences of accidents, thus averting complex litigation in their aftermath.

The Paris Convention and the Brussels Supplementary Conventions (BSC) were revised significantly in 2004. They included various technical amendments, but the revisions mainly aimed to increase liability limits to more realistic levels. It clarified a tiered system of compensation, with the first Paris Convention tier provided by the station operator (not less than EUR 700 million via its own resources and backstops from private insurance pools and reinsurers), a second BSC tier guaranteed by the national government of the territory where the station was located (not less than EUR 500 million), and a third BSC tier of up to but not less than EUR 300 million provided by pledges of public funds from all contracting parties to the BSC according to a specified formula. Thus, the 2004 Paris Convention-BSC regime makes available up to but not less than EUR 1.5 billion to compensate for any incident of nuclear damage in the signatory countries. The Paris Convention as modified by the 2004 protocol encompasses Belgium, Denmark, Finland, France, Germany, Greece, Italy, the Netherlands, Norway, Portugal, Slovenia (formerly a member of the Vienna Convention), Spain, Sweden, Switzerland, Turkey, and the United Kingdom, while the BSC as modified by the 2004 protocol encompasses all of the Paris Convention states except Greece, Portugal, and Turkey. After Switzerland and Norway deposited their instruments of ratification, both the Paris Convention and the BSC as modified in 2004 became effective on January 1, 2022. (Austria and Luxembourg signed on but had not ratified by that date.)

THE PARALLEL EVOLUTION OF A THIRD-PARTY LIABILITY REGIME IN THE IAEA

Since the same essential risk issues associated with nuclear energy production apply outside the boundaries of OECD states, again it might have been more efficient to have drafted a global convention on third-party liability under the auspices of the IAEA. After all, President Eisenhower's 1953 speech at the UN had already kickstarted the development of a specialized agency tasked with managing the global aspects of nuclear technologies and by 1956, eighty-one nations had approved its statute. Based in Vienna, at the crossroads of member-states on opposite sides of the Iron Curtain, its principal efforts focused on discouraging the proliferation of nuclear weapons.[34] Since it was also dedicated to encouraging the safe development of nuclear energy for peaceful purposes, it could well have also taken the lead on international burden sharing in the event of accidents at generating stations.

But comprehensive international negotiations on technical questions have rarely been straightforward. Clubs of like-minded countries reach agreements more quickly. The Paris and Brussels Conventions were nearing completion when parallel negotiations within the IAEA began to move forward. Personal and institutional rivalries may well have impeded convergence, but the more likely sources of contention both within the IAEA and between it and the OECD arose from ideological tensions among member-states and from differences posed by their different stages of development. A broader normative as well as operational consensus would have to emerge more indirectly.

34 Fischer, *History of the International Atomic Energy Agency*, 231–232.

By May 1963, the Vienna Convention on Civil Liability for Nuclear Damage opened for signatures. Although it took many years for states with any nuclear capacity to actually ratify the agreement, it came into force in 1977, when enough signatories, mainly from Eastern Europe and Latin America, had signed on. The Russian Federation did not sign on until 1996, and it finally ratified the convention in 2005.[35] Although similar in design to the Paris Convention, this convention had differences in terms of liability and territorial limits as well as arrangements for the settlement of disputes. For example, although the liability of operators was technically considered unlimited in the Vienna Convention, contracting parties were able to specify actual limits at their own discretion. The results were wide differences among them. Although it was open to all UN members, forty had ratified it by 1977.

Both the Paris and Vienna regimes remained based on the principle of absolute operator liability. Still, in addition to actual liability amounts, they also embodied distinctive approaches and limits on accidents occurring during transport, time limits on bringing liability claims forward, and categories of losses covered.[36] For a global industry of technology suppliers, this was problematic. Specialists therefore had to hammer out compromises to render them compatible. Until the late 1980s, the two evolving regimes still operated in relative isolation from one another. In principle, this meant that an accident occurring in a member-state of the Paris Convention that damaged the territory and citizenry of a member-state of the Vienna Convention, and vice versa, would not be covered. The issues were not easily resolvable. Among the questions that richer members of the Paris Convention raised, for example, was why their own industries and treasuries should be liable for accidents potentially caused by weak management in poorer and less advanced countries. For their part, some members of the Vienna Convention asked why they should be liable for accidents in countries with much more expansive nuclear installations. The 1986 accident at Chernobyl concentrated many people's minds on such questions of distributive justice.

35 The Soviet Union paid no compensation to other states in the wake of the 1986 Chernobyl disaster. After its dissolution, Russia denied responsibility for an accident that had occurred in Ukraine. After 2005, it could claim that the accident happened before it signed and well before it ratified the convention.

36 Schmid/Weinstein correspondence, May 14, 1969. OECD/NUC-RC/03/009 Folder 201 498 359.

In the wake of the accident, the NEA and the IAEA convened a joint conference.[37] By 1988, a joint protocol was finally negotiated to bring the two agreements on third-party liability for nuclear accidents into a reasonable degree of mutual applicability. In eleven articles, the protocol specified the principles of third-party liability and reciprocity across the member-states of both conventions. The protocol assigned primary governmental responsibility for any accident to the member-state hosting the damaged installation or the installation that transported materials to it. In turn, the terms of the convention that the member belonged to would apply.[38] Liability amounts, which remained diverse, were as previously negotiated within the respective conventions. That was a start, but it only begged more practical questions, certainly for the United States, which was not a signatory to either convention even though it remained a leading source of technology as well as fuel supplies.

Specifically, some still wondered about the limitations inherent in conventions focused on the liability of the operators of nuclear plants, whether legally or economically channeled, and therefore about the limits of national civil laws. When those limits were reached, the international legal liability of states hosting such facilities remained ambiguous. In 1990, a standing committee of the IAEA was established to examine related questions. Seventeen meetings of experts over the next seven years led to a draft Protocol to Amend the Vienna Convention. The protocol increased the minimum financial security pledged for nuclear installations from USD 5 million to SDR 300 million. It was opened

[37] For excellent comparative and historical analyses of the conventions and their updates, see Julia A. Schwartz, "International Nuclear Third Party Liability Law: The Response to Chernobyl," in *International Nuclear Law in the Post-Chernobyl Period* (Paris: OECD, 2006); Norbert Pelzer, "Nuclear Accidents: Models of Reparation," in *Nuclear Non-Proliferation in International Law*, Vol. 3, edited by Jonathan Black-Branch and Dieter Fleck (The Hague: T.M.C Asser Press, 2016), 355–401; Michael Faure, "Liability and Compensation Mechanisms as Tools to Reduce Disaster Risks," *Stanford Journal of International Law* 52 (2016): 117–119; Raphael Hephron, Stephen Ashley, and William Nuttall, "The Global Nuclear Liability Regime post-Fukushima Daiichi," *Progress in Nuclear Energy* 90 (2016): 1–10.

[38] A separate and related convention remained in force: the Convention Relating to Civil Liability in the Field of Maritime Carriage of Nuclear Material. Agreed in 1971, it specified legal channeling to the installation operator for damage caused in the maritime transport of nuclear materials to that installation. The terms of the Paris or Vienna Conventions applied. The convention entered into force in 1975. A predecessor convention signed in 1962 covered damage caused by accidents on nuclear ships; its liability scheme and limits operate similarly to those that would apply to nuclear installations on land in Paris or Vienna Convention member-states.

for signature on September 29, 1997, and finally entered into force six years later after five signatory states had ratified their commitments.

An important change that was incorporated into both the 1997 Vienna Convention and later into the 2004 Paris Protocol was the extension of the prescription period for legal actions in respect of personal injury or death. Originally, the time within which a victim could claim damages for personal injury or death was only ten years in both cases. This was not very helpful when, for example, radiation-induced cancers might be expected to appear many years after exposure to radiation during a nuclear incident. The time limit in respect of such actions is now thirty years. Neither the 1997 Vienna Convention nor the 2004 Paris Protocol, nor any development since then, relieved a nuclear operator of liability for damage where a nuclear incident results from a terrorist act, as long as the act is not considered to be an act of armed conflict, interstate hostilities, civil war, or insurrection. The onus remains on operators to secure their facilities to prevent damage even in such imaginable circumstances.

When it came to both the risk of terrorism and the thirty-year prescription period, insurers were very reluctant, at first, to provide coverage up to the increased liability amounts largely because the risks were extremely difficult to assess and therefore posed difficulties for determining premiums. The same could be said about coverage for "preventive measures" and damage to the environment, or the "costs of reinstating an impaired environment" under the new protocols (both Paris and Vienna). Over the years, however, the insurance industry has adapted and found capacity for all of these risks, albeit in some cases with separate premiums. Actual premium determination, regardless of which risks are being considered, depends also upon assessments of the technical safety as well as the political risks (including the risk of terrorism) associated with any specific installation.[39]

Also in September 1997, parties to both the Paris and Vienna Conventions, together with the United States, agreed to a new Convention on Supplementary Compensation for Nuclear Damage (CSC). The CSC was intended to represent a distinctive step toward a unified global

[39] See Julia Schwartz, "Liability and Compensation for Third Party Damage Resulting from a Nuclear Incident," in *Principles and Practice of International Nuclear Law*, edited by Kimberly Sexton Nick and Stephen G. Burns (Paris: Nuclear Energy Agency/Organization for Economic Co-operation and Development, 2022), 409–444. In the same volume, also see Sebastiaan M. S. Reitsma and Mark G. Tetley, "Insurance of Nuclear Risks," 445–466.

regime. At its heart, it specified that it would supplement and enhance the two principal existing agreements as well as "complying national legislation." In this way, the United States was able to be listed in an Annex to the Convention and its Price-Anderson rules were deemed to be acknowledged ("grandfathered") as essentially in compliance with the intent of the CSC, even though they continued to differentiate between legal and economic channeling of liabilities for nuclear accidents. Installation operators were required to have on hand not less than SDR 300 million in capital resources or insurance cover. A second tier of coverage was also agreed to, although its actual amounts would depend upon the number of contracting states. Roughly speaking, about SDR 330 million in coverage was anticipated in that tier, half of which would compensate for damage in or outside the so-called Installation State and, if that did not prove adequate in specific cases, the additional half would cover damage outside the Installation State. If, however, the Installation State had "ensured without discrimination" that at least SDR 600 million in *ex ante* coverage was available, then the second tier of coverage provided jointly by the contracting parties would be available for excess damage both inside and outside the Installation State. In other words, the CSC did not establish a middle tier of liability coverage to be provided individually by installation states.[40]

When the Paris Convention was updated in 2004, it maintained the absolute liability of (and channeling of all claims to) installation operators, regardless of fault. It raised the required minimum limits of liability in time and amount and removed a former exception for accidents caused by natural disasters. As a concession to members focused on the issue of moral hazard, the update permitted contracting parties to impose unlimited liability on installation operators, provided that the actual financial security in place was not less than the new minimum level specified.[41]

[40] According to Julia Schwartz, under the CSC the SDR 600 million alternative to the two separate tiers was introduced simply because many countries held the view that dedicating 50 percent of the secondary fund to transboundary damage only was discriminatory in nature and against their generally accepted legal principles. Belgium and Germany, for example, both raised this issue during the negotiations to adopt that convention. Personal communication, April 12, 2022.

[41] However, a contracting party to the 2004 Paris Protocol may also determine that, "having regard to the nature of the nuclear installation involved and to the likely consequences of a nuclear incident originating therefrom" the risks are such (i.e., small enough) that it may reduce an operator's specific liability to EUR 70 million for each incident at an installation and EUR 80 million for the carriage of nuclear materials.

Additional tiers of coverage as originally negotiated in the Brussels Supplementary Convention remained, but at increased minimum levels.

Signatories to the CSC all claim that their national laws are in basic conformity when it comes to managing nuclear liabilities even if they continue to differ in important respects. Fourteen members of the Vienna Convention (including Ukraine but not including the Russia Federation) have signed. Italy was the first member of the Paris Convention to have signed. The United States ratified the agreement in 2008.[42] Japan followed in 2015. The convention came into force in April 2015. India ratified in 2016, and Canada in 2017. China, South Korea, and Pakistan remained outside.[43]

A TEMPORARY PATCHWORK QUILT, OR AN EMBRYONIC GLOBAL REGIME?

One might imagine a more efficient and just nuclear liability regime on a global scale. In principle, a universal treaty open to all states and with disputes resolvable under a clear public international law would have been possible. However, the nuclear-capable states at the core of the system since the 1950s divided on basic economic and political questions. Those in the communist camp went their own way, while the capitalist states chose to maximize the role of private industry in the production of nuclear energy. From the start, the private industry approach entailed recourse to civil law to govern prospective liability for damage caused

[42] In 2007, the US Congress also passed the US Energy Independence and Security Act. One of its provisions specified that if an accident of a commercial nuclear nature occurred outside the USA, nuclear suppliers would be required to reimburse the federal government for the amount the US government would owe under the CSC's second tier, which suggested a maximum contingent liability in the range of USD 150 million.

[43] IAEA officials concede that the signatories to the Paris Convention are expanding and deepening their relationships with one another at a faster clip than their Vienna counterparts. Concerns among the latter range from historical legacies connected with other environmental disasters, such as the 1984 Bhopal tragedy in India, to the costs of premiums for contingent liability protection expected even from non-nuclear countries. Some might also be relying implicitly on prevailing winds to carry accidental radiation away. Measures such as using UN rates of assessment to adjust premiums have assuaged some concerns, since relatively poor countries pay in much less than richer ones. Some counterarguments against not joining or against resisting lifting limits on coverage rest on the proposition that in the event of an accident, the processing of claims for convention members will be more efficient than any alternative. In this regard, convention proponents are therefore supporting routine exercises, akin to bank stress tests, to probe the capacities of existing private-sector claim and settlement procedures. Interviews, Vienna, May 5, 2022.

to third parties by accidents. The uncertainty surrounding that liability, especially in cases involving transboundary damage, and the special nature of radiation damage over time, implied unending conflicts between national tort regimes and inestimable future loss exposures. No global industry could develop under such a cloud of uncertainty.

It remains debatable whether the industry should ever have emerged and whether it should persist tomorrow. With the urgent need to reduce greenhouse gases coinciding with rapidly growing demand for electricity, however, it looks set for further development. In this context, the actual environmental impact of mining and enriching radioactive raw materials, the rise of terrorism and other sources of instability in controlling systems, and the increasing availability of alternative energy sources hardly paint a rosy scenario for the industry as it has actually evolved over the past century. In addition, the challenge of safely handling and storing spent fuel has been deeply problematic from its inception. Indeed, myriad measurable risks as well as profound uncertainties remain when it comes to understanding the impact of past, present, and future exposure to radioactive materials.[44] It remains to be seen if innovative designs and breakthroughs in waste disposal and storage will dramatically change risk perceptions. In any event, many more reactors look set to be operating by the end of the twenty-first century in China, India, and much of the developing world. What is certain is that all associated risks will not be contained within their borders.

It bears repeating that no private-sector involvement in this sector (wherever it was permitted) would have been or would continue to be possible in the absence of insurance mandates imposed by governments. Moreover, private insurance would not have been feasible without arrangements for channeling liability and then limiting it. On this basis, pragmatic, incremental steps over time have led many nuclear-capable states and their neighbors to weave a patchwork of regional and now intricate global arrangements for sharing the burdens of third-party liability for future accidents. Those arrangements engage and bind diverse public authorities while providing an adequate degree of legal certainty to open the door to private investment activities.

Although it's not yet universally shared, the essential impulse toward joint governance among the willing in this sector has come not only from the instinctive inner logic of insurance but also from the compelling

[44] Robert A. Jacobs, *Nuclear Bodies: The Global Hibakusha* (New Haven, CT: Yale University Press, 2022).

narratives and dynamic strategies of insurance and reinsurance providers in an unavoidably transboundary context. The result has been the pooling and diversification of risks once considered uninsurable, the harnessing of private-sector capacities to bear an increasing share of those risks, and, necessarily, experiments with practical regulatory instruments to manage associated moral hazards. One significant consequence has been the effective enlistment of private insurers and reinsurers by states in the cause of preventive governance. The existing conventions converge on one purpose. Once consistent policies are in place, the interests of insurers, nuclear installations, and host states are expected to align in that cause. Intrusive inspections, policy reviews, and legal conventions – all monitored and reinforced by both public and private action – aim at keeping those interests aligned.

The acknowledged dean of legal scholars in this field, Norbert Pelzer, sets out more fully the key features of the admittedly still partial regime as follows. "Liability without fault (strict liability) of the operator of a nuclear installation—exclusive (absolute) liability of the operator (legal channeling)—limitation of liability in amount and in time—mandatory financial security to cover liability—exclusive competent court (dispute settlement)—recognition and enforcement of judgements—equal treatment of all victims."[45] As Pelzer and Schwartz have both emphasized, moreover, the evolving regime still encompasses a range of ambiguities and as-yet-unmet aspirations for universal membership.[46] In addition, many current members have lodged reservations of one sort or another. Elements of the linked conventions also remain disputable, both because of physical questions regarding the effects of long-term radiation exposure and political differences on the justice of the strict legal or economic channeling of liabilities.

Nevertheless, unlike the dream of perfect redress for readily imaginable damage to all third parties deriving from nuclear accidents, this incomplete regime does promise the reasonable amount of compensation required for the public–private partnerships at the center of a globalizing industry to persist. Since the regime began its evolution, private investment in nuclear energy production has become feasible and arguably rendered that production safer. Indeed, private insurers and reinsurers (who are focused as ever on reducing the risks they're exposed to) are typically empowered by the terms of the contracts they accept to

[45] Pelzer, "Nuclear Accidents," 356.
[46] Schwartz, "International Nuclear Third-Party Liability Law."

inspect reactor sites and transport lines regularly and to put pressure on operators to improve safety.

The regime within which private firms play such delegated regulatory roles has actually been constructed at practicable midpoints on an economic spectrum between private power and public authority and on a legal spectrum between the purely national and the ideally global. As such, it provides an example of how preventive risk governance can work in the lower left-hand box of Figure 3.1 from Chapter 3, where the risks involved are reasonably well understood and the time horizon of potentially large liabilities is long. A transnational normative consensus evolves gradually in the background.

Private insurance and reinsurance facilitated by public mandates as well as collaborative public reinsurance can't prevent disasters with certainty, but together they can play vital roles in reducing plausible risks. With this hybrid insurance experiment in mind, flaws in the alternative scenario are easy to spot. In China and a few other places, the state apparently accepts full responsibility for accidents. What that actually means for people living near nuclear installations as well as for those in other countries living downwind is worth probing. Indeed, it raises the very questions that our technologically interdependent world must continue trying to answer directly.

Relatively small releases of radioactivity from nuclear generating stations have tested evolving liability arrangements ever since the dawn of the industry in the 1950s. The much larger disasters of Chernobyl and Fukushima Daiichi revealed their limits. The regime signified by the Paris and Vienna Conventions and the bridges between them represent steps in a necessary direction. Of course, it could collapse in the years ahead, or it could be improved and extended. But for our purposes, the developing regime stands out as a clear example of how the idea of insurance-as-governance can inspire globalizing political practice.

Realists may continue to depict the regime as yet another modest exercise in voluntary intergovernmentalism. In extremis, even sovereign signatories that have ratified the conventions can in principle walk away, though the costs they would then have to bear would likely be high and rising over time. At present, moreover, the amounts of cover provided by private insurers under the conventions remain modest. Plant owners and the governments behind them have also tended to resist the significant premium increases necessary to induce insurance and reinsurance providers to accept greater shares of potential future liabilities. Those same governments remain wary as well of reinforcing cartel-like behavior among insurance pools. Like most private insurance purchasers, perhaps they also tend to excessively discount the probabilities and costs of future accidents. It is true that all parties involved in this industry, including the consumers of nuclear-generated electricity, voluntarily confront readily understandable trade-offs.

But a more ambitious interpretation of the story recounted in this chapter is justified. Transnational nuclear law, like all public law, is advancing within complex social and economic environments. The tightest bonds underlying trust are now mainly found at the national level, but also increasingly at the regional level. Material ties that bind in this arena of risk governance are nevertheless becoming visible across regions. They reflect rapidly deepening mutual interests in burden sharing and resilience during and after imaginable future emergencies. They also reinforce mutual interests in prevention to forestall such emergencies. The process of regime building in this case is far removed in kind from fantasies of easily reversible policy integration across pristinely sovereign borders. With over half of the world's nuclear reactors now covered by the evolving liability regime, it is hard not to discern the integrationist impulse driving an innovative sectoral governing system forward in an ever more interdependent world. Despite the profound and as yet unmet challenge posed by existing and expected stockpiles of radioactive waste, pressures are rising for more nuclear generating capacity, especially because of rapidly expanding demand for electricity in a deteriorating global climate. In this context, the evolving liability regime looks set to become much more important.

Deep and dense political interests are working to expand the capacities of the private sector to bear more of the calculable risks associated with nuclear power generation. Serious political dynamics are also at work to discourage states from abrogating undeniable systemic responsibilities under conditions that may always be defined by irreducible uncertainties.[47] There is an intricate process underway to build and

[47] In this regard, industry leaders are focused on developments within China. As its society changes and the domestic nuclear energy sector expands, they sense rising concerns within China's central government about the costs of future accidents. They aren't worried about the basic safety of Chinese plants, which are being built in alignment with best industry standards and with excellent technology. Government regulators are said to be strong and assertive, but they are also increasingly aware of the risk burden the public sector alone is being asked to bear. In this context, global insurance providers are carefully watching for signals of durable market opening and a willingness to incentivize the deployment of other pressures for reinforcing safe practices at the plant level.

strengthen a global regime to govern the potential third-party liabilities of the generators of nuclear power. Private insurance markets, reinsurance pools, and, ultimately, national fiscal authorities are all implicated in a complex, adaptive, and inherently integrated system.

Long before it is perfected, however, the nuclear third-party liability regime may serve as an exemplar for other sectors inevitably exposed to transboundary risks and sources of uncertainty. Can helpful analogies be drawn? I address that question in Chapter 6 in the arena of globalizing capital markets.

6

Systemic Capital Market Risks and the Politics of Improvisation

> The decadent international but individualistic capitalism, in the hands of which we found ourselves after the War, is not a success. It is not intelligent, it is not beautiful, it is not just, it is not virtuous – and it doesn't deliver the goods. In short, we dislike it, and we are beginning to despise it. But when we wonder what to put in its place, we are extremely perplexed.
>
> —John Maynard Keynes, "National Self-Sufficiency"

Capital markets are the Achilles heel of global capitalism. They move the system forward, but their history repeatedly reminds us of the danger of leaving them unprotected. When individuals are free to move their capital through them and around the world, the tension at the core of the international system is exposed. Even capitalist states sometimes pursue interests that conflict with the idea of maximum liberty for individuals, firms, or other states endowed with capital. In the wake of World War I, Keynes put his finger on the tension in the epigraph that introduces this chapter.

States seek to control the capital markets upon which they depend. But they sometimes also open them up, both to attract foreign capital and to provide outlets for national investments abroad. This makes them harder to control, or, more precisely, to keep stable with national regulatory and supervisory policies and practices alone. Looking back on the turbulent markets of the 1930s, for example, Keynes was hardly the only observer to see international financial instability as a harbinger of war. However, since the end of World War II and despite crises and attendant backsliding, a trend toward capital market openness has gathered pace. Mindful of past sorrows, banks and other intermediaries, as well as the governments licensing and overseeing them, have sought new ways to cover the rising risks involved. Their joint project may accurately be viewed as an increasingly complex experiment in global reinsurance-as-governance.

OPEN MARKETS, BOUNDED POLITICS

Accelerating during the 1970s, the unfettering of international capital flows reflected a complicated and quite technical series of national policy decisions. The political strategies permitting them were not always easy to discern, as was the case in the first great financial globalization of the late nineteenth century. During both eras, however, periodic systemic crises always brought politics back to the fore.

Banks are at the core of vital national payments' systems. In the normal course of their operations, they confront a time inconsistency problem. They take in short-term deposits or investments and typically use them to make longer-term loans and investments. When depositors lose confidence, either because of specific institutional problems or because of a generalized panic, intermediaries can face demands for deposit redemption that they cannot readily meet on short notice. Well-run private (i.e., not state-owned) banks have therefore traditionally sought to self-insure to some extent by building up callable reserves. They also often put a second line of reserves in place through correspondent arrangements with trusted counterparties. But ultimately banks have long relied on insurance and reinsurance implicitly offered by the states that license them and permit them to expand. Since the 1930s, such arrangements have become ever more explicit around the world. States have then been forced to deal more clearly with inherent moral hazard problems.

As banking markets reopened to inward and outward flows of capital, as well as to the participation of foreign financial institutions in the postwar era, national regulatory and supervisory policies had to be better coordinated. The range of those policies, moreover, had to widen as the boundaries around "banking" became blurry. In Chapter 4, for example, we noted the development of catastrophe bonds in reinsurance markets, bonds that today could well be purchased or otherwise supported by banks. Bundled syndicated bank loans, their conversion into tradable securities, collateralized debt obligations, and more speculative instruments such as credit-default swaps are other examples of financial products now crossing lines between commercial banking and markets for tradable securities that were once relatively clear. The broadening scope of bank exposures has thus complicated the roles of national central banks and governments as lenders to or investors in banks facing liquidity or solvency problems. At the same time, the gradual opening of national markets to foreign banks and other providers of financial services gave those central banks and governments even more reasons to coordinate the policies that effectively insure and reinsure increasingly interlinked markets.

Today the external exposures of large financial intermediaries recognized as systemically significant require central banks and governments to act in concert when their potential failures threaten to cascade globally. Even the implied promise to do so effectively provides official and collaborative reinsurance policies to those intermediaries. Moreover, as systemically significant governments over the past half century became more dependent on attracting external capital to balance their own fiscal and current accounts as well as to diversify their own reserves, that same reasoning increasingly applies to them. Today, they are tacitly locked into reinsurance arrangements with one another. Indeed, the prospect of a "doom loop" between leading sovereign debtors and troubled private intermediaries is hardly novel or abstract. Central Europe experienced it in an incipient form in the 1930s.[1] Eighty years later, it was experienced around the world.

With its complex risk dynamics and short time horizons during crises, the contemporary politics of global finance represents the situation described in the upper right-hand box of Figure 3.1 in Chapter 3. Many of the risks involved are short term in nature, but the market structures those risks move through like quicksilver are increasingly complex. In this chapter, I elucidate the deeper process by which global reinsurance arrangements are evolving. Although a role for regional, national, local, as well as private insurance and reinsurance arrangements in stabilizing the system has not disappeared, we have repeatedly seen leading monetary and fiscal authorities assertively step in to reinsure the system in the midst of crises. The most dangerous systemic emergencies have been managed in this way – albeit in an ad hoc fashion. Politically destabilizing effects, even inside reinsuring states, have sometimes followed. The fundamental question for the immediate future is whether the governance of systemic risks in this sector can be set on the firmer

[1] Aurel Schubert, *The Credit-Anstalt Crisis of 1931* (Cambridge: Cambridge University Press, 1992); and Marcus Nathan, *Austrian Reconstruction and the Collapse of Global Finance, 1921–1931* (Cambridge, MA: Harvard University Press, 2018).

and fairer foundation of more explicit reinsurance and supervisory arrangements among a wider group of political authorities.

HISTORICAL CONTEXT

If Chernobyl and Fukushima clarified risks in the nuclear arena, financial crises – arising in Mexico in 1982 and 1994, in East Asia in 1997, in Russia in 1998 and again in 2014, in US markets in 2008 and 2023, in Western Europe in 2012, and in many countries during the COVID-19 pandemic as well as in the wake of Russia's invasion of Ukraine – brought systemic capital-market risks clearly to the fore. As ever, the world perceived those risks through clouds of uncertainty. Since 1945, a common memory of financial shocks linked to hyperinflation, depression, fascism, and world war during the first half of the twentieth century has stimulated a persistent search for better coordinated monetary and fiscal policy responses aimed at preventing worse catastrophes.[2]

During the Great Depression, the initial answer to the underlying systemic problem was to break the circuits through which financial shocks could readily be transmitted. In a world where leading states insisted on pegging their currencies to a fixed gold value, cascading financial instability was widely viewed as contributing to the spread of debt crises that began in central Europe. Many concluded that cross-border capital flows simply needed to be curtailed. As John Maynard Keynes would put it in the article cited in the epigraph to this chapter, "Let goods be homespun whenever it is reasonably and conveniently possible, and, above all, let finance be primarily local."[3] The difficulty of actually building and then controlling the volumes of capital necessary to rebuild a world economy and expand prosperity after World War II soon rendered such advice impractical.

The revival of more open capital markets posed collective action problems for national governments. In the early postwar era they were addressed by enshrining national regulators' ultimate right and responsibility to maintain the stability of domestic financial systems and to authorize a new multilateral authority, the International Monetary Fund (IMF),

[2] Michael D. Bordo, Barry Eichengreen, Daniela Klingebiel, and Maria Soledad Martinez-Peria, "Is the Crisis Problem Growing More Severe?" *Economic Policy* 16, no. 32 (2001): 52–82; and Michael Bordo and Catherine Schenk, "Unusual, Unstable, Complicated, Unreliable, and Temporary: Reinterpreting the Ebb and Flow of Globalization," NBER Working Paper 29114, National Bureau of Economic Research, July 2021.

[3] John Maynard Keynes, "National Self-Sufficiency," *The Yale Review*, Summer 1933.

to promote necessary collaboration among its members on the management of exchange rates and foreign exchange reserves.[4] In principle, capital movements conducive to freer trade and "productive" investment would be encouraged while speculative capital flows would be discouraged. Member-states hoped that fixed but adjustable exchange rate commitments monitored by the IMF would then promote policy adjustments that would incline the overall system toward stability.[5]

From the start, the IMF offered a kind of collective insurance facility to ease those adjustments as economic circumstances changed. Member-states paid into the Fund and received a share of votes on the executive board (weighted by the relative size of their economies). They were then entitled to draw on the Fund's capital resources with increasingly stringent conditions attached. As is the case for commercial insurance providers, a permanent staff was charged with overseeing the fair application of the terms specified in the Fund's Articles of Agreement and with monitoring compliance.

Despite the general acceptance of capital restrictions of various kinds, by the late 1960s national capital markets began expanding and opening up to investors, debtors, and intermediaries from around the world. Restricting capital movements became increasingly costly in administrative, economic, and ultimately political terms. Before long, the IMF was relegated to providing insurance mainly to members who didn't have ready access to private international capital markets. Often, those members, such as Pakistan, Mexico, and Argentina, were strategically pivotal to the stability of an American-led political order.[6] Through ensuing

[4] Eric Helleiner, *States and the Reemergence of Global Finance* (Ithaca, NY: Cornell University Press, 1994); K. Cohen and Benjamin J. Cohen, *The Geography of Money* (Ithaca, NY: Cornell University Press, 1998); Rawi Abdelal, *Capital Rules: The Construction of Global Finance* (Cambridge, MA: Harvard University Press, 2007); Jeffrey Chwieroth, *Capital Ideas: The IMF and the Rise of Financial Liberalization* (Princeton: Princeton University Press, 2010); Benn Steil, *The Battle of Bretton Woods* (Princeton: Princeton University Press, 2013); Eric Helleiner, *The Forgotten Foundations of Bretton Woods* (Ithaca, NY: Cornell University Press, 2014); and Stefan Eich, *The Currency of Politics* (Princeton: Princeton University Press, 2022).

[5] On how the system worked in practice, see Beth Simmons, *Who Adjusts? Domestic Sources of Foreign Economic Policy during the Interwar Years* (Princeton: Princeton University Press, 1994).

[6] Phillip Y. Lipscy and Haillie Na-Kyung Lee, "The IMF as a Biased Global Insurance Mechanism: Asymmetrical Moral Hazard, Reserve Accumulation, and Financial Crises," *International Organization* 73. no. 1 (2019): 35–64; Mark Copelovitch, *The International Monetary Fund in the Global Economy* (New York: Cambridge University Press, 2010).

decades, the Fund's resources were stretched, even as more members were able to borrow from rapidly growing private markets.

During the 1970s, one government after another loosened controls as the owners of capital complained, lobbied, and exploited opportunities for cross-border arbitrage. Over time, few would seriously resist policies encouraging private-sector competition in markets opening on a reciprocal basis. The return to capital market openness akin to that characterizing much of the world economy before 1914 began with industrial countries' decisions to finance macroeconomic imbalances and defer fundamental domestic adjustments. By the early 1970s, an exchange rate system rigidly linked to an unstable US dollar had become untenable. The system broke down and the value of many currencies began to float more or less freely. By the 1980s, functional barriers designed during the interwar era to separate banking from stock and bond markets were lowered.

The process of financial liberalization was gradual and often marked more by acquiescence than by enthusiasm for any libertarian ideology.[7] Most countries simply faced a dearth of politically palatable alternatives as they themselves came to rely on capital inflows and as leading financial intermediaries sought competitive opportunities at home and abroad. As a result, leading governments eased restrictions on the entry of foreign intermediaries as well as constraints on the international exposures of the intermediaries they continued to license. Ultimately, their shared hope after the collapse of the original Bretton Woods exchange rate system was that freer trade and investment, a "stable system of exchange rates" overseen by the IMF's enhanced "surveillance" machinery (now including in-depth examinations of developments in integrating capital markets) and the voluntary coordination of macroeconomic policy adjustments would henceforth maintain systemic stability.[8]

Temptations to revert to widespread capital controls during market crises throughout the late 1970s and early 1980s proved short-lived.[9]

[7] Paola Subacchi, *The Cost of Free Money: How Unfettered Capital Threatens Our Economic Future* (New Haven, CT: Yale University Press, 2020); Mark Copelovitch and David Singer, *Banks on the Brink: Global Capital, Securities Markets, and the Political Roots of Financial Crises* (Cambridge: Cambridge University Press, 2020); Orfeo Fioretos, "Retrofitting Financial Globalization," in *Explaining Institutional Development in World Politics*, edited by Thomas Rixen, Lora Anne Viola, and Michael Zürn (Oxford: Oxford University Press, 2016), 68–95.

[8] Louis Pauly, *Who Elected the Bankers? Surveillance and Control in the World Economy* (Ithaca, NY: Cornell University Press, 1997).

[9] IMF staff played a long-run role in rationalizing the drift of policies influencing the global flow of capital. In the beginning the orthodoxy leaned against liberalization. By

The infrastructure linking national economies became more integrated.[10] Global wealth chains across political and sectoral boundaries were rapidly forged.[11] Tax havens and a broad range of official incentives to take full advantage of them grew apace.[12] Immediately after crises, efforts to decouple from global banking markets sometimes occurred, only to fade away in time. Whether nascent regional infrastructures, such as the Cross-border Interbank Payments Systems launched by China in 2015, would eventually challenge the post-1970s system would become an ever more important question.

Although the IMF did at times play a prominent role in maintaining that system, especially when Mexico and other emerging-market economies found themselves facing severe debt repayment problems during the 1980s, the political struggle to manage more open capital markets shifted mainly to more informal and restricted settings. Clubs such as the G7 arose, and the vagaries of capital markets very often demanded attention and shaped the agendas of their meetings. To the extent that they provided the functional equivalent of insurance to the intermediaries they licensed as well as to the markets those intermediaries interacted through, the IMF's surveillance was still considered valuable. Its

the late 1980s, it had turned 180 degrees. After the Asian crisis of the late 1990s and especially after 2008, people briefly tolerated apostasy on this score, especially for developing countries in need of temporary breathing room in a turbulent system. The internal winds shifted once again in the postcrisis period. See Atish Ghosh, Jonathan Ostry, and Mahvash Qureshi, *Taming the Tide of Capital Flows: A Policy Guide* (Cambridge, MA: MIT Press, 2018); Ilene Grabel and Kevin Gallagher, eds., "Capital Controls and the Global Financial Crisis," *Review of International Political Economy* 22, no. 1 (2015): 1–6; Maurice Obstfeld, "Evolution Not Revolution," IMF Survey (Washington, DC: International Monetary Fund, June 2016). Also see James Boughton, *Silent Revolution: The International Monetary Fund 1979–1989* (Washington, DC: International Monetary Fund, 2001).

[10] Henry Farrell and Abraham Newman, "The New Interdependence Approach: Theoretical Development and Empirical Demonstration," *Review of International Political Economy* 23, no. 5 (2016): 713–736; Sylvia Maxfield, Kindred Winecoff, and Kevin Young, "An Empirical Investigation of the Financialization Convergence Hypothesis," *Review of International Political Economy* 24, no. 6 (2017): 1004–1029. On how deepening financial interdependence could later be weaponized via sanctions and other policies, see Henry Farrell and Abraham Newman, *Underground Empire: How America Weaponized the World Economy* (New York: Henry Holt, 2023).

[11] Leonard Seabrooke and Duncan Wigan, "Global Wealth Chains," *Review of International Political Economy* (Special Section) 24, no. 1 (2017): 1–86.

[12] Ronen Palan, *The Offshore World: Sovereign Markets, Virtual Places, and Nomad Millionaires* (Ithaca, NY: Cornell University Press, 2006); Raymond W. Baker, *Invisible Trillions: How Financial Secrecy Is Imperiling Capitalism and Democracy and the Way to Renew Our Broken System* (Oakland, CA: Berrett-Koehler Publishers, 2023).

actual effect, however, was mainly to discipline indebted poor countries. Creditors and rich countries were left to discipline themselves. By the turn of the twentieth century, the tension between integrating capital markets and dis-integrated regulatory authorities was high and rising.

OPENING MARKETS AND ENCOURAGING COLLABORATIVE GOVERNANCE

Governments throughout the postwar period could have made different choices about the instruments they'd use to meet or finance their external obligations. At Bretton Woods, for example, Keynes had proposed an official and mandatory clearing union built around a supranational currency. But after the unique Marshall Plan intervention, leading policymakers found that the easiest choices involved reopening and expanding financial markets – first banking markets and then securities markets. Broadening experiments in domestic financial liberalization went hand in hand with official efforts to encourage more competition *and* prudent risk-taking among "private" but still recognizably "national" champions, mainly chartered banks. Ever since the traumatic experience of runs in the 1930s, the most systemically significant banks now had access to insurance systems in their home markets that national governments effectively backed in one way or another. A prominent example is the Federal Deposit Insurance Corporation, which was established in the 1933 Banking Act.

Acquiescing in reciprocal market-opening and bolstering competitive impulses are relatively straightforward policy tasks. Fostering prudence is not, especially when implicit promises of official backstops bring with them readily understandable moral hazards. It's even more difficult to maintain public confidence when regulatory arbitrage leads to perceptibly unfair outcomes in a system without an authoritative referee.[13] Such issues were in the background when, as in the pre-1914 era, financial panics began to recur with some regularity. Moreover, new technological developments meant that the consequences spread more rapidly across both sectoral and geographic borders.[14] Governments' mutual awareness of renewed systemic risks slowly began prompting

[13] Ronen Palan, "Voice, Exit … Arbitrage: The Politics of the Modern Multinational Firm," *European Journal of International Relations* (2024): 1–24.

[14] Carmen Reinhart and Kenneth Rogoff, *This Time Is Different: Eight Centuries of Financial Folly* (Princeton: Princeton University Press, 2011).

them throughout the world to focus attention on transnational financial networks that were becoming much more complicated than their antecedents had been.[15]

Maintaining confidence in banking systems by providing the equivalent of both effective reinsurance and regulation long ago emerged as a core rationale for central banks' existence.[16] Finance ministries had led the Bretton Woods negotiations, but by the 1970s central bankers had risen to prominence in the internal governance of the IMF. Over the ensuing decades, they had learned how to collaboratively manage liquidity crises that spread quickly from troubled emerging-market economies.

Solvency crises, especially when they involved leading industrial countries, are a different matter. When it's difficult to differentiate liquidity shocks from emergencies threatening bankruptcy, when official back-up facilities prove inadequate, when banking operations can no longer be neatly separated from securities market activities, and when a cascading systemic collapse is plausibly imaginable, the lender of last resort function of central banks has to be backstopped by investors of last resort. That directly implicates governments with access to robust national treasuries and the ability to sell bonds in international capital markets. This inevitably brings us back to finance ministries, some of whom are in a stronger position than others.

Thirty years after the end of World War II, the widely shared desire for economic growth had accelerated the deepening of more open capital markets; it had also increased the risk of cascading financial instability. After every financial crisis since 1974, those same finance ministries preferred to keep their emergency powers in reserve and repeatedly to invigorate the cause of global financial stabilization by focusing less on the IMF and more on the risk assessment and containment functions of central banks and related supervisory agencies. Some also hoped that self-discipline by banks and other private financial intermediaries would limit systemic risks. When cross-border market conditions were

[15] Charles Kindleberger and Robert Aliber, *Manias, Panics, and Crashes: A History of Financial Crises* (New York: John Wiley & Sons, 1978); Hyman Minsky, *Stabilizing an Unstable Economy* (New Haven, CT: Yale University Press, 1986); Susan Strange, *States and Markets* (London: Pinter, 1988/94); Gary Gorton, *Misunderstanding Financial Crises: Why We Don't See Them Coming* (Oxford: Oxford University Press, 2012); Douglas W. Arner et al., eds., *Systemic Risk in the Financial Sector* (Waterloo, ON: CIGI Press, 2019);.

[16] Charles Goodhart and Gerhard Illing, eds., *Financial Crises, Contagion, and the Lender of Last Resort* (Oxford: Oxford University Press, 2002).

calm, such hopes seemed justified.[17] But cycles of euphoria and disappointment regularly repeated themselves.

THE CHALLENGE OF GOVERNING GLOBAL FINANCIAL RISKS

As financial markets opened and integrated across the political boundaries of both developed and developing countries throughout the 1970s, the basic governance deficiency anticipated at Bretton Woods became ever more apparent. Intergovernmental agencies such as the IMF can help recognize and measure related risks. They can identify the positive and negative spillover effects of national policy decisions and encourage prudence by regulators and intermediaries. They can provide surveillance over the wide range of policies now affecting foreign exchange reserves, and their financial assistance can help developing and emerging-market members adjust when their reserves prove inadequate. But they are not well equipped to formulate or enforce crisis-prevention policies or to manage systemic emergencies. They can provide some insurance to individual states, but they cannot provide serious insurance or reinsurance for advanced economies. They can be useful scapegoats after they provide conditional financing, but they cannot manage the often-fraught domestic politics surrounding the inevitable distribution and redistribution of crisis-driven financial losses.

Still, the construction of official instruments for collaboratively gathering reliable data and estimating risks before crises occur is no small historical achievement. Any insurance system depends upon such data. So this aspect of the work of the IMF and other specialized agencies after the 1970s bears emphasis. The League of Nations had pioneered such a data collection and assessment system at the international level in its World Economic Surveys, which the United Nations continued to produce after the war.[18] In the 1950s, the Marshall Plan agency that eventually became the Organization for Economic Cooperation and Development also began compiling and assessing similar data. For several decades now, the IMF's World Economic Outlook series and more

[17] Timothy Büthe and Walter Mattli, *The New Global Rulers: The Privatization of Regulation in the World Economy* (Princeton: Princeton University Press, 2011).

[18] Louis Pauly, "The League of Nations and the Foreshadowing of the International Monetary Fund," *Essays in International Finance*, no. 201, Princeton University, International Finance Section, December 1996, 1–47; Patricia Clavin, *Securing the World Economy: The Reinvention of the League of Nations, 1920–1946* (Oxford: Oxford University Press, 2013).

recently its Global Financial Stability reports have provided a framework for global risk assessment exercises. The World Bank and various regional development banks have also contributed to this effort. Even when such assessments and related forecasts miss the mark, the analysis behind them provides reference points for the private and public financial institutions that can provide lines of credit – insurance policies of a sort – mainly to emerging-market and developing countries.

From the early 1970s onwards, specific efforts to translate global risk assessments into workable risk-mitigation policies in key banking markets began to move away from the IMF to a more restricted group of central bankers. That group, often referred to as a club, was hosted by the Basel-based Bank for International Settlements (BIS) even before the collapse of the postwar pegged exchange rate system. (It initially overlapped with the central banking group established in 1962 to allow the IMF to supplement its capital resources through the General Arrangements to Borrow.) Established to manage reparations payments after World War I, the BIS survived attempts to close it down in favor of the IMF after the end of World War II. Having developed a profitable business managing central-bank reserves, it had the resources to host informal and low-profile meetings of monetary officials, as well as a staff of economists capable of gathering and assessing specialized data on key banking and capital markets.

The Basel Committee on Banking Supervision (BCBS), supported by BIS staff, emerged in the wake of the 1974 failures of Germany's Herstatt Bank, the US-based but internationally active Franklin National Bank, and two troubled subsidiaries of UK-centered intermediaries, Lloyds Lugano and the Israel-British Bank (IBB). The fact that Herstatt could not settle open foreign exchange contracts had knock-on effects around the world. The fraud-related Franklin National collapse around the same time clearly exposed critical gaps in supervisory responsibilities between home and host country authorities. Unanticipated fragility in the Lloyds and IBB networks did the same.

Inelegantly, and in an ad hoc manner, the central banks and bank supervisors involved in each crisis first responded by encouraging troubled banks and their correspondents at home and abroad not to cut their credit lines with one another. Central banks then provided additional liquidity to calm growing market panic and keep core payments' systems functioning. As discreetly as possible, they and sometimes their fiscal authorities also began sweeping up uncovered bank liabilities themselves. Scapegoating, the lengthy pursuit of recoveries through national legal systems, and much political theater ensued. But international markets always stabilized, and the pattern was set for the management of future systemic crises. A mix of private and public insurance arrangements would ultimately be backstopped by national lenders and investors of last resort. In other words, the monetary and fiscal capacities of implicated states would be coordinated on an ad hoc basis to provide interconnected capital markets with an ultimate layer of reinsurance. What changed over the following half-century was mainly the scale of that implicit commitment and the number of central banks and finance ministries necessarily involved at the point of systemic emergency.

By the end of 1974, in short, it was already evident that political collaboration was required in the cause of global financial stability. Emergency management would rest on it, but perhaps joint approaches to dealing with the moral hazard problem raised by market expectations of ultimate official reinsurance would also be possible. The BCBS began its work with precisely such an objective in mind. From the start, it tried to prepare for future systemic crises by engaging central banks with regulatory responsibilities and bank supervisors who in some countries walked a fine line between the public and private sectors. It provided a vehicle for pooling knowledge, sharing official data, and encouraging common supervisory standards. It also constituted a plausible political buffer for the monetary and fiscal authorities likely to be engaged in any serious future emergency. Not by coincidence, intensive private-sector work on building new, more reliable, and faster infrastructure for global payments accelerated at around the same time. For example, the Society for Worldwide Inter-bank Financial Telecommunication (SWIFT, a cooperative society licensed by Belgium) was inaugurated in 1973 to provide essential payment-messaging services to 239 banks with support from their regulators in fifteen countries.[19]

In the mid-1970s, one could still make the case that building global infrastructure for open and integrating capital markets remained at base an *intergovernmental* activity. But in practical terms, the underlying project aimed at constructing an effective *transnational* capacity to forestall serious future financial crises that would inevitably cross geographic and functional borders.[20] In essence, by collaborating on regulatory and

[19] Susan Scott and Markos Zachariadis, *The Society for Worldwide Interbank Financial Telecommunication: Cooperative Governance for Network Innovation, Standards, and Community* (Abingdon: Routledge, 2014).

[20] Charles Goodhart, *The Basel Committee on Banking Supervision: A History of the Early Years 1974–1997* (Cambridge: Cambridge University Press, 2011).

supervisory policies, club members were trying to collectively address the moral hazard problems that would confront them after every incident requiring them to deploy their joint crisis-fighting machinery.

The BCBS concentrated on the largest clearing banks' operations, which they referred to as systemically significant, and the payment linkages among them. It spawned a search for common or at least compatible bank regulatory and supervisory standards, and it pushed beyond the contentious politics of risk measurement and assessment. Today, other bodies convening in a loose Basel Process (also informally supported by BIS staff) seek to facilitate collaboration on risk assessment for the nonbanking parts of a globalizing financial system. They include groups made up of insurance supervisors, bank-deposit insurers, and stock exchanges. Harmonizing financial reporting standards, producing comparable data, and promoting stability in markets that cross geographic and functional boundaries provide the rationale for an increasingly dense and transnational web of overseers.

A quickly evolving capacity for assessing systemic risks and promoting prudent business practices initially gave the BCBS credibility. Following debt crises in Latin America in the early 1980s, its members negotiated a Concordat to clarify the respective responsibilities of cross-border banks' home and host country supervisors. It also began to draft protocols setting out minimum standards for capital reserves expected to absorb losses and reduce the likelihood that national monetary and fiscal resources would be called upon during periods of instability. The first such protocol was dubbed Basel 1.

The Basel 1 Protocol formalized an agreement to ensure that internationally active banks maintained a ratio of liquid assets necessary to meet potential obligations at 4 percent (so-called Tier 1 capital). It also commenced cooperative work programs between the BCBS and other national and regional bodies to bolster the effectiveness of prudential supervision within and beyond the banking sector narrowly defined. One of its legacies is the broadly accepted principle that regulatory rules and supervisory practices need not be identical, but that home country rules and practices should be roughly equivalent in effect and recognized as such by others. From the start, the application of that principle was bedeviled by the question of whether systemic stability defined in these terms ultimately required a mutual understanding not only of market behavior but also of what constituted fair and politically sustainable market outcomes. A key operational question would turn on how much capital systemically significant banks should hold as self-insurance against future losses, the buffer to be drawn down before official back-up facilities would have to be called upon.

The most extensive and detailed effort to rebalance the capital adequacy of cross-border market participants and to "level the playing field," the issues that were central to the BCBS standard-setting agenda, came in the Basel II accord. It was crafted in the midst of cascading crises in East Asia, Russia, Latin America, and in the United States, and came into effect in 2004. Its terms encouraged international lenders to bring sophisticated risk-management techniques more directly into their calculations of capital adequacy. The politics of policymaking through transnational clubs here reached a limit, for the national risk cultures, fundamentally reflected in banks' internal models, remained quite diverse. Internal capital adequacy modeling exercises authorized by national supervisors remained embedded in societies that continued to differ in their relative tolerances for risks of various kinds. More common rules were required to stabilize globalizing markets.

In a competitive environment that seemed routinely volatile but structurally stable, Basel II in practice encouraged excessive borrowing and speculation. The risk models at its heart turned out to be too complex and too variegated, and they exacerbated moral hazard problems. The experiment ended in tears in less than five years, but the Basel Process itself remained in place. It had established the dominant form of diplomacy by which systemic financial risks would be understood, measured, and debated. While the technocrats at its core never formally shed their national identities, they did constitute a classic "epistemic community," guided by a frustrating but continuing quest to develop common knowledge and mutual rules in the cause of global financial stability.[21] Meanwhile, the IMF continued to focus its surveillance activities on its members' foreign exchange reserves and access to regional reserve-pooling systems. In cases where such self-insurance and mutual insurance proved inadequate, as in many of its poorer members, the Fund continued to adapt its conditional liquidity facilities.

Immediately after each banking crisis since the end of the Bretton Woods pegged exchange rate system, in fact, experts claimed that more than technical innovations and insurance experiments were necessary to prevent future systemic crises. They insisted that better cross-national

[21] Abraham Newman and Elliot Posner, "Structuring Transnational Interests: The Second-Order Effects of Soft Law in the Politics of Global Finance," *Review of International Political Economy* 23, no. 5 (2016): 768–798.

coordination of fiscal and monetary policies remained necessary to mitigate the risks generated by the most important economic imbalances. But every effort to bring leading states into a deliberative process with serious incentives to coordinate key policies still ended with the international institution originally designed for such purposes, the IMF, on the sidelines. At the same time, the ideas of de-concentrating ever-more open and volatile financial markets, dramatically enhancing possibilities for diversifying the financial risks facing individuals, firms, and governments across different geographic and functional markets, and otherwise increasing the inherent resilience of freer capital markets – all proved politically unpalatable in practice.[22]

SYSTEMIC CRISES

Sixty years after the Bretton Woods Conference, the United States continued importing too much, saving too little, and relying on vast inflows of capital from China, Japan, Germany, and many middle-income and developing countries. Creditor states too came to depend upon being able to recycle their surpluses through US markets. At times, the situation looked like a happy one for cross-border financial intermediaries. Instead of encouraging macroeconomic adjustments, however, their expansion permitted imbalances to grow and regularly led to disastrous "sudden stops" in flows to vulnerable economies.

In 1999, with the so-called Asian crisis still unfolding, the leading states represented in the G7 recognized that they needed to bring large emerging-market states into dialogue on their shared interests in well-functioning capital markets. They established the G20, which soon reached an agreement to build an informal Financial Stability Forum (FSF). Central bankers, finance ministers, securities regulators, and bank supervisors from a dozen leading states, as well as representatives from various international organizations, including the IMF, were all represented in the forum. In the absence of a permanent secretariat, FSF meetings were supported mainly by a small staff borrowed from the BIS. (In 2008, delegations were invited from China and other large emerging-market economies.) The FSF's declared intention was to focus more

[22] Recall here Friedrich Hayek's historic warnings about the illusion of control in a world of profound uncertainty. Jon Danielsson, *The Illusion of Control: Why Financial Crises Happen, and What We Can (and Can't) Do about It* (New Haven, CT: Yale University Press, 2022); Friedrich Hayek, *Individualism and Economic Order*, Chicago: University of Chicago Press, 1948).

attention (in a still decentralized setting) on the systemic implications of large financial intermediaries' global operations. Less obviously, participants were also searching for a new balance in postcrisis risk mitigation strategies between the technocratic approaches favored by Europeans and the often schizophrenic free market/state regulatory approaches that the US promoted.[23] Many continued that search at the regional level. For example, Southeast Asian states developed the Chiang Mai Initiative, which eventually promised to pool foreign exchange reserves in a crisis. Similar if as yet less successful projects were launched in South America and among the members of the so-called BRICS group (Brazil, Russia, India, China, South Africa, Egypt, Ethiopia, Indonesia, Iran, and the United Arab Emirates).[24] Whether China on its own or with regional partners could build similar financial buffers with its Belt-and-Road Initiative remained to be seen.[25]

In addition to placing a spotlight on the responsibilities of local supervisors at the level of individual intermediaries, the FSF concentrated on the need for better "macroprudential policies." These included a range of instruments intended to foster the safety and stability not of individual intermediaries but of entire financial sectors from banking to insurance, which posed evident new global risks with their intensifying interconnectedness. As in every analogous effort since the early 1970s, the FSF's overarching aim was to prevent the next crisis while still allowing the system itself to encompass a diversity of national risk cultures, or, in other words, a range of fundamental values and social purposes expressed in terms of systemic-risk aversion or acceptance.[26]

The results of those discussions – consensus-based, advisory, informal, and resting on a long-run sense of reciprocity – could have been different. They could in principle have reinforced systemic financial stability

[23] Alexander Reisenbichler, "The Domestic Sources and Power Dynamics of Regulatory Networks," *Review of International Political Economy* 22, no. 5 (2015): 996–1024.

[24] Gregory Chin and Fahimul Quadir, "Rising States, Rising Donors – BRICS and Beyond," *Cambridge Review of International Affairs* 25, no. 4 (2012): 493–506.

[25] Hong Yu, *Understanding China's Belt and Road Initiative* (Singapore: Springer, 2024).

[26] Charles Lipson, "Why Are Some International Agreements Informal?" *International Organization* 45, no. 4 (1991): 495–538; Kenneth Abbott and Duncan Snidal, "Why States Act through Formal International Organizations," *Journal of Conflict Resolution* 42, no. 1 (1998): 3–32; Joost Pauwelyn, Ramses Wessel, and Jan Wouters, eds., *Informal International Lawmaking* (Oxford: Oxford University Press, 2012); and Kenneth Abbott et al., eds. *International Organizations as Orchestrators* (Cambridge: Cambridge University Press, 2015); Andrew Baker and Wesley Widmaier, "Macroprudential Ideas and Contested Social Purpose," *British Journal of Politics and International Relations* 17, no. 2 (2015): 371–380.

by establishing reliable insurance instruments backed by sufficient regulatory understandings to mitigate moral hazards. But they did not in fact prevent the sprawling systemic financial crisis of 2008 – the worst since the 1930s. Driving it were excessively loose monetary policies in key states, lax national-level regulation, remarkably high leverage ratios in key financial intermediaries, ill-conceived and poorly supervised financial innovations, and an underappreciated convergence in national business cycles. Its spark came from an unsustainable expansion in US housing markets, which US governments at all levels had excessively relied upon to fill their fiscal coffers, and deplorable risk management by a range of banks and other intermediaries that claimed to be innovating creatively in securities markets. The simultaneous exposure and collapse of the biggest and longest-running Ponzi scheme in recorded history, the Madoff scandal, did not help.[27]

Real estate-related bank failures were not new in American history. But after 2007, staggering numbers of such failures occurred. Other kinds of intermediaries also threatened to fail simultaneously, including insurance companies exposed to new kinds of financial derivatives. As the effects cascaded among counterparties around the world, the ability of existing multilateral arrangements to interrupt circuits of contagion proved inadequate. Informal intergovernmental understandings and inadequately equipped international organizations failed to prevent a full-blown systemic emergency. A second Great Depression seemed on the horizon.

Assertive ad hoc collaboration across the United States and other leading national central banks and finance ministries proved essential to containing the crisis of 2008. Whether that containment hinted at waxing or waning hegemonic power remained debatable.[28] At the crucial moment, however, cooperative efforts by others, including China, matched still-robust US financial power as basic interests in systemic stability converged. Among other things, this meant that the membership of the BCBS and other BIS-hosted clubs expanded quickly. By March

[27] Eric Helleiner, Stefano Pagliari and Hubert Zimmerman, eds., *Global Finance in Crisis* (London: Routledge, 2009); Andrew Ross Sorkin, *Too Big to Fail* (New York: Viking, 2009); Joseph Stiglitz, *Making Globalization Work* (New York: W.W. Norton, 2009); Herman Schwartz, *Subprime Nation: American Power, Global Capital, and the Housing Bubble* (Cornell: Cornell University Press, 2009); Adam Tooze, *Crashed: How a Decade of Financial Crises Changed the World* (New York: Viking, 2018).

[28] Carla Norrlof, *America's Global Advantage: US Hegemony and International Cooperation* (Cambridge: Cambridge University Press, 2010); Jonathan Kirshner, *American Power after the Financial Crisis* (Ithaca, NY: Cornell University Press, 2014).

2009, the number of countries around the Basel table grew from thirteen to twenty-seven. At the same time, the G20 restructured the FSF. The new Financial Stability Board (FSB) was now mandated to seek large increases in capital buffers, minimum liquidity ratios, and maximum leverage requirements for banks, investment funds, and other financial intermediaries bearing systemic risks.

Behind the scenes, regulatory forbearance was the order of the day, as finance ministries around the world put the key intermediaries under their ultimate control onto life support. In some cases, this entailed outright nationalization. In others, it meant providing unlimited liquidity injections and extending implicit guarantees of equity. In short, finance ministries, led by the US Treasury, had reasserted their last-resort emergency management and investing authority. Together with their central banks, their core market reinsurance functions once again became undeniable.

When the line between liquidity crises facing individual intermediaries and solvency crises implicating the system as a whole disappeared in 2008, fiscal capacity and national authorities' willingness to stand behind extraordinary and unusually coordinated monetary operations proved crucial. The United States in particular began lending and investing official resources lavishly. In early October 2008, the US Congress quickly passed and President George W. Bush immediately signed the Emergency Economic Stabilization Act, which authorized USD 700 billion mainly for institutional bailouts. The beneficiaries included most big banks, the American Insurance Group, many other financial intermediaries, and many foreign institutions operating within and across its borders. Between 2007 and 2010, 190 domestic and international firms benefited from special Federal Reserve liquidity facilities, rising to the level of USD 1.2 trillion. At the same time, massive currency swaps – some via emergency arrangements without any upper limits – were coordinated between the US, Swiss, and European central banks and eleven other advanced industrial countries.[29]

Between September 2008 and June 2009, finance ministries, related agencies, and central banks around the world announced some thirty-four systemic or institution-specific programs involving bank recapitalization, debt guarantees, asset purchases and guarantees, and increases in

[29] Timothy Geithner, *Stress Test: Reflections on Financial Crises* (New York: Crown, 2014); Daniel Drezner, *The System Worked: How the World Stopped Another Great Depression* (Oxford: Oxford University Press, 2014).

deposit insurance limits.[30] The politics of emergency management at the domestic level essentially permitted, even necessitated, informally coordinated assertive action by national fiscal authorities at the core of the system. And this time the action was backstopped by reserve-rich China, which leaned against any tendencies of intermediaries under its control to sell US liabilities in a panic and increased official outlays to stimulate economic growth. Leading governments, in short, asserted themselves informally and collectively to prevent systemic collapse.

After the emergency had subsided, the expanded size of their external balances – their financial exposure to one another – constrained any seriously independent action.[31] Over time, however, it encouraged many, including China, to gradually diversify their reserve portfolios and reduce their reliance on the US dollar. In doing so, leading states were confronted once again with the fundamental questions raised at Bretton Woods. In light of the systemic financial risks they were exposed to – effectively, in anticipation of less coordinated emergency management in the future – could they adequately build up their capacities to self-insure while still engaging in open trading and investing systems? If not, could they agree on more reliable collaborative reinsurance and supervisory arrangements to underpin those systems?

Those questions remained open after emergency conditions had subsided, and new, if still mainly informal, experiments in crisis prevention began to emerge. The BCBS and FSB, for example, moved toward more comprehensive supervision of individual cross-border financial institutions through multilateral "colleges" involving home and host-country supervisors. Following internal adjustments in voting power and staff representation that acknowledged the rise of China and other emerging-market members, the IMF also linked itself more completely to G20 discussions on what its executive board now called the global financial safety net. It clearly depicted that safety net as composed of international reserves, expanded central bank swap arrangements, regional financial support arrangements, and IMF resources often committed in tandem with funding from multilateral and national development agencies. Tied to its routine surveillance procedures, innovative IMF facilities now included insurance facilities bearing the titles of Flexible Credit Lines and Precautionary and

30 Fabio Panetta et al., "An Assessment of Financial Sector Rescue Programmes," *BIS Papers*, no. 48 (Bank for International Settlements, 2009), 8.

31 Iain Hardie and Sylvia Maxfield, "Atlas Constrained," *Review of International Political Economy* 23, no. 4 (2016): 583–613.

Liquidity Lines. The intention was to strengthen confidence in less powerful but basically well-managed member-states' markets. The idea was to quickly inject official funding early on during liquidity crises that might be generated by the unwarranted flight of private capital.[32]

At the same time, wider discussions under the continuing rubric of the Basel Process tilted away from Basel II-style discretionary supervision back toward Basel I-style capital adequacy requirements for cross-border banks. Basel III was announced in 2011, but even before its ink was dry contentious debates commenced inside national markets. Lists of intermediaries subject to the new rules were soon pared down, and some implementation deadlines were extended to 2023. Even in countries that had internally agreed to even tougher bank disciplines, most prominently in the United States, political winds soon blew in the opposite direction as competition across market segments and around the world heated up. Mounting pressures in the United States to unwind elements of the post-2008 reforms, a nearly catastrophic series of sovereign debt crises in Europe after 2012, and challenges to keep London competitive in the wake of Brexit all looked set to accelerate a new cycle of regulatory competition. Then, in late 2019, the global COVID-19 pandemic placed everything else on the backburner.

Big banks proved resilient during the early years of the pandemic, but financial portfolios around the world adjusted rapidly in response to staggering emergency government spending and unusual monetary programs pushing the cost of money to zero. US federal authorities alone allocated nearly USD 4.5 trillion to new expenditures. Others followed along the same line. With low interest rates prevailing in leading economies, a global search for yield prompted vast flows into emerging-market economies. When inflationary pressures later necessitated monetary tightening, those flows suddenly reversed. As in less dramatic but similar episodes in past decades, large debts, severe adjustment costs, and political turmoil were left behind in many countries.

With headlines focused elsewhere, BCBS members continued their dialogue and gradually agreed on a series of technical complements to capital adequacy rules designed to limit leading banks' ability to reduce their requirements through the kinds of internal risk-weighting modeling that had left many vulnerable in 2008. Systemically significant banks were expected to continue increasing their Tier 1 capital from 4 to 6 percent as well as to add supplementary capital buffers that raised their overall capital ratios to 13 percent. By 2027, a new regime some were calling Basel IV

[32] IMF, "Adequacy of the Global Financial Safety Net," Policy Paper, 26 July 2017.

was slated to include not only these explicit and generally higher requirements for bank capital, but also extra buffers during periods of high credit growth, explicit new operating ratios for leverage and liquidity, and commitments to routine stress testing. If the regime was designed and implemented wisely, equivalent strictures might also be imposed by regulatory authorities on other kinds of financial institutions – such as securities firms and private equity funds capable of competing with banks and generating similar systemic shocks. In the wake of the pandemic and the subsequent resurgence of economic nationalism and populist politics, wisdom looked to be in short supply. Bank lobbies, especially in the United States, pressed vigorously against the imposition of new capital and liquidity rules, and nonbank financial institutions as well as their clients were once again vocal about the need to loosen regulatory and tax requirements to strengthen their ability to compete.

In that context, an obvious problem persists. There is no formal systemic reinsurer and no formal systemic overseer. National decisions made during and after repeated financial crises constituted a system comprising discrete but relatively open markets interacting ever more intensively with one another. The hope remained that a future crisis across intimately entangled economies would evoke the improvised if uneven sharing of the burdens of adjustment, just as it did in 2009.

On the macroprudential questions surrounding evolving procedures for sovereign debt restructuring after the systemic crisis, serious reform proposals were grouped into two main categories.[33] In the first, creditors and debtors were left to their own devices to ensure the future sustainability of their debts. The second category included effective reinsurance arrangements – with multilateral institutions providing the functional equivalents of emergency lending, bankruptcy, and liquidation facilities. Two successive deputy managing directors of the IMF made proposals along these lines, one to empower the Fund to play the role of global lender of last resort, and the other to grant it an explicit mandate to do for the world what it has occasionally and informally done for some of its most troubled member-states by coordinating debt rescheduling and restructuring operations.[34]

Especially after investment funds operating globally made actual debt restructuring operations much more complex, actual practice evolved

[33] Edwin Truman, ed., *Reforming the IMF for the Twenty-First Century* (Washington, DC: Peterson Institute for International Economics, 2006).

[34] Sean Hagan, "Sovereign Debt Restructuring: The Centrality of the IMF's Role." *Peterson Institute for International Economics Working Paper* 20–13, 2020.

less elegantly. Under limited circumstances, ad hoc restructuring arrangements – that the Fund led in cooperation with the London and Paris Clubs after "collective action clauses" had been inserted into new debt obligation contracts – were occasionally feasible.[35] National authorities continued to differ, though, on the question of how to more reliably and legitimately manage both excessive sovereign debt and the broadly shared dilemmas posed by systemic financial risk. In consequence, the IMF would neither be adequately empowered nor decisively abandoned.

FINANCIAL RISKS, IMPLICIT INSURANCE, AND REGULATORY ADAPTATION

Policy spillovers now routinely occur across integrating but politically stratified capital markets. If the modalities of resolving repeated crises could be agreed *ex ante*, an overseer with a transnational mandate widely perceived to be legitimate would instill confidence. The IMF had an analogous mandate in the immediate postwar period. Its Articles of Agreement conferred legitimacy, even as systemic rules were sometimes honored in the breach. After the 1970s, regime complexity, informality, and normative ambiguity failed to have a similar effect. Ad hoc crisis management did succeed, but efforts to prevent the next and more serious crises typically faltered as competitive pressures gradually reasserted themselves. States once again sought to attract the same sources of jobs, wealth, and power. The private financial intermediaries they oversaw sought higher market shares and more profits. Underneath related technical debates over regulatory arbitrage lay deeper concerns within the societies governed by those states about distributive justice. Although they benefited in an aggregate sense from the deepening of competitive markets, globally mobile owners of financial assets seemed to be taking a rapidly growing share of those benefits. If the continuing integration of capital markets ultimately requires underlying official reinsurance arrangements and reliable sovereign debt restructuring facilities, the absence of coherent and undoubted collaboration among the governments of states threatens to become an increasingly acute problem.

[35] Chris Brummer, *Soft Law and the Global Financial System: Rule Making in the Twenty-First Century* (Cambridge: Cambridge University Press, 2012); Louis Pauly, "The Old and the New Politics of Financial Stability," *Journal of Common Market Studies* 47, no. 5 (2009): 955–975; Stephen Brooks and Eric Helleiner, "Debt Politics as Usual?" *International Affairs* 93, no. 5 (2017): 1085–1105.

In theory, there's an alternative "solution." Societies around the world with their own distinctive, if still interdependent, goals and preferences could welcome financial fragmentation and diversification. De-risking would not technically be the objective. The collective preference would allow freer and less concentrated markets to accommodate necessary economic adjustments, act as systemic shock absorbers, and enhance societal resilience in the face of uncertainty. The system would allow sovereign defaults to occur, permit unrestrained digital currency and crypto asset speculation, and let efficient market forces do their work without interference. At most, collaborating national authorities would simply be left to clean up after crises.

Despite the dimensions of the 2008 crisis, and despite some limited moves by host countries demanding that foreign firms hold more capital locally to reduce the probability of future runs, the fact remains that still-globalizing financial markets continue moving in the opposite direction of the libertarian dream.[36] Few markets have become less concentrated or less complex.[37] After the crisis of 2008 subsided, renewed prudential limits at the national level were not entirely rolled back, but competitive pressures on them built quickly.[38] The chimera of decentralized finance and free-market discipline disappears during every crash and rises again during every recovery.

The true dimensions of the deepening collective action problem that systemic financial risk poses are partly obscured by the specific policy arenas within which particular interests and priorities come into conflict. The technocratic politics of risk measurement, assessment, and insurance are more tractable and fluid right after crisis conditions subside. Cooperation on new standards and reciprocal supervisory practices can be reinforced at that point. But longer-term differences in risk cultures, supervisory traditions, and discrete social preferences reassert themselves as soon as cross-border competition heats up and regulatory arbitrage kicks back in.

Financial crises in the past have sometimes forced the restructuring of political institutions. The modern state itself is, in this sense, partly an outcome of systemic risk conflicts. Its fiscal core represents in

[36] Sebastian Mallaby, "Globalization Resets," *Finance and Development* 53, no. 4 (2016).

[37] Stephen Bell and Andrew Hindmoor, *Masters of the Universe, Slaves of the Market* (Cambridge, MA: Harvard University Press, 2015).

[38] Eric Helleiner, *The Status Quo Crisis: Global Financial Governance after the 2008 Meltdown* (Oxford: Oxford University Press, 2014); Ilene Grabel, *When Things Don't Fall Apart: Global Financial Governance and Developmental Finance in an Age of Productive Incoherence* (Cambridge, MA: MIT Press, 2017).

essence pooled resources and the promise to stand behind fundamental economic activity. Taxes, though typically involuntary, are like premiums paid for insurance cover. Something like a global tax system is already developing as a transnational, if informal, fiscal and monetary capacity effectively reinsures large intermediaries in open markets – and the creditors and debtors represented on both sides of their balance sheets. The citizenships of firms and individuals may remain segmented, but financial crises since the early 1970s have forged a wide-enough realization of our shared fate to sustain deeply collaborative arrangements for risk assessment and the decisive management of emergencies. Decisively preventing such emergencies, however, remains very much a work in progress. It may well prove impossible to complete that work in an uncertain and more complex world. But the quiet consensus that paying insurance premiums and absorbing regulatory costs to cover macro risks seemed politically tolerable, as long as they were not called "taxes" and as long as the determination of their levels would remain subject to competitive national contests. The situation suggests the continuing practical and rhetorical functionality of reinsurance-as-governance, now extended informally beyond the historical limits of strictly calculable risk and sovereign authority.

Adapting the IMF's mission, bolstering the Basel Process, building up FSB, and encouraging dynamic central banking networks might then accurately be viewed as representing important aspects of a movement toward official reinsurance and reliable collaboration at global scale. But there's an obvious backlash to the mutual obligations implied when issues of jurisdiction, representation, justice, and fairness must be addressed formally. Indeed, inside the United States legislative and judicial moves in the aftermath of the 2008 crisis, triggered in substantial part by justified perceptions that the benefits of official intervention had mainly and excessively benefited the richest people in the country, threatened to rein in executive discretion during future crises. Countermovements elsewhere toward strengthening self-insurance through more reserve accumulation, and toward deeper regional arrangements signal similar frustrations. As understandable as they may be, such measures threaten to exacerbate systemic risks and compromise financial stability by undermining the modicum of political solidarity required to preempt or manage future emergencies.[39]

[39] C. Randall Henning, *Regional Financial Arrangements and the International Monetary Fund* (Waterloo, ON: Centre for International Governance Innovation, 2020).

With each systemic financial crisis over the past fifty years, national and regional authorities have not only acquiesced in the continued opening of capital markets but also tacitly acknowledged that they could sustain those markets only on a collaborative basis. The incipient emergence of a kind of macro-reinsurance system backed by effective transnational governing capacity is readily observable, but it cannot yet be fully recognized or rendered immune from backsliding. It remains informal, opaque, and even plausibly deniable.[40]

Depending on one's ideological position, the idea of global central banking facilities and binding reinsurance facilities backed by fiscal guarantees – the ultimate foundations for deeply integrated capital markets – remain either a utopian dream or a dystopian nightmare. Today we live on the middle ground. Again, the contagion emanating from US markets in 2008 was finally stopped by collaborative but ad hoc arrangements among finance ministries and central banks in an authoritative hierarchy. They were able to provide the countershock necessary to restore the confidence of global market participants and stabilize the system.[41]

In the aftermath of the 2008 crisis, international capital markets clearly expected that systemically significant financial institutions, and the larger experiment in global integration they signified, would persist. That informal public insurance arrangements implied subsidies for those institutions, not only during emergencies but also in "normal" times, thus became as obvious as the unavoidable moral hazard problem.[42] Inadequately coordinated supervision also threatened to push more risk into less regulated and more opaque markets, such as markets centered on hedge funds and private equity firms. That those subsidies and that opacity would also again encourage imprudent risk-taking and make global markets more, not less, fragile would lead governments (and organized interest groups) straight back to the now more complex agenda of technocratic risk assessment and crisis prevention. More quietly, it would

[40] Jacqueline Best, *The Limits of Transparency: Ambiguity and the History of International Finance* (Ithaca, NY: Cornell University Press, 2005).

[41] David A. Lake, *Hierarchy in International Relations* (Ithaca, NY: Cornell University Press, 2009); and *Indirect Rule: The Making of U.S. International Hierarchy* (Ithaca, NY: Cornell University Press, 2024).

[42] According to IMF staff, "In dollar terms, if applied at the total liabilities of the banks [designated by the FSB as global systemically important] net of equity, the implicit subsidies in 2011–12 represent around $15–70 billion in the United States, $25–110 billion in Japan, $20–110 billion in the United Kingdom, and up to $90–300 billion in the euro area." IMF, *Global Financial Stability Report* (Washington, DC: International Monetary Fund, 2014), 104.

lead them as well back to asking fundamental questions about stability in a system organized around open capital markets with no common rules governing executive compensation, no formal agreement on when to deploy discretionary supervisory judgment, and inadequately shared agreements on the pathways through which the overall gains and losses from financial openness and integration should be distributed.

As usual, the gap between what officials in leading states know they need to do and what they actually do was exposed after each relatively manageable banking crisis in the years after 2008. The failure of Silicon Valley Bank and Signature Bank in the United States early in 2023 again sent shockwaves through the global system. But they proved short-lived after rapid and politically controversial governmental intervention. Around the same time, the Swiss government engineered the faltering Credit Suisse Group's merger into the stronger UBS AG.[43] After the fiscal and monetary aspects of the bailout operations retreated from the headlines, technical discussions on collaborative supervision were energized yet again, not least within the IMF.[44]

The geographic and functional spillovers in policy debates over core values came into view, debates that cannot be contained in national or regional silos and cannot be finally resolved by existing governing institutions. Nationally based insurance and reinsurance instruments can be provided and monitored. Ad hoc official bailouts can facilitate short-term resilience in fragile systems of financial intermediation. Delicate policy coordination can continue to manifest itself at moments of emergency. But ultimate political authority cannot rise to the level implied by the very term "global finance." The resulting complexity, as well as people's widening perceptions of unfairness, provide fuel for populist movements around the world. The irony is that only deeper collaboration among their countries holds the promise of fairer outcomes. The alternative will only stoke the fires of exclusionary nationalism.

The path ahead is filled with moral hazards and political contestation, but the path back is blocked by the structural consequences of prior policy decisions. For now, the credible prospect of catastrophic loss periodically seems enough to motivate just adequate interstate collaboration during crises. The consequent diversification of cross-border and cross-market

[43] Ignazio Angeloni et al., *Geneva 27: Much Money, Little Capital, and Few Reforms: The 2023 Banking Turmoil* (Paris and London: CEPR Press, 2024).

[44] Tobias Adrian et al., "Good Supervision: Lessons from the Field," *IMF Working Paper Series* WP/23/181 (Washington, DC: IMF, September 2023).

portfolios by private and public investors propels the continuing expansion of the missions that the G7 and G20 have effectively assigned to the FSB, the constituent elements of the Basel Process, and other forums. They also continue to justify the technical mandates of the IMF and the World Bank to monitor systemic risks generated by relatively strong states and to directly support relatively weaker states, mandates dating back to the Financial Sector Assessment Programs of 1999.[45]

Bound together by markets they cannot decisively close or adequately regulate, leading states generally remain unwilling to embrace bold reforms.[46] At most, they allow existing international institutions to tinker at the edges of risks that might trigger future financial emergencies. IMF staff, for example, have been encouraged to coordinate with other agencies in exploring the impact of climate change and other 'macro-critical' drivers of tomorrow's financial, monetary, and fiscal shocks. The Fund's adaptive history suggests that behind such activities lies an awareness of the need rapidly to scale-up official multilateral reinsurance operations, but only when and if such shocks actually occur.[47] Within restricted groups of states, however, there are indications of more ambitious preemptive moves in the logically necessary direction. Nowhere are they more evident than among the member-states of the European Union. More explicitly than elsewhere, insurance practices and metaphors appear to guide the development of more deeply collaborative policies.

FINANCIAL RISKS AND BURDEN SHARING IN THE EUROPEAN UNION

The many dimensions of global risk governance in the financial sector make it exceedingly complex, while the time horizon for decisive action

[45] Stephany Griffith-Jones, Eric Helleiner, and Ngaire Woods, eds., *The Financial Stability Board* (Waterloo, ON: Centre for International Governance Innovation, 2010); Kevin Gallagher, *Ruling Capital: Emerging Markets and the Reregulation of Cross-Border Finance* (Ithaca, NY: Cornell University Press, 2015); Susanne Lütz, "From Washington Consensus to Flexible Keynesianism: The International Monetary Fund after the Financial Crisis," *Journal of International Organization Studies* 6, no. 2 (2015): 85–98.

[46] Kathryn Lavelle, *Money and Banks in the American Political System* (Cambridge: Cambridge University Press, 2013); Charles Calomiris and Stephen Haber, *Fragile by Design: The Political Origins of Banking Crises and Scarce Credit* (Princeton: Princeton University Press, 2014); and Emilios Avgouleas, Charles Goodhart, and Dirk Schoenmaker, "Bank Resolution Plans as a Catalyst for Global Financial Reform," *Journal of Financial Stability* 9, no. 2 (2013): 210–218.

[47] Independent Evaluation Office, *The Evolving Application of the IMF's Mandate* (Washington, DC: International Monetary Fund, June 2024).

during emergencies requires decisiveness in the short term. Again, the upper-right quadrant in Figure 3.1 of Chapter 3 situates the challenge. Progressive globalists might readily conclude that liberal governance reaches its limit here. Markets can play a role, but some global risks are finally governable only by public authorities acting quickly in a collaborative fashion. Utopians might hope to someday see the emergence of a binding world government capable of managing the tough political trade-offs implied by the term "global capitalism." Libertarians conversely conclude that only complete political surrender to the concept of market-based automaticity has any chance of actually succeeding in managing the difficult distributive dilemmas involved. If there is a middle ground among these unrealistic ideological positions where such issues are now seriously being hashed out, it is in Europe.[48]

The case of European economic and financial integration was at the core of the field of international political economy as it developed in the West, beginning in the wake of World War I. As I noted in Chapter 2, though, the vision of a viable midpoint between deep social solidarity and desirable political autonomy goes back much further in European history than post-1918 dreams of a stable federal system underpinned by deep economic interdependence. The Westphalian system gradually emerging in the wake of catastrophic war in the seventeenth century set the stage. The activation of the insuring instinct and the resurgence of liberal thought as now-sovereign states pragmatically began developing rules for constructive cross-border engagement was hardly coincidental. The first mutual fire insurance pools as well as the ambitious recovery and expansion of maritime insurance, discussed in Chapter 4, occurred then and in that same central European region.

After 1945, following another cataclysmic era, a much more ambitious political experiment aiming to harness the insuring instinct and support deeper economic linkages across national borders. The experiment would again use liberal means to attain common collective ends, but this time with persistent leadership coming from a newly assertive United States. The rising threat of invasion by the communist empire to the east simultaneously helped sustain that leadership and reinforce a renewed liberal turn in Western Europe.

[48] Research on the EU's international and comparative relevance is extensive and growing rapidly. For essential orientation, see Andrew Moravcsik, *The Choice for Europe: Social Purpose and State Power from Messina to Maastricht* (Ithaca, NY: Cornell University Press, 1998); and Thomas Risse and Tanja A. Börzel, eds., *From Europeanisation to Diffusion* (London: Routledge, 2014).

The legacy of the dynamic post-1945 settlement can still readily be observed in Europe's continuing, frustrating, conflictual, and still tentative efforts to build a solid federation, not as a bulwark against the United States but as a vehicle for helping to sustain a liberal world economy. Europeans today are enveloped across overlapping and variegated spheres of social life by cross-border risk-pooling systems aimed at managing and reducing common threats and sharing the costs and benefits generated by integration. Russia's invasion of Ukraine in 2022 expanded the implied scale and scope of such systems, not least those underpinning cross-border capital markets.

The European Union, now encompassing twenty-seven member-states, rests on various intergovernmental treaties. Supranational elements have evolved on the basis of those treaties, yet the overarching political structure remains more decentralized and arguably less cohesive than its founders might have hoped. Nevertheless, within certain areas of exclusive competence, as defined and continually refined by its members, its Commission today exercises some important executive functions that would be exceedingly difficult to dissolve. Until recently, the inroads of the EU Commission into the core functions of its member-states – most significantly fiscal (taxation) policy and foreign and defense policies – have been limited but not precluded.

After decades of debate, nineteen member-states launched within the European Union an Economic and Monetary Union (EMU) in 1992. They also sowed the seeds for much deeper integration. For them, a still-intergovernmental arrangement combining a customs union, a currency union, and a monetary union constituted a governing system that inclined toward unity but still accommodated internal power differentials and a diversity of approaches to financial risk management. The fact that the complex union could still fall apart under an imaginable set of domestic and external shocks precludes straightforward claims that irrevocable and common risk pools have been created. Indeed, until a common policy framework and reliable fiscal transfer system characteristic of strong federations exist, it will remain plausible to contend that the collective expression of the insuring instinct has only partially manifested itself in contemporary European history.

Decisions made in the wake of the 2008 global financial crisis, the sovereign debt crises in the years immediately following, and then the COVID-19 and Ukraine crises nevertheless testify to the persistence of the imperative to reinsure against the risk of catastrophic loss in Europe and to share in the associated responsibility of constraining moral hazards. Deepening arguments over burden sharing testify to the process's intimate nature. What the European Commission calls cohesion policy measures – the regional redistribution of resources to buffer economic troubles in weaker member-states, and the establishment of various special purpose solidarity funds over time – only vaguely resemble the common systemic risk pooling characterizing true federations. But look more closely at the evolution of financial markets within the union as a whole, and especially within the Eurogroup now grounded in a deeply coordinated central banking system. One can clearly see the mounting pressures akin to those encouraging the construction half a millennium ago of risk pools in European towns and cities confronting the prospect of repeated natural and man-made catastrophes.[49]

Why should it be surprising to find the geographic home of half of the world's insurance companies and the center of global reinsurance markets awakening to the logic of risk pooling at the most appropriate, efficient, and just level of governance? Why should we imagine that a stable division between solidaristic interests and aspirations cannot coexist with clearer understandings of reasonable demands for subsidiarity? In very practical terms, the story of the European Stability Mechanism (ESM) is especially suggestive.

As its most prominent founders, including Jean Monnet, Robert Schuman, and Konrad Adenauer, anticipated, shared risks and shared crises propelled the European project forward from the start. The breakdown of the postwar Bretton Woods pegged exchange rate system in the early 1970s threatened to pull the European customs union apart as fluctuating national cross-rates within it skewed trading patterns and disrupted supply lines. Monetary union was the answer, but it took a long time to come. In 1992, the Treaty on European Union was formally agreed in Maastricht, Netherlands, but the euro it created as well as the European Central Bank (ECB) to manage the common currency of willing member-states were finally launched only in 1999. It came as no surprise that this had knock-on effects in banking markets. Eurogroup members were unanimously reluctant to cede full control over their national payments' systems, nor were they willing to commit to fiscal union.[50]

49 Matthias Matthijs, "How Europe Got Its Mojo Back," *Foreign Affairs*, 17 January 2023.

50 Jesús Ferreiro, Giuseppe Fontana, and Felipe Serrano, eds. *Fiscal Policy in the European Union* (London: Palgrave Macmillan, 2008).

National central banks continued to operate within a federal-like European System of Central Banks loosely coordinated by the ECB. Bank regulation and supervision, and the fiscal flexibility that comes from having "your" banks purchase and hold state-issued bonds, remained under national control. The contradictions of an asymmetric union, with some member-states better able to manage internal political trade-offs as well as exogenous shocks, soon became intolerable as crisis-driven bank failures and potential defaults on certain sovereign bonds threatened to spread. In relatively open financial markets – which over time came to encompass banks as well as bond and stock underwriters – savers and investors always run to safety when shocks generate uncertainty and erode confidence in the future. The phenomenon occurred repeatedly within the EMU throughout its first decade, and especially after the global financial crisis of 2008.

In 2010, Greece hovered on the verge of insolvency. The country's main banks as well as the central authorities in place to lend to or invest in them during periods of distress appeared locked in a "doom loop." If the entire national system had failed, capital market contagion could have kicked in and taken heavily indebted Italy, Portugal, and Spain down as well. The plausible fear of such a catastrophe set in motion a series of reluctant and somewhat secretive moves by the ECB, the net creditor states within the European Union, and a group of private bankers to keep capital flowing throughout the region.[51] The boundaries between public and private as well as between monetary and fiscal policy became hazier.

The intergovernmental Council of the European Union initially tried to stabilize pan-European markets by establishing the European Financial Stability Facility (EFSF). Member-states capitalized the EFSF and authorized it to raise funds on international capital markets under guarantees provided by the European Commission. Amid increasing controversies, both internal and involving the IMF and external creditors, bailout and adjustment programs (later under the rubric of the European Financial Stabilisation Mechanism) would eventually be negotiated for Greece, Latvia, Hungary, Ireland, Cyprus, Portugal, Romania, and Spain.[52]

[51] Charles H. Dallara, *Euroshock: How the Largest Debt Restructuring in History Helped Save Greece and Preserve the Eurozone* (New York: Rodin Books, 2024).

[52] Marcus Brunnermeier, Harold James, and Jean-Pierre Landau, *The Euro and the Battle of Ideas* (Princeton: Princeton University Press, 2016; C. Randall Henning, *Tangled Governance: International Regime Complexity, the Troika, and the Euro Crisis* (Oxford: Oxford University Press, 2017); Ashoka Mody, *Euro Tragedy: A Drama in Nine Acts*

In 2012, Eurozone members moved to strengthen the euro's foundations by establishing a similar but more robust and permanent reinsurance facility, the ESM. Cooperating closely with both the ECB and the IMF, the very act of constituting the ESM brought under control a sovereign debt crisis that had widely been perceived to be capable of taking the European project back several decades.[53] At the center of that construction was a straightforward guarantee from Eurogroup members that would enable the ESM to issue triple-A rated bonds in international markets. With adequate liquidity promised by the ECB, long-term back-up reserves available if needed from the ESM, and policy adjustment conditions in debtor members enforced by both the ESM and the IMF, savers and investors soon regained enough confidence to allow European banking and capital markets to resume "normal" operations.

In short, the technical coordinating machinery reluctantly constructed under pressure proved minimally acceptable to Germany and other net-creditor member-states. In the absence of more attractive options, net debtors perhaps reluctantly acceded to the conditions tied to the assistance they received. But creditor and debtor alike agreed that the long-run objective was to restore debtors' access to private capital markets. Regional financial risk pooling did what it was expected to do for creditor countries. Stabilization, adjustment, and recovery gradually occurred in debtor countries, though with ill-distributed pain that might have been lessened. In the end, no one emerged from the crisis entirely satisfied. But the monetary union survived. Less obviously, the long-term vision of an eventual and smoothly functioning fiscal federation also survived.

The embedded asymmetries of postcrisis governance machinery and the continuing tentativeness and partiality of monetary and now fiscal coordination within the Eurogroup and the larger European Union fell short of a permanent solution. In fact, the inconsistency and incoherence involved in a "system" that combined a single market for goods and services, a common currency, enhanced capital mobility, and ultimate national control of monetary policies had been clearly diagnosed even as

(Oxford: Oxford University Press, 2018); European Stability Mechanism, *Safeguarding the Euro in Times of Crisis* (Luxembourg: Publications Office of the European Union, 2019); Harold James, *The IMF and the European Debt Crisis* (Washington, DC: International Monetary Fund, 2024).

[53] Klaus Regling and Maryann Haggerty, "Lessons Learned Oral History Project Interview," *Yale Program on Financial Stability*, No. 2021-04, Yale University School of Management, 3 March 2021.

the Maastricht Treaty was being negotiated. The prescription then was to complement the currency union with a banking union and eventually a pan-European capital markets union, both backed by an irrevocably coordinated fiscal capacity.

Momentum toward a banking union again gathered in the wake of the sovereign debt crises culminating in 2012. As the ESM was selling its triple-A-rated bonds and struggling to restore confidence in the euro by using the bond proceeds to support adjustment programs in Greece, Cyprus, Portugal, and Spain, the European Commission made plans to prevent a repetition of the disorderly bank bailouts and national barrier building of the post-2008 period. Two initiatives followed: a Single Supervisory Mechanism overseen by the ECB in 2014; and a Single Resolution Fund (SRF) in 2015. Both instruments would ultimately rely on a single rulebook for banking regulation across the union. As the European Commission asserted, when finally completed, the Capital Markets and Banking Union "will promote a stable and integrated financial system in the European Union. It will increase the resilience of the EMU towards adverse shocks by substantially facilitating private risk-sharing across borders, while at the same time reducing the need for public risk-sharing."[54] Despite the best of intentions, the initiatives remain incomplete.

Aspiration may have long outpaced compliance, but the story of what Monnet called the United States of Europe is still being written. The board that manages the mainly bank-funded SRF, for example, rests on the assumption of a significant degree of cooperation across national and especially local levels when bank resolutions are required. Banks across the union did prove to be better capitalized and more robust when the COVID-19 shock hit in 2019 and the Ukraine war soon followed. Both crises stimulated intense coordination within the Eurogroup. Emerging in 2022, amendments to the ESM Treaty significantly expanded its financing capacity and allowed it to directly backstop the SRF. In principle, a declaratory consensus existed across the entire membership on the necessity of common supervision of all financial institutions whose failure might destabilize cross-border markets and of common crisis management when such stability was under threat. There was also agreement that the European Union needed a common system of deposit

[54] European Commission, *Communication to the European Parliament, the Council, The European Central Bank, the European Economic and Social Council and the Committee of the Regions on Completing the Banking Union*, COM (2017) 592 final, Brussels, 11.10.2017, p. 3.

insurance for banks at the core of those markets. After all, ever since the bank runs that ushered in the Great Depression, the idea of deposit insurance combined with stability-oriented bank regulation had been accepted as conventional wisdom. But putting such a system into place across remaining borders within the European Union was never going to be easy. Its halting progress sheds much light on the impediments effective risk governance continues to confront, and not only in Europe.

In the broadest sense, the networks of technical agencies evolving ever since EU members agreed to work toward the objective of a single market, and especially since most of them decided to join a currency union, constitute an insurance system. They essentially pool trading and financial risks and try to manage and reduce them in anticipation of future internal and external shocks. They also tend to do as little as necessary to restore stability after emergencies. The hope clearly persists among market participants that the ECB will continue to provide enough liquidity to distressed banks as necessary to preempt future panics in international capital markets, and that various regulatory agencies will routinely work to encourage prudence. As in 2012, the guarantees of emergency funding from creditor states might then never actually have to be activated.

Similarly, the enhancement of the ESM and its backstopping of the SRF might be enough to reinforce market confidence and promote societal resilience within troubled member-states. Conditions attached to ECB loans or ESM investments, in turn, might then continue to be designed to mitigate moral hazards without setting any draconian conditions. National authorities would also retain room for political maneuver. The overall result could effectively be a minimally adequate reinsurance system intricately linking significant private intermediaries, national central banks, the ECB, and finance ministries.

"In the longer run," Harold James argues, "Europe will need a more formal program that operates through intergovernmental, rather than monetary, institutions ... The core of a reform would need not simply more fiscal integration, but also more precise and transparent rules on how it might be achieved."[55] Enhancing the ESM's mandate and capacity already moves in this direction. So too does slow progress toward a unified system of deposit insurance to complement banks' own reserves in securing a completed banking union.

In many countries, deposit insurance programs require banks, and indirectly their customers, to pay premiums into a common pool. The

[55] Harold James, "A Decade of 'Whatever It Takes'," *Project Syndicate*, 26 July 2022.

customers of a distressed bank can then call on the SRF, typically within prespecified limits. The backstop's very existence is meant to make such calls unnecessary. The regulatory role assigned to the deposit insurance agency is also designed to reduce the probability of actual bailouts. In the United States, for example, the Federal Deposit Insurance Corporation has a reputation as a tough enforcer of liquidity and capital adequacy rules. What remains vital for the FDIC as well as most other deposit insurers around the world is the perception that standing behind the bank-funded insurance pool is the full faith and credit of the national government. In short, the understanding is that fiscal resources gathered from taxpayers or borrowed as required from either central banks or private capital markets will be available in whatever amount is required to prevent cascading bank collapses and economic depressions. An EU-wide deposit-insurance system – a necessity if capital is truly to flow freely and encourage, not compel, necessary adjustments across the system – implies an ultimate pooling of fiscal risks *and* fiscal resources.

As if to suggest the impossibility of states moving forward and undermining their own monopoly on fiscal power within their territorial domains, many commentators now emphasize Germany's and other EU net creditors' reticence to formally promise future bailouts for net debtors such as Greece, Italy, Portugal, and Spain. But this emphasis ignores several realities. In a currency union, sovereign debt plays a necessary buffering role for members facing asymmetric shocks. Over time, imbalances will not simply reflect fiscal profligacy or mismanaged banks. Capital will move in response to perceptions of structural constraints, political preferences, and opportunities. In addition, if markets deem several national deposit insurers as more or less robust than others, banks from stronger countries will reap competitive advantages. A single market for financial services will not exist. Less obviously, remaining differences in national banking structures within Europe make even net creditor states reluctant to give up their abilities to differentially support institutions of local importance, like certain over-leveraged but politically vital regional financial institutions within Germany. In such a context, gradual compromise in the direction of deeper integration seems more likely than reversion to the earlier status quo.

If the path to common deposit insurance arrangements resembles the earlier winding paths toward monetary and banking union, it will be marked by reluctant decisions to shift more policy capacity toward central institutions. It will happen despite that reluctance, especially as risks migrate out of banks into other kinds of intermediaries and investment vehicles in integrating capital markets, some of which will undoubtedly become systemically significant. In exchange, stronger controls will be necessary to provide political leaders in creditor states with cover against the accusation that they are forcing their national constituents to sign "blank checks."[56] The specter of the moral hazards linked to any explicit or implicit insurance program has already reared its head.

Wolfgang Schäuble, the late and formidable German finance minister with a reputation for tight-fistedness, set the tone by advocating not the "mutualization" of sovereign debts but the establishment of a "sinking fund." Such a fund would be capable of supporting the refinancing of members' future debt-servicing obligations with enforceable conditions, including presumably any obligations resulting from deposit insurance guarantees. Between the lines, the logic and political sensibility of his position evoked familiar metaphors. Schäuble quite clearly understood the practical implications of reinsurance. He was pushing in the direction of eventual integration of ultimate fiscal supports for sharing burdens that must be shared. But he wanted to see them evolve in a federal, not unitary, form.

More clearly than in the case of nuclear insurance, the limits of insurability in Europe's Banking Union and eventually Capital Markets Union can expand outward only to the edges of coordinated fiscal capacity. Private insurance and insurance-like securities can take initial slices of pooled financial risks, but no ultimate alternative exist to joint public backstops for higher-risk tranches. In the midst of a future regional financial crisis, Germany and other net creditor member-states will have to be prepared to provide the ultimate round of reinsurance coverage.

This political logic is compelling, but various states' resistance to formally acknowledging that reality remains predictable. When the COVID-19 pandemic was still underway and Russia had invaded Ukraine, European politics was heavily inflected by populist reactions to the earlier sovereign debt crises and coincident waves of unwanted immigration. In the background, doubts about the United States' post-2008 commitment to systemic leadership and continuing economic openness combined with questions about the trajectory of relevant Chinese policies. Observing the uneven effects of economic integration in Europe and the growth of populist parties in both the core and periphery of the monetary union, observers of European affairs have begun to question the endurance

56 David Howarth and Lucia Quaglia, "The Difficult Construction of a European Deposit Insurance Scheme: A Step Too Far in Banking Union?" *Journal of Economic Policy Reform* 21, no. 3 (2018): 190–209.

of the "permissive consensus" that had permitted a half-century of movement toward an "ever closer union."

The Great Recession that followed the global crisis of 2008 hit European economies hard. Markets for exports contracted and resources available for imports declined. After the sovereign debt crises of 2010 and the insistence on fiscal austerity in the euro area periphery, recessionary forces deepened and public opinion became increasingly skeptical of the European project, in both periphery and core EMU countries.[57] Postfunctionalists then emphasized the move from "permissive consensus" to "constraining dissensus."[58] But some doubted the strength of any constraint, especially when fiscal solidarity was required.[59]

Combined with the post-2012 resurgence of identity politics, best exemplified by the United Kingdom's decision to leave the European Union, more people expected that the integration project would be rolled back. In particular, many doubted the markets' utility in promoting that integration. Liquidity provided by the ECB and the ESM appeared to some as not just tamping down debt crises, but also as allowing governments – especially creditor governments – to postpone necessary fiscal decisions.[60] In the wake of the crises of 2011–2012, much of the debate on the future of the fiscal, banking, and capital market unions intended to follow monetary union turned on just such a proposition. As in any insurance system that doesn't include incentives for prudence and future disaster prevention, EMU members found themselves dealing with rising moral hazards and a weakening sense of trust in one another. The system still needed external support, but the fact is that it did not break down.

What was the feasible alternative? Perhaps the populist, neo-mercantilist, and ethno-nationalist movements rising around the world in the wake of

57 Harold James, *Seven Crashes: The Economic Crises that Shaped Globalization* (New Haven, CT: Yale University Press, 2023), chapter 6.

58 Frank Schimmelfennig, "European Integration in the Euro Crisis: The Limits of Postfunctionalism," *Journal of European Integration* 36, no. 3 (2014): 321–337.

59 Athanasios Orphanides, "The Euro Area Crisis: Politics over Economics," *Atlantic Economic Journal* 42 (2014): 243–263.

60 See, for example, Yvan Lengwiler and Athanasios Orphanides, "Collateral Framework: Liquidity Premia and Multiple Equilibria," *Journal of Money, Credit and Banking* 56, nos. 2–3 (2024): 489–516. On the political importance of EU-level reinsurance systems in this context, see Waltraud Schelkle, "The political economy of reinsurance," in Dariusz Adamski, Fabian Amtenbrink, and Julian de Haan, eds., *The Cambridge Handbook of European Monetary, Economic and Financial integration* (Cambridge: Cambridge University Press, 2023), 125–138.

financial crises and the COVID-19 pandemic that began in 2019 were unanticipated reactions to a global political project inspired by dreams of peaceful interdependence backed by the insuring instinct. In any case, the regional risks necessitating collaborative governance would not disappear if the project suddenly went into reverse. To the contrary, they would probably increase exponentially. If there is a less risky and more reliable alternative to "failing forward," no one could quite see it.[61]

As the COVID-19 pandemic was subsiding in 2022, the European Union proposed a solidarity fund that came to be called NextGen EU. By issuing Eurobonds it pledged to gather EUR 750 billion to be used for collective infrastructure rebuilding across the continent. As with previous moves, this joint borrowing operation was widely interpreted as a small step toward fiscal union. It also, predictably, stimulated resistance to advancing that objective. European leaders again faced the task of resetting the economic balance between efficiency and resilience as well as the political balance between integration and autonomy.

Conflict and contestation remained the hallmarks of that complex task. Most leaders still remain mindful of their countries' contemporary history, and under pressure they continue to opt for sharing a necessary minimum of the burdens of collective adjustment. Without idealizing a profoundly complicated process of mutual accommodation activated by shared financial risks, the persistent question is whether lessons for the world can be drawn from halting European experiments inspired by insurance practices and metaphors, which ultimately rest on the frequently expressed promise of ever closer union.

THE PROTECTION GAP IN GLOBAL FINANCE

Although they were often amended and "softer" than its originators had hoped, the IMF's Articles of Agreement continue to reflect a shared affirmation of "the advantages of the joint exercise of sovereignty."[62] In the arena of financial policy today, that may remain an aspiration. With regard to the challenge of maintaining stable capital markets, we now live in a world organized around national political authority that must be

[61] David Howarth and Lucia Quaglia, "Failing Forward in Economic and Monetary Union: Explaining Weak Eurozone Financial Support Mechanisms," *Journal of European Public Policy* 28, no. 10 (2021): 1555–1572.

[62] Joseph Gold, *Legal and Institutional Aspects of the International Monetary System* (Washington, DC: International Monetary Fund, 1979), 11.

shared to be effective. Over the course of the past half-century, we have witnessed this phenomenon during every point of financial emergency.

When moments of crisis have passed, the continuing integration of markets regulated mainly at the national level has prompted the deepening of transnational and technocratic capacities for systemic risk assessment and analysis. This is the seedbed for what could someday become a more durable public reinsurance system in this vital sector. Such a system might well transcend the pioneering analogue centered on the IMF in the early post-1945 era. It might represent a step toward a kind of fiscal federation where still-distinct polities would be more firmly bound together while retaining a significant autonomy. It might depend on more formal collaborative machinery for sharing future burdens of crisis recovery and prevention. A far-fetched idea? Not to thirteen independent colonies in North America in 1783, not to most members of the European Union today, and not to anyone attentive to the expansive historical trajectories of cross-border risk pooling and diversification at the heart of many contemporary public and/or private insurance systems.

I return to this theme in Chapter 8. But for now, recall Berliner's principles of insurability noted in Chapter 4 and imagine them applied to the kinds of risk examined in this chapter. For insurance to be relevant, anticipated losses at the level of the insured unit would have to be random. Maximum losses would have to be bearable by the ultimate public insurer. Average losses and the average time between occurrences would have to be capable of estimation. Feasibly payable, but not necessarily "profitable" premiums for adequate insurance cover would have to be capable of estimation. Moral hazards would have to be limited by regulatory/surveillance systems overseen in ways broadly perceived to be both effective and legitimate.

Nothing here is beyond the realm of imagination at the global level. But every point admittedly stretches our thinking at a time when the systemic leadership provided by the United States after 1945 looks increasingly tenuous and when a rising great power in Asia may be reaching the limits of its interests in collaboration under rules that began evolving before its rise. In this context, one must ask whether integrating capital markets can forever be sustained in the absence of some kind of negotiated agreement on monetary and fiscal burden sharing – and collaborative supervision – in advance of even more serious emergency conditions than those recounted in this chapter.

History provides plenty of hints concerning the alternative: costly disintegration as the world experienced after 1931, and, *in extremis*, systemic collapse. So why should the next generation – in the United States, China, and everywhere else – not expect their leaders to continue trying to build more solid foundations for this crucial sector of the global economy? In response, it is worth repeating the essence of the story leading to this very question. During ever larger financial crises, tacit and collaborative public reinsurance arrangements continue to come out of the shadows at the system level. Less dramatically, and despite short-sighted resistance from vested interests, in the aftermath of those crises governments continue to experiment with technical instruments intended to keep increasingly complex capital markets open and stable.

In fact, the larger experiment in governing ever more integrated national markets extends back a century. It links the history of the Economic and Financial Organization of the League of Nations to that of the FSB of the G20. The seminal compromise struck at Bretton Woods in the middle of that tumultuous century tried to extend the rule of law to a multilateral exchange rate system. It rested on the assumption that minimally linked financial markets would be reinsured and regulated nationally. Then came a series of complicated currency, banking, and debt crises across opening and integrating markets. The governing practices witnessed in response fall mainly into the upper right-hand corner of Figure 3.1 in Chapter 3. The systemic risks crystallizing at points of emergency became increasingly complex, and liabilities had to be covered in the very short term. Emergency management continues to rely on an informal public reinsurance system ultimately backed by powerful states' monetary and fiscal capacities. That system called forth repeated follow-up efforts to coordinate regulatory and supervisory initiatives to rein in inevitable moral hazards. In the aftermath of crisis, uncertainty and distrust obscured the path toward more formal monetary and fiscal integration, except in Europe. Heightened geopolitical rivalries simultaneously intensified that uncertainty, even as deep economic linkages remained undeniable. The Basel Process and related, if informal, transnational public–private partnerships and pragmatic political judgments sustained and continued to sustain those linkages.

Participants in the Basel Process continue to focus on inextricably shared technical problems and unavoidable practical trade-offs. Can the basic "plumbing" through which cross-border payments flow be made more secure without complete integration? Can public as well as private digital currencies usefully complement traditional stores of value? Can agreed standards for new financial instruments derived from conventional forms of investment be maintained? Can reliance on relatively costly financial reserves by private intermediaries be reduced? None of these questions is really new at a fundamental level. Despite persistent and even enlarged geostrategic rivalries, all but the most autarchic national authorities remain engaged with one another in working through necessarily collective governing arrangements. A more assertive China, for example, retains its place at various tables constituting the Basel Process. Someday soon, perhaps, Russia will again take its place there too.

As in Keynes's day, the "decadence" of finance capitalism remains as obvious as the generally shared sense of perplexity concerning what could feasibly replace it. The chimera of reliable self-insurance – the persistent dream conjured when states build up excessive reserves of gold, exchangeable currencies, and stocks of various commodities – reappears and then dissolves during actual systemic emergencies. Informal and mainly public reinsurance arrangements thus continue to evolve in a political setting where competitive and collaborative impulses remain in tension.[63]

Formalizing preventive financial governance at the global level in a way that elegantly matches reliably coordinated fiscal capacities with adequately regulated cross-border capital movements may remain out of reach for a time. Straightforward *ex ante* burden-sharing agreements to underpin interdependent financial markets might continue to prove elusive. After all, they always do suggest the possibility of having to transfer taxpayers' resources both internally and externally in ways and for reasons not easy to understand. Repeated ad hoc arrangements implicitly acknowledging a sense of shared fate during and immediately after systemic emergencies nevertheless do give rise to reasonable expectations of more reliable and mutually beneficial risk pooling and diversification in the future. Assertive governance by liberal democracies may become more difficult as uncertainty deepens, particularly in the wake of the ascendancy of populist movements. The political and economic costs of not persisting with collaborative experiments in systemic reinsurance in this policy arena, however, promise to rise exponentially. Policymakers may be tempted to fall back on the ahistorical fantasy that conflicts in this arena can be resolved by automatic market mechanisms or with the aid of new apolitical technologies. But digital currencies, fintech products introduced into payments systems, novel instruments promising "open" banking

[63] Charles B. Roger explores a similar contention in *The Origins of Informality: Why the Legal Foundations of Global Governance Are Shifting, and Why It Matters* (Oxford: Oxford University Press, 2020).

markets, the expansion of alternative financial and monetary blocs – none of them evolve beyond politics. They all simply test the fading capacity of any individual state to go it alone.

As systemic financial risks become more complex, insurance – in practice and as guiding metaphor – plays a vital role in generating long-run confidence and pushing integrative processes forward. During actual emergencies, public coverage of losses capable of breaking the evolving world system remains essential. Basic political questions then inevitably arise: Who pays and who benefits? Here complex risks and short time horizons entail a continuing role for private-sector judgment and discipline, but an essential role for the occasional assertion and justification of public authority. Across the entire post-1970s era, that authority has increasingly been reconstituted informally as collaborative. The sovereign debt problems that typically followed systemic crises during that period underline the need to recognize how only deeper and more extensive collaboration can secure a planetary system significantly reshaped by relatively open capital markets.

In such a system, one thing is certain. Crises will recur. Variations on Ponzi schemes will manifest themselves, often just before crashes. First comes the failure of regulatory power, then comes the panic. Leading governments then become reinsurers intervening to restore confidence and subsequently to rein in moral hazard. Creative governmental decisions may work to ensure that associated costs are fairly distributed, but increasingly they will have to collaborate if such efforts are to succeed. Accusations of corruption, fair or not, will fly. But if and when the abyss of radical uncertainty opens up, as it did in 2008, public authorities will again struggle together to close it, ultimately by shifting losses to their fiscal accounts and struggling against the political forces demanding moves back toward economic closure. They may fail, but they haven't done so since the early days of the Great Depression. And no one has an excuse to forget the catastrophic global war that came next.

No one can eliminate the risks of hubris, stupidity, miscalculation, and miscommunication – or the risks posed by letting a select few harvest most of the benefits of efficient capital markets. Such risks can be managed and shared only at the level logically required. Complex risks, often short term in nature and only roughly calculable, manifest themselves during financial crises. Their management requires government that is equally complex and collaborative. Chapter 7 looks at crises in other policy arenas that are also complex but slow-moving.

7

Global Challenges and the Frontier of Insurability

> Order within the great society of all mankind is not only wider than international order or order among states, but also more fundamental and primordial than it, and morally prior to it. The system of states has constantly to be assessed in relation to the goal of world order.
>
> —Hedley Bull, *The Anarchical Society: A Study of Order in World Politics*

We return to where we started. Even famous conservative skeptics ("realists" as they are called in the field of International Relations) such as Hedley Bull and Hans Morgenthau, agreed on the necessity of anticipatory collaboration in certain policy arenas. Most explicitly, they contended that natural human survival instincts that depend on distinctions between "in" groups and "out" groups simply had to be reconciled with fundamental species-level interests in the cause of controlling the proliferation of nuclear weapons. They never conceded that the challenge was insuperable.

RISK, UNCERTAINTY, AND THE PROBLEM OF SOLIDARITY

As I noted in Chapter 1, bold dreams of world government somehow rendered legitimate and effective seem to coincide with the ascendancy of a great power that seeks to remake world order in its image. Such dreams were quite apparent, for example, in the United States after 1945. As Townsend Hoopes put it in his famous memoir of American policy-making during what now looks like the heyday of US hegemony: "To the President's men in 1965, there seemed no stopping point between isolationism and globalism."[1] Alas, that stopping point was soon found on the killing fields in Vietnam. The idea of striking a sustainable balance between the two extremes then reasserted itself.[2]

Today, what is the realistic alternative to human beings somehow beginning to see themselves in solidarity in at least some crucial policy arenas – where they inevitably make up a society that must harness just enough binding and durable power to manage common risks? Just as the prospect of nuclear Armageddon after 1945 reinvigorated, however briefly, a spirit of universalism, the insuring instinct today prompts reengagement with certain necessarily system-wide experiments in risk assessment, preventive governance, and emergency management.

Although shared instinct might open a door, the actual practice and organizing narratives of insurance and reinsurance rest on convincing people that risk pooling and collective risk management are in their individual interests. Throughout history, as Geoffrey Clark and Gregory Anderson note:

> Left to its own devices, the public has preferred to avoid confronting the certainty of fatality or the probabilities of catastrophe. It has therefore been the particular task of insurance promoters to create a demand for their products, first, by persuading the public to see the world as ruled less by divine judgments and more by statistical patterns, and second, by proclaiming a moral imperative of hedging against death and disaster by the prudential recourse to insurance.[3]

In previous chapters, I described the key roles that governments have played in this realm, from town level to national level. Recognizing that private markets left to their own devices will underproduce public goods, governments backstopped some insurance markets. In the arena of commercial nuclear power, as we saw in Chapter 5, they took on long-term and extreme risks but left private firms with short-term incentives to help prevent disasters. They also sometimes directly organized insurance arrangements, as in the arena of public health. Over time, public authorities worked to convince their constituents that it was worth paying for the expansion of such arrangements. Persuading people to pay

[1] Townsend Hoopes, *The Limits of Intervention: How Vietnam Policy Was Made – and Reversed – During the Johnson Administration* (New York: David McKay Company, 1969), 16.

[2] Again, as Eric Helleiner reminds us in *The Contested World Economy* (Cambridge: Cambridge University Press, 2023), visions of world order did not emanate solely from European and American sources.

[3] Geoffrey Clark and Gregory Anderson, "Introduction," in *The Appeal of Insurance*, edited by Geoffrey Clark, et al. (Toronto: University of Toronto Press, 2010), 3.

premiums for social and medical insurance often proved to be an easier "sell" than persuading them to pay new taxes. Something similar seems at play in demands for official property and casualty insurance in places perceived by private insurers to be too risky. Might this kind of reasoning apply to more challenging cross-border risks?

Reconceiving global risk governance against the backdrop of the insuring instinct is an ambitious, difficult, and essential project. In this realm, both official insurance as well as reinsurance for market-based insurance practices ultimately imply fiscal collaboration. Harmony and cosmopolitan bliss may not appear on the horizon anytime soon. But a combination of conflict, struggle, and the absence of feasible alternatives with regard to some risks just may prepare the domestic and international terrain for the expansion of just-adequate insurance and reinsurance-as-governance arrangements. The practical political challenge is to match them with enough consent or tacit acquiescence that they remain sustainable. And here, at the very least, insurance metaphors may come into their own.

Systemic problems more intractable than those encountered in the production of nuclear-generated electricity and the taming of global finance clearly exist. Thinking about them, pragmatists find it hard to avoid drawing the conclusion that a limited set of governing instruments capable of preventing the obliteration of world society must be designed and implemented, not necessarily immediately but definitely in the not-so-distant future. These are the kinds of problems highlighted in the lower right-hand quadrant of Figure 3.1 in Chapter 3. They include climate change, biodiversity loss, the threat of future pandemics, and various challenges associated with rapid technological innovation. While the insurance arrangements and narratives evolving in the other three boxes are suggestive here, such challenges by their nature push us past conventional limits of insurability.

THE EVOLUTION OF GLOBAL PREVENTIVE GOVERNANCE

For decades now, many observers have leaned into the view that the most difficult global challenges of our times foretell the end of national self-governance. Ulrich Beck certainly held to this position at the time of his death. But even pioneering contemporary realists such as Robert Gilpin, doubting the possibility that global governing experiments would soon replace nation-states, hoped that collaborative regional governance and links across regions could constructively facilitate a necessary degree of interstate cooperation.[4] If he were still with us, Gilpin might even today contend that at least some cross-regional policymaking elements are proving scalable to the extent that great powers at the core of the world's main regions perceive and act on a restricted set of mutual interests. Peter Katzenstein's work on regionalization moved along this same line, but also emphasized dynamic forces moving across the world's main regions.[5]

In Chapter 4, we saw how innovative instruments in cross-regional capital markets are already helping to manage a widening array of relatively simple risks over short- to medium time horizons. Chapter 5 showed how those same markets can also raise increasing amounts of capital to cover the expanding risks associated with nuclear energy production, as long as governments acting jointly guaranteed coverage for large-ticket and long-term liabilities. As noted in Chapter 6, leading governments, necessarily collaborating, have also proven themselves capable of managing foreseeable systemic emergencies linked to the globalization of finance. It is not a stretch to conclude, therefore, that insuring states have lately – and contrary to experience during the 1930s – practiced joint risk governance, albeit often on an ad hoc basis. They have backed up their internal insurance systems and tacitly affirmed their willingness to go far beyond providing minimal guarantees conducive to systemic stability. Arrangements among leading central banks to swap currency reserves when needed to stabilize cross-border payment systems, for instance, are now understood to be normal. They are also now understood to be rapidly expandable during emergencies.

Unlike in the nuclear liability arena, the states at the core of global finance have proven unwilling to bind themselves explicitly. Grappling with the inevitable moral hazards implied by their tacit understandings, they and the markets they oversee are nevertheless learning to live with ambiguity. The fact that they cannot formalize what is essentially collaborative reinsurance for integrating risk societies does not mean that deeper *ex ante* understandings are impossible. Experience over the past half-century instead suggests the opposite. Even between "strategic competitors" such as China and the United States, some level of mutual understanding on the management of shared financial risks was evolving

[4] Robert Gilpin, *The Political Economy of International Relations* (Princeton: Princeton University Press, 1987).

[5] Peter J. Katzenstein, *A World of Regions: Asia and Europe in the American Imperium* (Ithaca, NY: Cornell University Press, 2015).

in the early years of the twenty-first century. Populist backlash rooted in the unnecessarily unequal outcomes of recent official actions threatened that understanding, but it could not change the fact that the economic fates of the two countries were now intimately linked.

Masking the dimensions of burden sharing and preventive governance developing among a group of states extending far beyond the United States and China may well facilitate the gradual legitimation of collaborative risk governance. In light of history extending much further back than the early twenty-first century, however, it would be naïve to contend that a reversal is impossible. Nevertheless, the specter of mutual assured destruction from mismanaging either nuclear energy or global finance has certainly concentrated sensible minds during the decades following 1945. Why stop there?

The dynamics of climate change, biodiversity loss, pandemics, and other system-spanning challenges are now forcing pragmatists and skeptics alike to think creatively about overcoming the constraints imposed by extreme commitments to the idea of national self-reliance. It is becoming difficult not to sense the inevitability of a profound socioeconomic transformation eventually forcing deep structural political change at the system level.[6] The consequences of fossil-fuel-driven economic development, combined with strategically and technologically driven openness to other increasingly obvious global dangers, suggest an impending transformation in what Bull called the anarchical society of states.[7] Complex and slow-moving or "creeping" crises with transnational dimensions will not be managed successfully by nation-states assigning unwavering priority to their own autonomy.[8]

Unlike the historical situation that once consolidated peak governing power in nation-states, no exogenous force lies just over the horizon

[6] Matthew Paterson, "Climate Change and International Political Economy: Between Collapse and Transformation," *Review of International Political Economy* 28, no. 2 (2021): 394–405.

[7] Citing the rise of "global" international society and the need for responses in this arena that test the limits of both pluralist and solidarist understandings of policy development in a state-centered system, Robert Falkner updates and adapts a worldview derived from Bull's work. See *Environmentalism and Global International Society* (Cambridge: Cambridge University Press, 2021).

[8] Brett Christophers, Patrick Bigger, and Leigh Johnson, "Stretching Scales? Risk and Sociality in Climate Finance," *Environment and Planning A: Economy and Space* 52, no. 1 (2020): 88–110; Arjen Boin, Magnus Ekengren, and Mark Rhinard, "Hiding in Plain Sight: Conceptualizing the Creeping Crisis," *Risks, Hazards and Crisis in Public Policy* 11, no. 2 (2020): 116–138.

adequate to the task of convincing groups of human beings voluntarily and soon to reimagine the scope and scale of their communities.[9] Nationalism continues to reign supreme as the functional source of legitimation for governments all over the world. At the same time, we're all seeing mounting evidence of rapid deterioration in the systems required to sustain human and animal life in that world.

The straightforward question I noted at the outset of this book thus comes back to the fore. Might the "insuring instinct" today be harnessed in zones that stretch the limits of risk calculation quickly enough to enable more ambitious forms of government to develop? In his last book, Beck asserted that a deeper societal metamorphosis was in sight.[10] Reasons for skepticism about his claim abound, but they do not justify resignation or exhaust the possibilities of feasible political reform.

Can existing political authorities in vital and inherently complex policy arenas effectively deploy insurance narratives to begin moving beyond easily reversible intergovernmental arrangements? Might some combination of private and public insurance analogies reflecting a longer-term sense of mutual interests – and also the justice of sharing basic burdens – help to preempt populist backlashes and underpin reliable global instruments of preventive governance? Hopeful answers in the affirmative rest on the history of human ingenuity under pressure.[11]

The very idea of global risk governance opens itself naturally to considering the challenge of pushing beyond standard accounts of the limits of insurability. In policy arenas such as those I have discussed in previous chapters, more expansive solidarity networks – or risk pools – seem feasible at systemic scale. In other arenas, analogous demands for recognizing and managing cross-border risks, coping with rising sources of uncertainty, and preparing for emergency management in practical terms are rising. Progress in meeting those demands is maddeningly slow, but it is not invisible. Deeply informed commentary treats many of the complex challenges involved as existential threats.[12] But useful knowledge suggesting possibilities for moving back from the brink is rapidly

[9] Benedict Anderson, *Imagined Communities: Reflections on the Origin and Spread of Nationalism* (London: Verso, 1983/2006).

[10] Ulrich Beck, *The Metamorphosis of the World* (Cambridge: Polity Press, 2016).

[11] For early work on this theme, see Thomas Homer-Dixon, *The Upside of Down: Catastrophe, Creativity, and the Renewal of Civilization* (Toronto/New York: Knopf, 2006), and *The Ingenuity Gap* (Toronto: Knopf, 2000).

[12] Nathan Sears, "International Politics in the Age of Existential Threats," *Journal of Global Security Studies* 6, no. 3 (2021): 1–23.

mounting inside government agencies, universities, and think-tanks, as well as inside global insurance and reinsurance firms.

Another book would be required to even begin synthesizing that knowledge. In brief outline, however, it is already possible to discern promising ideas and policy experiments aimed at addressing such challenges that draw on the experience of insurance. The limits of insurability in some arenas of cross-border risk are also today being pushed steadily outward. Underlying forces are obscured by many sources of uncertainty, but the nature of plausible dangers requires the capacity to make long-term plans. The history of insurance practices and related metaphors outlined in previous chapters opens a path forward, even as it clarifies boundaries that soon need to be crossed. A brief overview of developments in the multidimensional policy arenas of climate change, biodiversity loss, and pandemics shines a light on that path.

CLIMATE CHANGE

The UN's Intergovernmental Panel on Climate Change is the preeminent forum for scientific research and authoritative negotiation on the policies needed to reduce the risks posed by the accelerating warming of the physical environment within which our species flourishes. The signatories to the 2015 Paris Agreement accepted the collective mission to meet that challenge, even as most soon seemed to resign themselves to accepting a near-term breach in the original temperature limits they'd agreed to.[13] Denial of the rising probability of future catastrophes has become both increasingly unjustifiable and stubbornly evident in many domestic political settings. Material and ideological constraints hamper decisive progress in leading states, even as scientists approach unanimity in adopting the term "climate emergency." But such constraints exist elsewhere as well, thus creating what analysts call the quintessential super-wicked policy problem at the systemic level.[14] Collaborative risk management and preventive governance appears in

[13] Jen Iris Allan et al., "Making the Paris Agreement: Historical Processes and the Drivers of Institutional Design," *Political Studies* 71, no. 3 (2021): 914–934.

[14] Kelly Levin, Ben Cashore, Steven Bernstein, and Graeme Auld, "Overcoming the Tragedy of Super Wicked Problems: Constraining Our Future Selves to Ameliorate Global Climate Change," *Policy Sciences* 45, no. 2 (2012): 123–152. On the different meanings of "uncertainty" in this context, see Art Dewulf and Robbert Biesbroek, "Nine Lives of Uncertainty in Decision-Making: Strategies for Dealing with Uncertainty in Environmental Governance," *Policy and Society* 37, no. 4 (2018): 441–458.

the real world of politics to be both an urgent necessity and a hazy dream, with bursts of perceptual clarity and limited institutional experimentation coming only at discrete moments in time.[15]

Leaders in both industry and government have begun planning for adaptation to this climate emergency under increasingly likely scenarios. They wonder how long it will actually take for residual uncertainties to be replaced by the certainty of systemic cataclysm. As they wait, the insuring instinct focuses itself on the possibilities of risk pooling. The modeling and scenario testing currently underway inside and among large insurers and reinsurers, as well as their regulators, seek to illuminate what this means in practice. A basic question, though, is whether climate "risks" and the disasters they portend are radically different from other global risks, such as the risks posed by financial openness. It's hard to answer that question, given that the temporal dimension of the challenges posed by climate change, for example, is quite different.[16] The cumulative effects of climate change may disrupt the basic conditions of life on the planet human beings now call home. Even if those effects can be rendered more gradual, they may not be reversible.

The ideas of postcrisis resilience then become less relevant, and the conventions and metaphors of insurance here become less useful. Increasing awareness of those limits may still leave room for some degree of risk pooling, burden sharing, and "protection" that benefit some people for a time. But the systemic challenge remains, and it begs a more profound kind of adjustment. The larger challenge may even be exacerbated by measures that aim to separate out or even privatize specific risks by building up targeted buffers. As Steven Bernstein argues, it is not stabilization that seems required but transformation. In this policy arena, with its boundaries impossible to establish, with diverse and multidirectional relationships, with repeated interactions, and with unpredictable feedback loops, uncertainty not risk seems the essential background condition.[17]

To assess scholars' and governments' related assertions and judgments concerning the ultimate relevance of insurance practices and metaphors

[15] Michael Manulak, *Change in Global Environmental Politics: Temporal Focal Points and the Reform of International Institutions* (Cambridge: Cambridge University Press, 2022).

[16] Thomas Hale, *Long Problems: Climate Change and the Challenge of Governing across Time* (Princeton: Princeton University Press, 2024).

[17] Steven Bernstein, "IR, Climate Politics and Change: Opportunities for Productive Engagement?" *International Relations* 38, no. 3 (2024): 349–368.

in such a context, we need first to recall the discussion from Chapter 4. Private insurance providers are in the business of managing risks. They accept and pool them, transfer them from those most averse to those most acceptant, and they also diversify their own ultimate exposures. Their capital bases permit them to initiate this process, and their pooling operations have the effect of expanding their markets' capacity to absorb expected losses. Access to reinsurance, and lately to insurance-linked securities markets, also facilitates the absorption of more unexpected losses. For their services, insurance and reinsurance providers may retain a share of underlying risks in the expectation that the value of premiums paid will exceed the value of probable losses. They also take fees on risks they transfer to others. On their balance sheets, they sometimes hold assets in excess of what they and their regulators deem necessary to cover losses, and they manage their risk-bearing liabilities to reduce the chances that losses will actually crystallize. If they succeed in adequately pricing the risks they transfer as well as the risks they retain on their balance sheets, they earn a net profit. Public insurers perform similar functions, but they typically call their premium charges *taxes*, and their aim is often simply to break even.

Global warming complicates life on both sides of insurers' balance sheets.[18] The value of their assets will vary with a deteriorating climate, and the scale of their potential liabilities may rise – including from indirect losses associated, for example, with rising disease burdens. The key question is whether tolerable degrees of uncertainty prevail and reasonable levels of reserves can be maintained. The more certain it becomes that big surprises will become routine – that natural catastrophes and other disasters will become both more severe and more predictable – the less private insurance as a more or less market-based system of risk distribution remains feasible on its own. And here is where consideration of public backstops reenters.

In political settings such as those prevailing in advanced industrial economies, private-sector insurance practices rest on consumers, intermediaries, and investors sharing a basic understanding of liberal risk regimes. The underpinning assumptions make sense of the idea of insurance *as* governance. An early study on the subject concluded:

[18] Similar effects are occurring and will occur in many other places, with social and political implications only beginning to be explored. See Jeff Colgan, Jessica Green, and Thomas Hale, "Asset Revaluation and the Existential Politics of Climate Change," *International Organization* 75, no. 2 (2021): 586–610.

"Insurance is a core institution in governing modern societies ... [that] encourages a minimal state and governance based on local knowledge of risk."[19] What makes this possible is sufficient self-restraint within a market framework, a modicum of trust and a willingness to accept some personal responsibility, a willingness to share knowledge, a basic sense of social solidarity, acquiescence in the face of some official rebalancing of social outcomes, and the acceptance of a basic capacity for monitoring and dispute-settlement. Global risks such as those linked to climate change necessitate pushing such limits outward.

Even within the classic liberal framework, private insurance obviously already plays a role in managing the effects of global warming and fostering resilience, at least for certain privileged individuals and firms in some societies. In the property and casualty sector, for example, rising premiums for natural catastrophe cover send clear signals into the arena of public policy. Even clearer signals are sent when private insurers and reinsurers withdraw from certain markets, either because customers resist paying adequate premiums or because the probability of disasters such as wildfires and floods has moved closer to certainty. At that point, private insurance provision becomes implausible. The classic underwriter's role in leaning on premium-paying clients to reduce the scale and scope of insured risks also disappears. Lost too is the societal resilience that comes from the pooling and transfer of risks to those adequately endowed to hold them and to bear losses when they materialize. However, as we have seen in previous chapters, a middle ground may exist before we reach that point.

Recall here the critical risk-channeling role that specific energy-producing installations play in the nuclear arena. They concentrate risks, retain a share, transfer a share to private insurers, another share to reinsurers, another share that may turn out to be trivial or extremely large to their host states, and a final share to treaty signatories who again may be either very small or very large. Yes, extreme catastrophes overwhelm the capacity of private insurers and reinsurers. But in everyday circumstances, they can bear most of the risk and play their normal role in helping to mitigate the overall risks of nuclear energy production.

When climate change raises the prospect of especially dramatic disasters for specific regions, who might play a similar role? Not too long ago, that very question prompted a group of experts and heads

[19] Richard V. Ericson, Aaron Doyle, and Dean Barry, *Insurance as Governance* (Toronto: University of Toronto Press, 2003), 360.

of national nuclear insurance pools to examine the subject. They tried to think through how the private–public partnership model in the nuclear field might be applied to help manage the risks posed by global warming. Their effort foundered on the issue of risk concentration and channeling. In the absence of a focal point, they concluded, underlying responsibilities could not easily be discerned or assigned.[20]

Fossil-fuel-fired electricity generating stations, in some countries privately owned and in others considered public utilities, could be considered equivalent to nuclear plants, but governments would have to force them to bear the increasing weight of insurance premiums. A generalized carbon tax, or other measures to embed the polluter pays principle in a broad set of policies, would be simpler. But these are policy tools, not insurance, to manage risks or reduce them. In practice, they also face varying degrees of resistance, even among states with similar political cultures. In any case, the fact is that insurance industry experts observing the long-standing impasse on such issues at the global level hold out little hope that the private sector alone can play a leading role in addressing the underlying challenge. As Figure 3.1 in Chapter 3 suggests, the political and economic complexity of the risks involved as well as the incrementally rising scale and scope of realized damage over the long haul place the core issues squarely in the public realm.

That said, private insurers and reinsurers are already involved in markets buffeted by winds that seem obviously driven and accelerated by climate change, and some are making a great deal of money. In 2022, major reinsurers such as Munich Re predicted that recent losses would bring about a hardening market for natural catastrophe insurance for at least a couple of years, during which it would seek to expand its underwriting book while less deeply capitalized insurers and reinsurers would exit.[21] Their prediction proved accurate, and the strategy was quite lucrative. At the same time, investors both in the insurers and reinsurers of peak risks and in capital market instruments such as catastrophe bonds and so-called weather derivatives (financial contracts speculating on specific weather events) sent mixed signals. Profits were likely to be made in the near to medium terms where clients could afford to pay higher premiums for fire and flood insurance or for insurance-linked securities with parametric payouts. California and much of the United States as well as Western Europe fell into that category. But even in

[20] Confidential interview with the former head of a nuclear pool, Zurich, May 2022.
[21] *Artemis Newsletter*, www.artemis.bm, accessed July 5, 2022.

places such as Florida, the increasing certainty of costly coastal disasters soon meant that little private insurance would be available in the absence of public subsidies.

Elsewhere, more creative solutions were enabling private insurance contracts without directly implicating local taxpayers. As we saw in Chapter 4, for example, regional climate-risk pooling was being encouraged by innovations in parametric insurance instruments. They now include the Caribbean Catastrophe Risk Insurance Facility Segregated Portfolio Company, the Pacific Catastrophe Risk Insurance Company, the Southeast Asia Disaster Risk Insurance Facility, and the African Risk Capacity Group. At base, all of these "facilities" depend on assistance and incentives of some kind provided by the World Bank or other development agencies and by local governments. The challenge is to make them sustainable. In every case, if the expertise, risk-modeling, and capital of private insurers and investors is to remain involved, it means driving down premium costs while still delivering competitive returns. The challenge becomes ever more daunting as the number and severity of climate-related disasters increases.

Continuing debate on the private sector's future role in this arena thus revolves around the essence of insurance systems as they have evolved over time, whether delivered directly by underwriters or indirectly by investors in alternative reinsurance transfer instruments. They take risks from clients and then diversify and manage them in internal or external pooling arrangements. Such activities depend upon functioning markets and robust information sharing. It is therefore no coincidence that the insurance industry is paying more attention to data collection and demanding more transparency on the drivers of climate change.

In the absence of historical data and conventional models, insurers and reinsurers must rely on the best scientific analysis they can muster. They can then place bets to the extent their capital bases permit. If they extend coverage on this basis, their risk mitigation role kicks in as usual. In addition, they can and are taking into account the probable short- and long-term effects of climate change on the asset side of their balance sheets. Investing in green technologies and favoring securities issued by environmentally sound companies are widely seen as constructively helping to stimulate more general corporate mitigation and adaptation activities. In the end, however, the limits of private insurance markets come ever more clearly into view. As one company put it, "Traditional models and loss experience will not be predictive.

Obligations will change, requiring new techniques of portfolio management. And there will be more non-linear effects at play. For example, what is the correlation between more frequent floods and economic activity in a given region? Underwriting will need to become even more strategic."[22]

Attempts to elaborate more holistic responses to the complex challenges posed by global warming continue to adapt the conceptual and practical tools of insurance. In 2021, for example, inspired by policies advocated by the Bank of England to take into account the risks of climate change in bank regulation and supervision, the Institute for Sustainability Leadership of Cambridge University released a major report on global risk pooling.[23] It summarized much of the research undertaken by the Insurance Development Forum, a public–private partnership established in 2014 by the government of Great Britain, the UN Development Program, other international organizations, and many of the world's leading insurers and reinsurers. In essence, the report called for a vast expansion in risk-sharing systems now in place but mainly concentrated in advanced industrial countries. Asserting that the climate emergency is now global and deepening fast, it proposed a risk-sharing continuum ranging from more encompassing tax-based social protection programs to multi-trillion-dollar premium-based systems of micro-insurance to cross-national insurance pools that foster disaster prevention and postdisaster resilience.

Aligning with the UN's Sustainable Development Goals, the report's authors foresaw collaborative actions among UN member-states, the International Association of Insurance Supervisors (IAIS) involved in the Basel Process (discussed in Chapter 6), and the Financial Stability Board (FSB). That collaboration, they held, needed to rest on clear, quantifiable, and standardized assessments of local and regional climate risks. It then required agreed preventative adaptation or risk reduction policies for all potential losses deemed intolerable, contingent and cost-effective arrangements to manage or transfer tolerable risks, and loss-acceptance instruments when predictable damage is less than the costs of risk reduction.

[22] McKinsey & Company, "How Insurance Can Help Combat Climate Change," *Reimagine Insurance* podcast text, July 6, 2021. Also see Maryam Golnaraghi et al., *Bringing Climate Tech to Market: The Powerful Role of Insurance* (Zurich: The Geneva Association, 2024).

[23] University of Cambridge Institute for Sustainability Leadership, *Risk Sharing in the Climate Emergency: Financial Regulation for a Resilient, Net Zero, Just Transition* (Cambridge: University of Cambridge Institute for Sustainability Leadership, 2021).

The Cambridge study ultimately came down to the essential questions climate change poses for individuals, firms, and government. "What is the risk; what is valued; what should be protected; what should be insured, how should it be shared, and what should be left to fate?"[24] Given the problem's borderless nature, only a global framework seemed likely to generate the risk-sharing pools that would "govern, fund, and deliver" satisfactory outcomes. Only within it would fully adequate contractual relationships and payment mechanisms emerge to reveal in clear detail the costs and benefits allocable to different "stakeholders" necessary to make risk pools sustainable and useful. The implication is that insurance regulation and supervision as well as insurance legislation would need to be much more coordinated, at least among the states producing most of the global problem itself. This means estimating potential losses from climate-related disasters, and also building up, stress-testing, and then protecting loss-absorbing capital buffers across both public and private sectors. It also means collaborating on governing the conditions under which those buffers are deployed, risks are shared (including systemic financial risks), and related investment decisions are made.

Such messages are certainly clear in principle and are now coming from all sides. The extent of the global risk domain is also coming into view. In 2022, it was estimated at USD 80.1 trillion, equivalent to one-third of global gross domestic product (GDP), most of which remained uninsured. But then comes the hard part.

Despite this growing awareness, focal points for delimiting physical climate risks that can readily be used by policy and financial practitioners remain elusive. Without them, the largest risks will effectively be hidden because they are not measured and communicated. This creates a structural asymmetry between the scope of risk management systems and the driving threats to sustainability and human well-being. The disconnect has been recognized. The increasing priority of adaptation and resilience within mainstream policy processes, combined with related concerns from financial authorities and markets, is starting to bring shared attention on this issue. Governments, international institutions, and financial firms are converging towards approaches using insurance-aligned methods and metrics at larger scales.[25]

Perhaps convergence at least on risk assessment is actually happening through the work programs of the IAIS, the FSB, and national climate

24 Ibid., 21.
25 Ibid., 33.

agencies preparing for continuing negotiations under the UN Framework Convention and elsewhere. Private-sector initiatives, such as the prominent Glasgow Financial Alliance for Net-Zero (GFANZ), a 2021 consortium initially claiming 450 financial firms across forty-five nations as members – all pledging to align their lending and investing operations with net-zero objectives – certainly helped to raise awareness. But those firms still had to compete in markets that are inadequately primed by governments to achieve collaborative goals. Within three years, most of the world's top insurers and reinsurers had opted out of the insurance component of the GFANZ, called the Net Zero Insurance Alliance. Under obvious market pressures, some claimed now to be concerned about violating anti-trust and anti-cartel statutes. Others claimed that their individual commitments to helping clients adapt to climate change would be better achieved outside a formal alliance. What had become clear, though, was the lack of support coming from political authorities in key markets. Perhaps such initiatives will eventually turn out to be more than exercises in enhancing institutional reputations. Perhaps local contests between financial institutions and interest groups will eventually lay the groundwork for a sustainable balancing of environmental and economic policy objectives.[26] Their ultimate impact, though, looks set to depend on the willingness of governments acting collectively to induce changes in the behavior and expectations of the nonfinancial clients of leading lenders and investors, including insurance and reinsurance providers.

Massive losses from weather-related disasters around the world are already being recorded. The idea that global warming has nothing to do with the trend seems, in many jurisdictions anyway, increasingly untenable. Those losses are still mostly uninsured, and this means that the protection gap everywhere is opening, not closing. The resource gap is also increasing between (still potentially profitable) advanced markets and the sites of most floods, earthquakes, and fires in developing and emerging-market countries.

The idea of building resilient-because-insured societies becomes irresistible. It means paying the costs of insurance, even as those costs gallop ahead, while issues of fairness in risk distribution as well as moral hazard become more complex. The specific problems of identifying

[26] See Christian Morin Elliott, "Hedging the Planet: The Demand for Global Governance in Sustainable Finance," PhD Dissertation, Department of Political Science, University of Toronto, December 2023.

responsible parties and encouraging them to purchase private insurance become more difficult but also less avoidable. The same can be said about the provision and coordination of public subsidies, the collection of necessary revenues, and the regulation of associated moral hazards. Expressions of the increasingly common wisdom, if not blueprints for concrete action, abound.

> To match this scale and fully manage climate risks, we have to share them by significantly expanding the availability of sustainable risk pools. To do so, the Climate Emergency needs all actors of the risk-sharing domain (tax-based and premium-based, from community programs to multinational level) working together in a public–private and mutual risk-sharing continuum. In the Climate Emergency, everything and everybody should be a member of risk-sharing pools. We must ensure this happens on a large scale, across both public and private sectors.[27]

In principle, strict limits on insurability when it comes to climate-related natural disasters are being pushed outward by the "climate process" outlined in such documents as the Cambridge report. In practice, the political struggle intensifies to harness the insuring instinct to build appropriate risk pools and effectively mitigate the risks of catastrophic climate change. At the system level, existing public insurance instruments are stimulating imaginations. Proposals to adapt and expand multilateral and regional development banks are also proliferating. Related incremental changes are already on display within the International Monetary Fund and World Bank. More ambitious ideas, such as the Loss and Damage Fund agreed in-principle at COP27 and a Global Climate Finance Facility could play important roles. Despite rising resistance and populist countermovements, later official and unofficial meetings moved along the same line. Governments were called upon collectively to be more ambitious on funding, distributing, and dividing responsibilities for systemic stabilization between public and private sectors.[28]

In the absence of conditions reminiscent of wartime, the bulk of the vast sums required for a global "green transition" will have to be raised in private capital markets, with coordinated support from governments. It is already happening, and negotiations to increase such funding significantly received a boost in 2019 from the Secretary-General of the UN.

[27] "Risk Sharing in the Climate Emergency: Financial Regulation for a Resilient, Net Zero, Just Transition" (Cambridge: University of Cambridge Institute for Sustainability Leadership, 2021), 42.

[28] Håvard Halland, Justin Yifu Lin, and Alan Gelb, "What the Paris Development Finance Summit Missed," *Project Syndicate*, July 10, 2023.

A Coalition for Climate Resilient Investment proposed a framework for pricing climate risks with the aim of promoting investment in protective infrastructure. Comprised of thirty insurance and other financial firms, the coalition sought to limit an estimated climate-related loss of USD 1 trillion between 2019 and 2024. They hoped that many multiples of that amount could be made available by 2030, 70 percent of which could be directed toward developing countries. A related initiative launched in 2019, the InsuResilience Global Partnership, which sought to ease climate change's financial impact on the world's poorest and most vulnerable people. The governments of Germany and the United Kingdom promised to provide enough support until 2025 to enable up to USD 5 billion in risk-bearing capacity from private insurers.

By the time COP28 commenced in Dubai in November 2023, negotiations between the finance ministers of the so-called Vulnerable 20 (V20) and their G7 counterparts were well advanced. They now called their initiative the Global Shield against Climate Risks, which essentially promised resources that could be rapidly deployed after particular climate-related disasters. Starting contributions topped EUR 210 million, including about EUR 170 million from Germany. According to V20 estimates, almost all of the 1.5 billion people residing within these countries had no insurance, and climate-related losses in recent years had already exceeded USD 525 billion. The Global Shield was clearly long on ambition but short on cash. Numerous related initiatives were similarly premised on private insurance and reinsurance arrangements guaranteed, subsidized, or otherwise supported by creditworthy governments operating collaboratively. The promise was there, but the dedicated public resources were not yet visible at the scale required.

Key questions remain to be answered about the modalities of insurance systems and the actual roles that private insurers and reinsurers could constructively play under the rubric of "loss and damage." At one level, private firms can offer to localities in developing countries likely to be harmed by future climate-related shocks more insurance coverage with the kinds of parametric triggers pioneered in insurance-linked securities markets. The ultimate providers of postdisaster private capital might in principle then have the incentive to encourage risk reduction by all parties concerned. Such activities could help structure and provide market-based discipline to overarching adaptation and mitigation programs. To the extent that private insurers and reinsurers can assist, the premiums paid by disadvantaged countries will have to be subsidized by official providers of foreign aid. Then the question would be whether the tangible and intangible benefits of the involvement of private firms outweigh the costs. The answer will likely vary across specific cases.

As the planet heats up, common interests are becoming difficult to hide or ignore. Since the 2015 Paris Agreement, sophisticated risk-modeling adapted from the cutting-edge technologies of the world's top insurers and reinsurers has helped set the negotiating table. Every five years, states agree on more ambitious targets to reduce carbon emissions. But decisive action by leading public authorities lags behind. As one reinsurance executive I interviewed noted, "Staggering losses are being booked every year from weather events, and they are increasing annually. At the same time, it is incredible that we collectively won't invest comparable or even lesser amounts in mitigation and adaptation."[29] Nevertheless, the Paris Agreement and the COP process continue to drive necessary negotiations. They also provide targets for social and political pressures and incentives for technological innovation and political experimentation.[30]

Fundamental struggles persist over the distribution of liability and compensation for damage anticipated or already realized. The insuring instinct points persistently toward systemic collaboration among public authorities. In the end, universal risks are shared and cannot be diversified. Complexity and uncertainty only render more difficult the inescapable necessity of governing them jointly. Social justice as well as the efficacy of any serious response requires that the better off of the world's residents support the rest in dealing with contemporary consequences of past environmental damage and the absence of plausible systemic alternatives. Faced with the increasingly credible prospect of future losses, even rich, well-insured individuals cannot in the end count on reliable or fully adequate personal coverage from private or even conventional public sources.

Private insurance markets and their justifying narratives may still play significant roles in addressing specific climate-related issues, but only reliably collaborative public authority can back them up in the long run. The fact that central banking and financial regulatory networks are beginning to focus on the linkages between their mandates and the effects of climate change is indicative of rising awareness.[31]

[29] Interview, Zurich, April 27, 2022.

[30] Charles F. Sabel and David G. Victor, *Fixing the Climate: Strategies for an Uncertain World* (Cambridge: Cambridge University Press, 2019).

[31] See Dirk Schoenmaker and Hesse McKechnie, "What can central banks do to take the Paris Agreement seriously?" *Policy Brief* 26, Bruegel, 2024.

Indirect fiscal supports and direct transfers of some kind will ultimately prove essential even if private markets are fully enlisted in the struggle, and technocratic coordination can only help prepare feasible pathways. Insurance market signals have already helped set the stage for more intensive official responses and more ambitious multilateral collaboration. Metaphors of solidarity, burden sharing, and resilience drawn from the history and practice of insurance and reinsurance may also continue to motivate preventive measures aimed at ameliorating the dangers of a warming planet. Similar conclusions may be drawn in the related policy arena focused on biodiversity loss.

BIODIVERSITY LOSS

Biodiversity's importance to the sustainability of human life should be intuitively obvious. The potential role of insurance practices and metaphors is less so, since they focus on specific risks and potential losses. Even so, serious work across both public and private sectors is underway to measure certain elements of biodiversity loss, convert them into risks that can be insured, and develop instruments to manage and redistribute costs.

We already know that more than three-quarters of the world's wetlands are gone, that nearly half of its peatlands have disappeared since 2000, that over a third of our forests is lost, that topsoil is rapidly depleting, that over half of the ocean's coral reefs have been destroyed, and that the oceans themselves are filled with plastic and are quickly acidifying. We also know that 85 percent of freshwater fish species have declined, while the known populations of vertebrates around the world have declined by 60 percent.[32] Traditional measures of economic and social progress have not taken into account the costs of the depleting supply of the natural resources upon which life itself ultimately depends.[33] If those costs were able to be estimated in advance, the insuring instinct may well have kicked in.

Innovative ecologists are in fact now developing what they call biological insurance theory. It starts with the simple assumption that biodiversity itself provides an essential risk management and mitigation

[32] World Economic Forum, *The Global Risks Report*, 16th edition, 2021; and World Wildlife Fund, *Living Planet Report*, 2020.

[33] Partha Dasgupta, *The Economics of Biodiversity: The Dasgupta Review* (London: HM Treasury, 2021).

instrument for ecosystem stability.[34] This has set the foundation for making distinctions between potentially beneficial selection effects and the kinds of buffering efforts that are critical for systemic welfare. Feedback loops and the dynamics of adaptive processes remain complex, but being able to measure the specific costs and benefits of biodiversity in actual physical settings is key to allowing the practical development of financial instruments of risk transfer and risk mitigation.

In principle, the risks of biodiversity loss have been widely recognized for quite some time. The multilateral Convention on Biological Diversity, after all, has been in force since 29 December 1993, with only the United States of 168 signatories not having ratified it. Its declared motivation was sustainable development and equitable sharing of the planet's genetic resources. Despite a long series of global and regional negotiations since then, initial studies from insurers and various international agencies on why and how such instruments might actually develop have only recently begun accelerating. A good example came from the Sustainable Insurance Forum hosted by the UN Development Program in 2021.

Using the familiar distinction between the underwriting and investing sides of insurers 'and reinsurers' balance sheets, the study highlights the two main sources of risk associated with biodiversity loss, both potentially quantifiable: physical risks to economies, societies, and businesses from existing trends of degradation; and transition risks as localities, regions, and the global system take practical steps to move toward remediation and sustainability.[35] Citing work rapidly advancing under the auspices of the United Nations' Intergovernmental Science-Policy Platform on Biodiversity and Ecosystem Services, which is itself directly linked to the climate change agenda, the study zeroes in on risks capable of generating widely dispersed financial shocks in the near future. These stem from findings already gathered in regard to known ecological damage from, for example, land-use changes and stratospheric ozone depletion. Estimates should probably be significantly higher because of profound uncertainties related to the effects of genetic loss and changes in the biochemical composition of the atmosphere initiated during the earliest days of the Industrial Revolution. Unfortunately, a bleak conclusion

[34] Michel Loreau, Matthieu Barbier, Elise Filotas, et al., "Biodiversity as Insurance: From Concept to Measurement and Application," *Biological Reviews* 96, no. 5 (2021): 2333–2354.

[35] Sustainable Insurance Forum, *Nature-Related Risks in the Global Insurance Sector*, UN Development Program, November 2021, vii.

already seems well supported. "We have entered an era of 'ecological emergency,' which could be bigger than the 'climate emergency' by an order of magnitude."[36]

Swiss Re reports already have some rough estimates of what this means in systemic financial terms. Over half of the world's GDP in 2021, or nearly USD 50 trillion, was moderately or highly dependent on nature, but we do not yet have reliable measures of how this translates into specific impacts on key economic sectors.[37] Agriculture, tourism, pulp and paper manufacturing, mining, metal manufacturing, and others are understood to be facing rapidly increasing risks in the near term. Rising losses in the property and casualty sector are also on the horizon, although they are difficult to separate from the effects of climate change. With surveys indicating that less than 50 percent of reinsurers are currently taking known nature-related risks into account in their general pricing, it's not difficult to scope out what all of this could soon mean for both private insurers and reinsurers.

To get beyond such general observations, the problem is not only to determine what specific losses might arise within a reasonable time frame for specific sectors and firms, but also to ascertain whether anyone will offer viable insurance policies or pay requisite premiums. If nature-related risks are underpriced by the entire insurance industry within a given jurisdiction over a period of time, the solvency positions of affected insurers could deteriorate. In response, the industry is likely to seek support to increase its capital buffers. In times of severe nature-related losses in an already challenging economic environment that constrains profit-making, the setting aside of additional capital can have a dual impact on the insurance industry. Underwriting losses combined with stressed capital reserves can have knock-on effects in broader financial markets. Furthermore, should a large number of insurers abruptly raise premiums or withdraw coverage from assets exposed to nature-related risks within a jurisdiction, this can bring about systemic financial shocks through self-reinforcing business failures. In extreme cases, state and local governments might be required to intervene to limit damage to the larger economy when rapidly growing debts and cascading failures among underinsured businesses begin to appear. As tax bases are eroded by economy-wide disruptions, governments may face

[36] Ibid., 6.

[37] Swiss Re Institute, *Biodiversity and Ecosystem Services: A Business Case for Reinsurance* (Zurich: Swiss Re Institute, 2021).

increasing fiscal pressures and become less able to service their own. This could result in a higher probability of defaults on national and local bonds and impair capacities to borrow in the future.[38]

A comprehensive World Bank study released in 2022 amplified the same themes.[39] It asserted that governments need to put more incentives in place to encourage insurance firms to develop better data and models as well as to bring new products to market. It noted that biodiversity risk is not yet linked to the core public accounts – a necessary condition for future public–private partnerships and cross-border risk pools. It then spelled out the ways in which insurance underwriting and investing operations can promote biodiversity-positive activities and discourage the opposite. Its sobering conclusion, however, was that private insurance may play an increasingly important but limited role in "incentivizing adaptation and providing financial protection for when an acute climate or biodiversity shock happens."[40]

In anticipation of just such a scenario, preemptive governmental responses are emerging, but they are slow, disjointed, and mainly informal. They include a "Nature Compact" agreed by G7 leaders in June 2021 and a commitment from G20 environmental ministers in July 2021 targeting measures to preserve land and ocean integrity. Related initiatives from the European Commission, other governments and central banks, and the International Association of Insurance Supervisors were expected to accelerate work on data gathering and dissemination.

In this policy arena the hour is late. Financiers, international organizations, and leading governments have been aware of the opportunities as well as the risks of biodiversity loss for many decades. After all, the first debt for nature swap in the context of developing country debt-restructuring operations took place in 1987.[41] Others soon followed, but their pace faltered as an array of domestic impediments compromised many local conservation efforts and as the liquidation price of developing country debt rose when bank creditors were replaced by less easily corralled private

38 Sustainable Insurance Forum, *Nature-Related Risks in the Global Insurance Sector* (New York: UN Development Program, November 2021), 22.

39 World Bank/Disaster Risk Financing & Insurance Program, *Insuring Nature's Survival: The Role of Insurance in Meeting the Financial Need to Preserve Biodiversity* (Washington, DC: World Bank Group, 2022). (Supported by the Swiss Confederation.)

40 Ibid., 9.

41 Stein Hansen, "Debt for Nature Swaps: Overview and Discussion of Key Issues," *Working Paper* 1, World Bank Environment Department, 1988.

equity firms and hedge funds. The insuring instinct manifests itself, but in increasingly complex markets. The future roles of private insurers and reinsurers in this context are again circumscribed by the need to concentrate risks limit the scope and duration of their responsibilities.

One can imagine such concentrated risks, but one would also immediately note that adapting market instruments accordingly would still require cross-national as well as intranational negotiations on both the generation and the distribution of public subsidies. Think, for example, of the rainforests in developing countries needing to be sustainably exploited or left alone. Or think of the plastic waste-disposal systems of tomorrow that may or may not be well managed. If private-market forces are to be relied upon, they also require the credible expectation that governments will bear risks potentially materializing just beyond the foreseeable future – and governments' only hope of success in ameliorating those risks rests on the deeper expectation that all relevant parties will cooperate. The deep complexity and long-term framing noted in the lower right-hand quadrant of Figure 3.1 is unavoidable. Some role for the private sector may well be necessary, but only within an overarching structure grounded in collaborative public authority. The same is true in the arena of public health, where we have often been reminded that political borders and functional boundaries provide only the illusion of protection.

PANDEMICS

The COVID-19 pandemic that began in 2019 did not force theorists or practitioners to break new ground. It followed a long history of plagues and airborne viral outbreaks, marked only occasionally by successful collaborative responses. The lethal transmission of a novel coronavirus from animals to human populations had long and accurately been predicted. The fact that this viral agent could spread rapidly through human respiration and that vaccinations on a massive scale complemented by standard containment techniques would be needed to interrupt the spread was well understood. Adverse economic effects were also widely anticipated in a world reshaped by people's vastly expanded mobility and the interdependence of the economies and societies they live in. Perhaps the only real surprise was the rapidity with which new vaccines emerged. The fog of uncertainty surrounding the potential spread of bacterial, viral, and parasitic infections lifted long ago. Even the imminent specter of antimicrobial resistance underlines not uncertainty but the same basic and interconnected challenge facing us with regard to climate change and biodiversity loss: we constructed a reasoned foundation for estimating the probability of disaster, but we have not come to grips with the social and political requirements it implied. Appropriate risks pools were necessary but not constructed fast enough. And we knew it. The insurance instinct was not absent. It was deliberately suppressed.

Ten years before the outbreak of COVID-19, the path-breaking work of Andrew Price-Smith on the contemporary political implications of pathogenic disease transmission came to crystal clear conclusions. The globalization of pathogens generates complexities, however, for the ways the dominant school of international relations conceptualizes world order. Realists, according to Price-Smith, assert that "states will engage in strategies of self-help to contain pathogens within their borders, [which] may require sealing borders to trade and migration, mass quarantining of infected individuals, and continued effective surveillance. [But] many states lack the endogenous capacity for surveillance, diagnosis, effective prophylaxis and treatment, and means of quarantine and border control."[42] Even great powers will thus find it necessary to negotiate arrangements of mutual assistance. Ethnocentric visions of global health that exclusively advocate self-help, to the exclusion of building universal capacity, will thus be ineffective in the global containment of emergent pathogens, for example, a novel and lethal influenza viruses. "The development of endogenous capacity for containment must be supplemented by cooperative international initiatives, as the means by which to effectively maintain surveillance and containment of pathogens on a global scale. Such cooperation is essential to the protection of the material interests of all states." As Price-Smith concluded, "Problems at the domestic level may generate externalities that destabilize the international system."[43]

He was prescient. Adding to the plausibility of both his diagnosis and his prognosis was the lengthy history of global efforts to manage specific disease outbreaks, starting with cholera and the International Sanitary Convention of 1892.[44] Admittedly, it took sixty-two years to reach that point from the first meeting of European governments during the cholera

42 Andrew Price-Smith, *Contagion and Chaos: Disease, Ecology, and National Security in the Era of Globalization* (Cambridge, MA: MIT Press, 2009), 232.

43 Ibid.

44 Michael McCarthy, "A Brief History of the World Health Organization," *The Lancet* 360, no. 9340 (2002): 1111–1112.

epidemic of 1830. But scientific advances soon accelerated a similar agreement to cooperate on the containment and eradication of the plague (1897). In 1902, the International Sanitary Bureau was established in the Americas; it soon became the Pan American Health Organization. L'Office International d'Hygiene Publique followed in 1907, and in 1919 the Health Organization of the League of Nations was established. Among its accomplishments were the 1926 and 1938 expansions of the International Sanitary Convention to target smallpox, typhus, and other communicable diseases. Its work was interrupted by World War II, but its personnel and agenda formed the foundation for the UN Relief and Rehabilitation Administration and eventually the World Health Organization (WHO), which was formally chartered at the World Health Assembly in 1948.

With a modest initial budget of USD 5 million, the WHO and its six regional sub-organizations were charged with the tasks of managing contagion risks related to malaria, tuberculosis, yaws, leprosy, trachoma, and endemic venereal diseases as well as to improve maternal and child health, sanitary engineering, and nutrition. Over time, its capacities to promote mass vaccination campaigns and surveillance regarding emerging pathogens were improved, even if its major member-states continued to focus the vast bulk of their own public health resources on domestic protection. The point, though, is that for almost 200 years those same member states have demonstrated a realization that the health of their own citizens could not be assured in the absence of a rising level of global cooperation. Nevertheless, as the panicked and inadequately coordinated responses to the COVID-19 pandemic clearly demonstrated, states continued, tragically, to fall short in delivering both effective emergency management and comprehensive risk reduction. Nowhere was the shortfall between instinctive aspiration and actual governance clearer than in the private insurance markets that had evolved in tandem with public policies over that same two-century period.

Within the first year of the long COVID-19 pandemic, private insurers and reinsurers worldwide were reporting losses exceeding those associated with the most severe weather-related catastrophes of the past century. Life and health insurers were surprised by the scale of mounting losses, which upended established actuarial tables. Property and casualty insurance providers were also caught off guard by the underestimates of potential liabilities related to business interruption claims. Litigation promised lengthy periods of uncertainty, even as wave after wave of mutating viruses overwhelmed surprisingly rapid if incomplete and uncoordinated vaccination campaigns. Just one year into the pandemic, for example, the world-leading Lloyd's reinsurance market estimated its underwriting losses at USD 4.3 billion, on a par with losses associated with the 9/11 terrorist attacks and the combined impacts of three massive hurricanes in 2017. Looking at both its underwriting and investment operations, Lloyd's executives claimed that "once the scale and complexity of the social and economic impact of COVID-19 is fully understood, the overall cost to the global insurance non-life industry is likely to be far in excess of those historical events."[45] In 2020 alone, history-defining underwriting losses for the entire global insurance industry were estimated to approach USD 107 billion, while investment losses were estimated to be USD 96 billion. Even more surprising was the fact that the industry and their regulators were unprepared.

Field-wide handbooks are typically published long after the conventional wisdom of a generation has been firmly established. They summarize important findings, highlight key areas for future work, and draw out implications for specialized scientific and policy audiences. In 2017, the *Handbook of Unconventional Risk Transfer* offered an assessment of cutting-edge issues at the frontier of insurance, reinsurance, and insurance-linked securities' markets. A key chapter covered pandemic risk modeling.[46] It began by noting that a 2013 survey of 30,000 insurance industry executives placed a global pandemic as "the biggest extreme risk facing insurers." After reviewing pandemic impacts from the Black Plague through the 1918 Spanish Flu and the Ebola, SARS, and MERS crisis of more recent years, the chapter gave special attention to air- and aerosol-borne viruses. It noted in passing Swiss Re's experimental Vita bond in 2003, which paid out if mortality claims exceeded a certain high level, and it highlighted a World Bank proposal to build on its previous disaster-management work with the establishment of a Pandemic Emergency Facility. It concluded as follows:

> Modelling infectious diseases remains an active area of scientific research and plays an important role in maintaining public health and resilience to catastrophic mortality events. It also underpins appropriate management of excess mortality risk by life insurers and reinsurers, including providing the means to quantify such risks for the purpose of risk transfer. Thus, insurers' mortality and

45 "COVID-19 Will See Historic Losses Across the Global Insurance Industry," Lloyd's Press Release, May 14, 2020. www.lloyds.com/about-lloyds/media-centre/press-releases/covid19-will-see-historic-losses-across-the-global-insurance-industry, accessed May 15, 2020.

46 Dominic Smith, "Pandemic Risk Modelling," in *The Palgrave Handbook of Unconventional Risk Transfer*, edited by Maurizio Pompella and Nicos A. Scoridis (Cham, CH: Palgrave, 2017), 463–495.

morbidity tables and modelling work would require significant and continuing updating as the novel and mutating coronavirus became endemic. Beyond the pure mortality impact, the emergence of a highly transmissible infectious disease could have a major impact on the global economy by way of less willingness to travel, reduced economic participation and confidence.[47]

So, when the COVID-19 pandemic hit two years later, no one with a stake in global insurance markets could credibly claim that they were operating in a context of radical uncertainty.

To be sure, the pandemic changed the global insurance landscape. In 2021, surveys and analysis sponsored by the Geneva Association affirmed that the fragility of modern life had been exposed and that the "new normal" faced by individuals and businesses would likely feature robust efforts to fill "protection gaps." But who would do most of the filling, at least in rich countries? Insurers and reinsurers expected a larger role for themselves in absolute terms, but they also expected that the main trend that was evident during the pandemic would continue. Yes, individuals who could afford insurance might face incentives to purchase more, and more expensive, insurance. But most individuals, in both rich and poor countries, would rely ever more assertively on their governments to provide them with disaster-risk coverage.

Heightened awareness of vulnerability led to a rise in mindfulness. For insurers, this shift offers additional opportunities to expand traditional business models predicated on paying claims and providing benefits to broader and more engaging customer propositions, such as prevention services. The pandemic also reinforced the pivot to sustainability across businesses and society, creating new opportunities for insurers. In light of the massive societal imbalances caused by the pandemic, insurers will have to pay more attention in the future to the social dimension. The pandemic prompted a broad reevaluation of the social contract, that is, the division of risk bearing among individuals, employers, and the state. This could herald a new chapter for the welfare state and the role of private-sector insurance in complementing it.[48]

The most immediate implication, as litigation continued to mount in the United States and most other profitable markets, was that insurers and reinsurers would henceforth be much more careful and much clearer in their assumption of liability for business interruptions caused

[47] Ibid., 495.

[48] Kai-Uwe Schanz, *The Global Risk Landscape after COVID-19* (Zurich: Geneva Association, June 10, 2021).

by pandemics and other disasters. As anticipated, associated strategic adjustments would soon begin to be made in "hardening" markets, where both the prices and the volumes of post-disaster insurance policies were rising. Of course, the same landscape would encourage both individuals and businesses to call on their states for increasing support.

As much as idealistic economists might bemoan such developments, and depict them as undermining entrepreneurial zeal, this logic would prove compelling. Despite rising debt loads around the world, neither democratic nor authoritarian states demonstrated much interest in pulling back in the post-COVID-19 environment. The protection gap between insured losses and total economic losses continued to expand after all, especially in emerging and developing economies.

All the more tragic, then, were the many internal mistakes that policymakers made during the first year of the COVID-19 pandemic, mistakes exacerbated by inadequate transparency. Openness early on would certainly have saved lives. And when the best vaccines became available, leading and following countries would have benefited from more solidarity, efficiency, and clarity. Policymakers clearly understood the need for mass vaccination beyond national borders to bring the virus under control. In April 2020, just a few months into the pandemic, the WHO, the European Commission, and the Government of France initiated a collaborative project called the Access to COVID-19 Tools Accelerator. A key element in the project soon became COVID-19 Vaccines Global Access (COVAX), which aimed to provide tests, treatments, and vaccines equitably around the world. Since 2017, the WHO and UNICEF had already been committed to developing vaccines that the poorer regions of the world needed (along with the Bill and Melinda Gates Foundation, the Wellcome Trust, and the World Economic Forum). By October 2020, almost all UN member-states had joined COVAX. But two years later, donor states had fallen far short of initial vaccine pledges. National self-centeredness was widely blamed, and the virus continued to mutate. And just as with the development and deployment of other vaccines, private pharmaceutical manufacturers fought over their appropriate level of compensation and property rights protection. The insuring instinct remained in evidence, but it was never strong enough on its own to mobilize required resources.

Journalistic accounts of what went wrong or right were plentiful, even as the COVID-19 disaster was still unfolding.[49] The task of excavating the

[49] See, for example, Lawrence Wright, *The Plague Year: America in the Time of COVID* (New York: Knopf, 2021).

underlying impediments to fully effective and fair responses will occupy natural and social scientists and historians for years to come. Even early on in the pandemic, responsible international consultative groups offered clear diagnoses of what was going wrong at local and global levels, and specific proposals on what needed to be done in the near term as well as the long term.[50] What seemed obvious as the pandemic wore on was that the simple call for "international cooperation" to confront an undoubted "human security threat" failed to tap fully into an insuring instinct narrowly conceived in nationalist terms. However understandable the need for national governments to give priority to the demands of their own citizens, no serious policymaker would deny that those demands could only actually be fully met on a global basis. Governmental and business actors alike downplayed the common sense of well-developed multilevel insurance practice, and millions of premature deaths occurred. Not only did preventive governance experiments nurtured in the prepandemic decades fail to flourish, their seemingly natural evolution in the direction of greater social solidarity went into reverse. Many observers wondered whether the pattern would be repeated a short time later, when avian influenza (H5N1) began to spread. The fundamental contradiction between inevitable openness and political fragmentation was again starkly exposed. With regard to irrepressible risks, an undeniably global society cannot be governed effectively by nation-states valuing their political autonomy above all other human values.

ACROSS AND BEYOND THE BOUNDARIES OF RISK

The complexity of risk management in the overlapping arenas of climate, biodiversity, and health is hardly unique. Rapid technological advances in such intimately related fields as generative artificial intelligence (AI), cybersecurity, and genetic engineering now pose similarly urgent questions, both for risk managers and those expected to govern them.

[50] Among the best was *Covid-19: Make It the Last Pandemic*, by the Independent Panel for Pandemic Preparedness and Response, commissioned by the director-general of the World Health Organization and convened by Helen Clark and Ellen Johnson Sirleaf, 2021. Specific recommendations were sensible and detailed, including serious proposals for a new International Pandemic Financing Facility with a ten- to fifteen-year time horizon, and the establishment of a permanent Global Health Threats Council to provide oversight for more open and transparent surveillance systems. The only reference to insurance in the report emphasized the importance of robust national health insurance programs for individual citizens.

Across all of these fields, experiments in authoritative regulation and supervision seem way behind developments that seemingly every day expose new risks. To the extent those risks can be roughly anticipated, they are stretching existing structures of risk management and governance. But many appear to be unanticipated and impossible to calculate, which again points toward the hazy realm of uncertainty.

Private insurers and reinsurers, for example, were developing a reasonable collective understanding of the risks associated with early advances in AI. After all, it affected their businesses' entire value chain in the early decades of the twenty-first century. The common wisdom saw most of the technology as simply accelerating the value added to normal business propositions and posing known management challenges. From improving and marketing new products to underwriting procedures to claims management, AI and early-stage machine learning were accelerating innovation, reducing costs, and improving efficiency.[51] As in other industries, however, the dawn of generative AI soon raised an array of concerns – some were entirely new, while others were complex variations of traditional problems to be managed. In principle, for example, AI tools could help insurers discriminate and limit future claims by cherry-picking clients. In practice, such discrimination could undercut the very rationale for an industry designed to provide a product and a service that ultimately depends upon its capacity to build broadly diversified risk pools. Even if resulting questions of affordability and exclusion were exaggerated or foreclosed by existing or planned regulations in most countries, the landscape of perceptions both inside and outside the industry changed quickly as innovations in AI technologies rolled out and forced political responses.

For industry regulators, discerning and then implementing rules and norms that balance consumer protection and socially beneficial technological innovation has never been easy. The dynamic challenge in cybersecurity and related areas is not dissimilar.[52] AI-related developments at once increase pressures for effective microlevel governance as well as for coordination across jurisdictional lines. To complicate matters, policy targets are constantly moving, sometimes into reverse. While it is natural for industries spanning borders to call for agreed principles of

[51] Geneva Association, *Regulation of Artificial Intelligence in Insurance* (Zurich: The Geneva Association, 2023).

[52] Ronald Deibert, *RESET: Reclaiming the Internet for Civil Society* (Toronto: House of Anansi Press, 2020).

regulation, clear guidelines, and harmonized policy frameworks, suppliers of innovative new technologies are constantly driven by competitive impulses to transcend any such limits.

Authorities around the world are trying to adjust and adapt in real time. The already deeply collaborative rule-making institutions of the European Union promoted certain regulatory principles for AI in the insurance sector and enacted them into law in July 2024 when, for example, the European Parliament and the European Council promulgated the AI Act.[53] Their counterparts elsewhere consequently faced the now-standard question of whether European attempts to preempt probable and unwanted social outcomes were stifling innovation and simply forcing innovators to practice their craft elsewhere. The same question soon began to roil regulatory politics within the United States, where most insurance rules emanated from state-level authorities.

Debates over similar policy responses arise as AI and the prospect of generative AI stimulate real-world advances in genetic engineering, gene therapy, drug discovery, and design. As boundless opportunities for life-enhancing innovations present themselves, immediate policy concerns typically focus on ensuring the fair distribution of benefits and costs and securing databases to prevent violations of privacy. For insurers and reinsurers, familiar issues arise, as do cross-cutting pressures to limit exposures to high risks and inadequately diversified risk pools, while maintaining resilient balance sheets. Again, in the realm of measurable risk, AI challenges firms and their regulators to move more rapidly.[54] To the extent it also appears to expand the realm of uncertainty, it prompts both firms and governments to limit their financial and political exposures. But what if there is no escape?

As earlier chapters have noted, increasingly complex challenges in the past certainly stimulated the kind of political solidarity required to establish effective and legitimate insurance mechanisms to develop *within* many civil societies. Think here of the forces pushing all advanced

[53] For an overview of the Artificial Intelligence Act of the European Parliament and the European Council, see https://artificialintelligenceact.eu/high-level-summary/, accessed April 7, 2025. On the specific issues presented by AI to European insurers, see European Insurance and Occupational Pensions Authority (EIOPA), Consultative Expert Group on Digital Ethics in Insurance, "Artificial Intelligence Governance Principles," www.eiopa.europa.eu/document/download/30f4502b-3fe9-4fad-b2a3-aa66ea41e863_en?filename=Artificial%20intelligence%20governance%20principles.pdf, accessed April 7, 2025.

[54] See Eric Best, Pedro Robles, and Daniel J. Mallinson, "The Future of AI Politics, Policy, and Business," *Business and Politics* 26, no. 2 (2024): 171–179.

societies toward some kind of public health insurance system. Similarly, cross-border challenges have sometimes prompted solidarity among distinct civil societies. The evolution of modern federal states can be understood in such a light, with variations in the kind of reinsurance arrangements available to constituents units often depending on specific circumstances.[55] Something akin to this kind of development, as we have seen, is occurring within the eurozone, as repeated emergencies forge just enough of a sense of community – a wide enough realization of solidarity – to sustain incipient regional capacities for resolving some emergencies and preventing relapses.[56] In the face of challenges such as those discussed earlier, there is no obvious reason that such a logic cannot ultimately apply universally as societies are forced to adapt and develop minimally necessary joint governing instruments. Indeed, a global economy and society organized around seemingly inexorable processes of financial deepening, technological integration, and environmental change suggest no feasible alternative.[57]

It was, perhaps, easier to think along such lines when many imagined the persistence and inexorable global extension of liberal hegemony, whether centered on the United States or on impersonal markets conjoining all powerful societies. Now that political power is shifting beneath a still-globalizing economy, the logic of functional and geographic spillovers meets the hard politics of legitimating ad hoc collaborative capacities extending across liberal as well as illiberal societies. New and necessary governing instruments must be built to manage inherently borderless risks and increasingly certain dangers. The system as a whole inclines toward deeper integration *and* more difficult political contestation. Not for the first time in history do such tensions foreshadow the legitimation of at least some governing capacity at higher levels of political aggregation.

[55] See, for example, Arthur Benz, "Governing under the Condition of Complexity," in *Configurations, Dynamics and Mechanisms of Multilevel Governance* edited by Nathalie Behnke, Jörg Broschek, Jared Sonnicksen (New York: Palgrave Macmillan, 2019), 387–409.

[56] Frank Schimmelfennig, "European Integration in the Euro Crisis: The Limits of Postfunctionalism," *Journal of European Integration* 36, no. 3 (2014): 321–337; Chris Brummer, *Soft Law and the Global Financial System* (Cambridge: Cambridge University Press, 2012); Dirk Schoenmaker, "The Quest for Financial Stability in Europe," Utrecht, SUERF Colloquium, 3 September 2009; and Geoffrey Underhill and Erik Jones, "Optimum Financial Areas: Retooling the Governance of Global Finance," *The World Economy* 46, no. 6 (2023): 1582–1608.

[57] Barry Eichengreen, *Capital Flows and Crises* (Cambridge, MA: MIT Press, 2003); Edward Truman, ed., *Reforming the IMF for the Twenty-First Century* (Washington, DC: Peterson Institute for International Economics, 2006).

But the process often witnessed in the past to resolve intractable conflicts of interest or ideology is or should be ruled out, especially among great powers in a nuclear era. Not for the first time in history is creative and pragmatic political imagination required.

Long ago, Stephen Krasner demonstrated convincingly that state sovereignty itself was always an "organized hypocrisy."[58] For the time being, emerging collaborative practices of risk assessment, crisis prevention, and emergency management at the technical level justify the same label in many policy arenas. In the arenas I've sketched in this chapter, as well as in others characterized by intensifying complexity and the need for long-run burden sharing and policy planning, conflict is sure to persist across and within political boundaries. If it can be contained within negotiating frameworks, however, it may also eventually generate innovative, effective, and legitimate governing instruments.

For this to happen, institutional experiments involving diverse interests across interdependent markets must continue eroding the boundaries around existing zones of communal solidarity and political responsibility.[59] While massive fiscal commitments will be required to sustain such experiments, perhaps the ultimate insurance metaphor can help rationalize them. The world system is singular and bounded. As prospects of climate and other worldwide disasters become more certain and the diversification of risks impossible, only a kind of unitary insurance system makes sense. Every organized element of world society pays whatever premium it can to save itself and the system that it cannot escape. Every member of that society then relies on the effectiveness of the collaborative governing instruments supported by those premiums.

There will be no winners if burden sharing and collective preventive measures in such policy arenas prove impossible to negotiate or implement. The ultimate political challenge therefore is not to govern risks in complex policy arenas where probability calculations break down. It is to cope collaboratively with rising probabilities of disaster and the uncertainty generated by political legacies of the past.

58 Stephen D. Krasner, *Sovereignty: Organized Hypocrisy* (Princeton: Princeton University Press, 1999).

59 Alexander Wendt, *Social Theory of International Politics* (Cambridge: Cambridge University Press, 1999); Wendt, "Why a World State Is Inevitable," *European Journal of International Relations* 9, no. 4 (2003): 491–542; Mathias Koenig-Archibugi and Michael Zürn, *New Modes of Governance in the Global System* (Basingstoke: Palgrave Macmillan, 2006); Michael Zürn, *A Theory of Global Governance: Authority, Legitimacy, and Contestation* (Oxford: Oxford University Press, 2018); and Heikki Patomaki, *World Statehood* (Cham, CH: Springer, 2023).

8

Complex Risks and the Reconstruction of Government

> Transformation means ... an evolutionary path from closed to open, from national to global, from poor to rich, from isolated to more involved. Metamorphosis of the world means ... epochal change of worldviews.
>
> —Ulrich Beck, *The Metamorphosis of the World*

For many decades now, experience and study after study have drawn clear lines between globe-spanning risks and rapidly approaching emergencies. Climate change, biodiversity loss, and pandemics hardly cover the universe of cases. Our daily media discuss the prospect of ever more damaging cyber-catastrophes and other technology-driven crises. In a time of rapidly advancing innovation, the need to think about and prepare for known and unknown risks triggers the insuring instinct but frustrates straightforward policy planning. Is it once again time to rethink the ways in which the world is governed?

INSURANCE AND CROSS-BORDER, SYSTEMIC, AND GLOBAL RISKS

When the insuring instinct resonates in a receptive social environment, it stimulates the practical development of risk pools that then need to be managed. When probabilistic models are deployed to forecast future developments, they provide a baseline to guide disciplined speculation. Unanticipated losses sometimes then lead to adaptations in those models as well as to increases in premiums. The process of repeated and incremental adjustment can produce a template for private insurance and reinsurance providers to begin imagining protective instruments even for risks that might initially seem uninsurable. As noted in Chapter 7, this is already happening with regard to business interruption claims caused by cyberattacks and by diseases exacerbated by climate change.[1]

Whether this kind of innovation actually leads to behavioral change or not depends upon insurance purchasers becoming both aware of the underlying risks they face and convinced of the value of burden sharing. Whether private or public or in some combination, the risk pools that could feasibly be imagined on this basis and the plausible models underpinning them require a gathering sense of solidarity. The same is true when we think of governance as insurance. Functional and sustainable governing instruments can find their footing on no other ground.

Private-sector insurance arrangements can and already do play increasing roles in effectively managing certain global risks. To recall the main lesson of Ericson and his far-sighted sociological explorations, insurance *is* a type of governance. Private insurers and reinsurers operating through legal and stable markets in fact extend the reach of states. When danger lurks, official coercive measures can stimulate resistance and make necessary social adjustments more difficult. Letting legal insurance markets nudge may be a wiser policy choice. Think again, for example, of the desired effect of skyrocketing insurance premiums for ocean-front houses as climate change brings rising sea levels. If market signals are ignored, of course, a no-bailout commitment would have to be plausible, if a reversion back to more coercive means of risk management, say via new zoning rules, is to be avoided. The point is that permissible operations of insurers and reinsurers can both reflect and influence the choices states and societies make with respect to the distribution of adjustment burdens.

The global expansion of such operations promises similar effects at the system level. Under current conditions of interdependence and great power competition, relatively open capital markets are implicated in the evolution of both deeper cross-border risk pools and yawning gaps in potential coverage. Insurers and reinsurers, for example, with or without public subsidies, can sometimes accelerate processes of international adaptation to climate change by underwriting estimable risks and investing in green technologies. The scale and scope of unsubsidized risk pools now evident in the reinsurance sector testify to the potential expansion of opportunities on both sides of relevant balance sheets. Of

[1] Kai–Uwe Schanz, *The Value of Insurance in a Changing Risk Landscape* (Zurich: The Geneva Association, November 2023).

course, they also testify to the geographic concentration of risk-bearing capacities in advanced, capital-rich markets. Government regulation and supervision may help sustain them. But the more profound systemic challenges become obvious when insurers and reinsurers signal the need for nonmarket crisis-prevention measures by refusing to offer coverage when risks cannot be estimated or priced affordably. Direct subsidies from public authorities are then likely to be required if private intermediaries are to play any role at all. When transfers intermediated by private markets become impossible but essential, as in poor countries, there is no alternative to such subsidies.

As I discussed in Chapter 6, unequal outcomes from any private insurance operations are a feature, not a bug, of an already evolving system. Public subsidies or public commitments to take on burdens that exceed what private markets can bear may usefully harness and stretch out the logic of insurance. But more ambitious and necessary decisions involving the redistribution of the burdens of preempting future losses (implied by many extreme global risks or sources of deep uncertainty) today expose limits posed by the fiscal capacities of states as they are currently constituted. Effectively governing many boundless risks today and tomorrow thus entails reliably breaching those limits.

When it comes to any complex risk, private insurers' and reinsurers' decisions can usefully signal imperatives for more extensive and more equitable actions by governments acting independently or jointly. Again, for example, rapidly rising premiums for ocean-front property insurance can indicate the necessity for better zoning, for smarter adaptation to a changing climate, and for more progressive burden sharing. But even in such readily observable arenas, market forces do not promise automatically to establish more efficient or fairer pooling or payouts.

The limitations of market signals become even more obvious when systemic risks that must be managed inevitably cross diverse legal jurisdictions and are shrouded by various sources of uncertainty. If the ultimate goal is not only to redistribute adjustment burdens and foster societal resilience, but also to promote prudence and prevent imaginable catastrophes, cooperating policymakers can try to encourage insurers and reinsurers – private or public – to accept liability in advance of such catastrophes and to set up public backstops with just enough uncertainty built in to encourage prudence and self-discipline. As if any such construction was not delicate enough, they would also be wise quietly to plan for collaborative responses if the damage caused by an actual cataclysm proves worse than imagined or if that self-discipline breaks down. Again, however, there are inherent limits to deploying private measures in the service of public purposes.

Private insurers and reinsurers typically depend upon reliable records of past events to facilitate their profitability calculations. As we saw in Chapter 4, the most advanced firms commonly use various techniques to compensate for incomplete information and justify more speculative underwriting and capital-market syndication operations. At the limit, when no deep market exists for risks that still must be managed, the classic space opens that governments alone can fill. They must be willing to accept liability preemptively if they are unwilling or unable to address their sources. For example, if the potentially cross-border risks created by the waste products of nuclear power generation escape the capacities of private insurers and reinsurers, governmental protocols are essential to facilitate large increases in the production of nuclear energy. The risks cannot be avoided, but such protocols may be judged cost-effective when they are set against the staggering losses likely if global warming continues apace.

When leading insurers and reinsurers take advantage of sophisticated risk-estimation techniques to scope out the landscape for risk-pooling opportunities on a global basis, they expose the limits of private markets backed by single governments. As the nuclear energy case suggests, private insurers and reinsurers can cover only near-term and medium-term tranches of risk.[2] The coverage of long-term tranches and potentially large losses plausibly imaginable in the zone of uncertainty beyond calculable risk requires nothing less than collaborative governmental arrangements. Even in such cases, liability limits are specified, although everyone knows they may well be exceeded during an actual emergency. Experts who have tried to stretch and apply the analogy in the global warming case have identified the main problems – not official collaboration per se but the issue of concentrating climate risk and responsibility in legal entities that can be sued or otherwise held liable for near- and medium-term losses and the difficulty of predetermining the scale of long-term losses. The analogy itself, though, opens a door to confronting those problems.

As signal work by Daniel Yergin emphasizes, despite rapid increases in the production of "clean" energy, including nuclear, 80 percent of the world

[2] For thinking along this line, see Virginia Haufler, "Producing Global Governance in the Global Factory: Markets, Politics, and Regulation," *Global Policy* 9, no. 1 (2018): 114–120.

economy still depends on hydrocarbon-based sources of power.[3] At the same time, Vaclav Smil points out that four main industrial sectors provide the essential pillars for all countries actively participating in that economy: steel, cement, plastics, and ammonia (for fertilizer), which are all reliant on the energy sources producing greenhouse gases.[4] Why can't every large, systemically significant plant producing steel, cement, plastics, and ammonia be held responsible for their immediate and quantifiable externalities?

If taxing such plants on a comparable basis poses legal challenges, what about developing collaborative, cross-national governmental mandates to hold them liable? If they could theoretically be sued for measurable local damage, they might turn voluntarily to local insurance markets, which might then naturally develop and expand reinsurance cover, albeit within limits beyond those that public-sector supports would apply to. As in the case of nuclear plants, insurers and reinsurers might eventually provide even more cover for limited tranches of risks, and governments might then find themselves under increasing pressure to develop deeper collaborative measures to manage wider tranches. Market-based incentives would then be in place to encourage decarbonization; insurance companies would find it in their interest to encourage risk mitigation as well as to invest in new technologies; and governments might find such arrangements easier to swallow (and sell to their constituents) than tax-based alternatives. Public acceptance of a duty to collaborate may then evolve over time.

While such ideas are hardly novel, their contemporary elaboration will take new thinking about plausible inducements for policy change. As we saw in Chapter 4, similar ideas permeated the history of insurance in the earliest days of industrialization. Despite daunting complexities, pragmatic risk-management innovations have developed throughout history. A similar process is conceivable today.

It might start with intensive negotiations among public and private insurers, but that is only the starting point. Of course, local and national governments are primarily responsible to their constituents. However, with regard to inherently *global* risks, they cannot now meet their basic responsibilities without seriously taking into account the interests of others. Beyond governments' local duties are moral and fiduciary

[3] Daniel Yergin, *The New Map: Energy, Climate, and the Clash of Nations* (New York: Penguin, 2021).

[4] Vaclav Smil, *How the World Really Works: The Science behind How We Got Here and Where We're Going* (New York: Viking, 2022).

responsibilities that can only be understood on a global scale. They unavoidably and ultimately entail duties to bargain in good faith, comply with final decisions, and submit to reliable dispute settlement procedures. Differences in fundamental approaches to social welfare and methods of resource distribution and redistribution across diverse jurisdictions must be respected, but they cannot be impervious to change.

To the extent that ambiguous moral hazards arise, some minimal understandings are required on how the costs of preemptive regulation are to be allocated, and on how individuals and firms will be incentivized to reduce the risks being covered collectively.[5] Executives of intermediaries that conceive of themselves as operating in an amorphous space between state and market will find it useful to nurture such understandings – as long as destructive rivalries are not unleashed by unequal treatment. Indeed, the leaders of the world's largest insurers and reinsurers already understand quite clearly that such norms define their domain. They are also fully aware that their decisions to pull coverage or exit particularly risky markets put pressure on governments to rebalance their own priorities.

In the past, hybrid market mechanisms have sometimes proven capable of holding local communities together and expanding the boundaries around them. I'm thinking here of the innovative European Stability Mechanism that was able on the basis of official guarantees from stronger states to gather resources from global capital markets to assist weaker states. Not only did it hold the European Union together, it also set the stage for expansion. Instinct and practice converged to provide an exemplary collaborative model. Since the vast majority of the capital needed for the green transition, sustainable biodiversity, and global public health is expected to come from private sources, plausible systemic reform might involve similar kinds of collaborative instruments at the appropriate scale.

Could underlying cooperative norms and pragmatic ideas be rejected? Of course. But what happens then?

DISCERNING STRUCTURAL CHANGE

In Chapter 4, we recalled how various forms of fire insurance developed in discrete settings almost 500 years ago. In regions of Germany, for example, it took a while for farming communities and urban neighborhoods

[5] Richard V. Ericson, Aaron Doyle, and Dean Barry, *Insurance as Governance* (Toronto: University of Toronto Press, 2003), 7.

to conclude that strictly localized mutual insurance, separate firefighting companies, and specialized reinsurance practices made no sense when everyone unavoidably shared risks. To allow an unprotected house to burn down and take others with it was foolish. Common risk pools required access to common risk-management tools. Joint arrangements for limited fiscal burden sharing followed. Private insurance plans were eventually sustained by public guarantees as well as by enforceable rules to mitigate moral hazards. The insuring instinct gradually came to be harnessed for the common good. With regard to planetary climate change, humanity-threatening biological degradation, and potentially pandemic diseases, are we not today in a similar situation in a global setting?

A comprehensive polity evolves as diverse societies begin to share with one another, however reluctantly, the burdens of collective risk management. Political identities might then be reimagined. The process doesn't work in reverse, and it is always contentious. The key question arises from necessity: How must the benefits and costs of the degree of risk sharing necessary to provide collective security be authoritatively distributed? As in all effective and sustainable governing structures at national and regional levels, fiscal capacities lie at the practical core of the answer to that question. Peak cross-border, systemic, and global risks today suggest the same question and the same answer.

As discussed in Chapter 2, debate over the feasibility of extending fiscal authority beyond the sovereign state runs like red thread through the tapestry of modern history. Eurocentric ever since the dawn of the Industrial Revolution, that debate traced a tutelary relationship between "core" and "periphery." As other perspectives reemerge today, most prominently among feminist, Indigenous, racialized, and decolonial thinkers, earlier critiques of the limits of fiscal solidarity naturally return.[6] What happens when established boundaries around national fiscal autonomy break down under the pressure of rapidly rising risks and sources of uncertainty that are both internal and external?

A version of that question received a thorough airing after World War I and World War II. Political visionaries imagined ideal plans. Some sought to build a federation of republics based on the principle of nondomination. Others envisaged a loosely organized set of separately constituted institutions ultimately centered on the principle of individual

[6] Hidemi Suganami, *The Domestic Analogy and World Order Proposals* (Cambridge: Cambridge University Press, 1989).

human dignity developing more or less automatically.[7] Still others argued for approaches emphasizing the practical realities and limits of public international law, treaty-based intergovernmental institutions, and routine interstate diplomacy facilitating transnational cooperation.[8]

By now, we can see quite clearly that formal intergovernmental arrangements have thus far fallen short on the management of certain global risks, such as those already evoked by climate change and the prospect of generative artificial intelligence. To the extent that such phenomena irreversibly erode the conditions under which our species has thus far flourished on this planet, they raise the specter not of risk but of radical uncertainty. For this very reason, Beck speculated freely in his last book, quoted at the start of this chapter, that a generational metamorphosis was already underway. For him, collective rationality promised somehow to cast aside obsolete ways of thinking and bring far-flung and distinctive communities into harmony with their inevitably shared fates. Alas, although I remain inspired by Beck and by his intellectual legacy, I do not share his faith in the innate power of reason. To be sure, rationality needs to be harnessed in the cause of political reform, but deep change only comes when it must.

At the end of his life, Beck joined other prominent scholars and observers committed to the view that the nation-state itself had become obsolete. He never denied that its claim to ultimate political authority had always been contested, even after it had consolidated that claim between the seventeenth and nineteenth centuries in Europe – and after waves of colonization and decolonization had extended it to the rest of the world. Like many of his critical colleagues in the academy, he was mindful of persistent evidence of that authority's explicit or implicit failure. Coming of age in postwar Germany, however, I think he struggled to balance pride in the late construction of his country's social democratic state with an objective analysis of its inability to embrace the regional necessity of transcending that success. To him, the need for a fundamentally new political structure was self-evident. Only it could meet myriad challenges now facing all of Europe and, most importantly, forestall a slide back into the abyss of the recent

[7] Ibid., 167. See also Daniel Deudney, *Bounding Power: Republican Security Theory from the Polis to the Global Village* (Princeton, NJ: Princeton University Press, 2007).

[8] Although focused on Europe, the theoretical foundations here are more broadly relevant: Mareike Kleine and Mark Pollack, eds., "Liberal Intergovernmentalism and Its Critics," *Journal of Common Market Studies* (Special Issue), 56, no. 7 (2018). Also see Christina Davis, *Discriminatory Clubs: The Geopolitics of International Organizations* (Princeton, NJ: Princeton University Press, 2023).

past. In the end, Beck thus took a very big leap of faith. I think he could not really see much of a future in Rosenau's larger world of governance without government. But he also could not abide the resurgence of an exclusionary nationalism that he observed during the final years of his life.

Actual political responses to one global crisis after another continue to serve as reminders of people's insistence on holding their own national leaders to account when they require immediate protection. Imagined national communities persist. Especially during times of manifest social stress, national leaders still find it easy to tap into shared images of dark external forces. They readily conjure walls, not well-regulated common spaces. This is an undeniable fact of life. Tribalism seems innate when human nature meets threats that individuals or small groups cannot master alone. The ideology of nationalism exploits this reality. Ironically, however, it now exacerbates threats that must be mastered. As Peter Katzenstein convincingly argues, power in our world is always fluid and shape shifting.[9] Today, national leaders and their communities may still think in terms of control power, but they now clearly chase only the illusion of control in an increasing number of actual policy arenas.

In one policy arena after another, aspirations of self-reliance and ultimate national control ring hollow everywhere. No functional ideology, however, has yet emerged to match the nationalist ideologies still underpinning the fading capacities of individual states. For the foreseeable future, though, the nation-state remains central to any serious global problem solving. Nationalism will not suddenly disappear. In the gathering shadow of uncertainty, the search is on for more ambitious collaborative institutions that nevertheless take it seriously.

Over the past few decades, regional and global intergovernmental experiments have opened some doors as well as some minds. Effective global governance must soon evolve beyond the confederal lines the more successful of those experiments have long implied. Systemic crises, in fact, have repeatedly brought something resembling federalist practices to the fore.[10] The global financial crisis of 2008 recounted in Chapter 6 moved along this line. When complex risks crystallized in the short term, and a coalition of states was capably though hardly

[9] Katzenstein, Peter J. and Lucia Seybert, eds., *Protean Power: Exploring the Uncertain and Unexpected in World Politics* (Cambridge: Cambridge University Press, 2018).

[10] Again, the global financial crisis of 2008 did the same, and in its aftermath we came to see more clearly how certain federations deepened and became more systematic in their policy interactions with one another. See, for example, Lucia Quaglia, *The European Union and Global Financial Regulation* (Oxford: Oxford University Press, 2014).

perfectly led, collaborative governance proved effective. For longer-term and even more complex risks, though, no feasible alternative exists to a pragmatic deepening of collaborative policy design and implementation. Gathering threats and the necessity of protection imply no alternative to at least one essentially transnational governmental commitment – a commitment not to walk away from a common policymaking table. In existing federations, ultimate authority rests on just such a commitment.

No great imagination is required to sense rising awareness of such pragmatic necessity around the world. Indeed, the rise of populist rejectionism testifies to it. Robust networks and technocratic policymaking mechanisms across national frontiers nevertheless continue to develop through risk-driven experimentation. Against the backdrop of governing deficits that I outlined especially in Chapter 7, the pragmatic emergence of global authority with both confederal and federal characteristics struggles to catch up with expanding demands.[11]

A clearer assessment of what can and must be done to accelerate that evolution comes into view when we think systematically about the interaction of time and complexity in the truly global challenges facing all of us. The history of private and public insurance systems becomes freshly relevant. Interstate *and* intrastate insuring practices within and across the world's main regions plausibly provide key elements in an increasingly complex, multi-level negotiation on risk governance – a process reasonably interpreted as endogenous to a global polity in formation. While that polity need not be viewed as unitary, even in the long run, it must address unavoidable threats and channel undeniably common interests.

Solidarity networks and risk pools develop slowly, tentatively, and partially, while discrete general policies must be painstakingly negotiated, somehow rendered legitimate, and effectively implemented at the most disaggregated levels possible. Conflicting interests are to be expected. Non-violent political reform evolves through dynamic and variegated processes of social learning, continuing economic interaction, and subtly pragmatic leadership. Uncertainty is always in the background, while risks not perfectly calculable provide the essential incentive for moving forward.

Far from blowing up the European Union, both financial crisis and the COVID-19 pandemic proved the point. Although the logic of

[11] Mathias Albert, *A Theory of World Politics* (Cambridge: Cambridge University Press, 2016); Michael Zürn, *A Theory of Global Governance* (Oxford: Oxford University Press, 2018).

solidaristic responses to a common threat held obvious appeal from a top-down point of view, demands for local-level accountability could not be denied. Policy performances and outcomes were less efficient than they could have been, and some external support proved helpful. Despite their inefficiency, the Union held together. It muddled through with new instruments designed under pressure that rebalanced changing expectations of solidarity and autonomy among its member-states.

A similar if more subtle dynamic seems evident more broadly. In the financial policy arena, from expanding club gatherings to more assertive efforts by many states to stretch the extra-territorial application of their own laws, transnational governance experiments are underway. Their success depends upon both combining effective power with the development of new understandings of distributive justice. The Basel Process is imperfect and incomplete, but it intensified as it confronted the intended and unintended consequences of earlier decisions. As new structures of monetary and fiscal power emerge, the struggle over legitimacy becomes more complex but also unavoidable. Ideological champions of self-reliance look ever more pathetic as they continue to seek the benefits of financial openness and deepening while trying to avoid the costs.

A vital analytical challenge across all inherently collaborative policy arenas is not to let the legacy of post-1945 intergovernmentalism, or dreams of "governance without government," restrict our imaginations. Governing structures that underpinned world order during the decades immediately following World War II reflected many factors, but most significantly the hegemonic position of the United States. Associated institutions, in fact, were relatively easy for Americans to accept, for the norms and practices of organizations such as the International Monetary Fund (IMF) promoted core US values and interests. They demanded no deep compromise in American governing practices. Indeed, they often deflected pressures for domestic policy adjustment.

That era is now coming to an end, and American policymakers sensed it even before a period marked by extreme polarization commenced in the early decades of the twenty-first century. This helps explain their renewed obsession with the long and winding national story aimed at a "more perfect" union less inclined toward intervention abroad. Some may certainly try to go back to pre-1945 and even pre-1914 practices of internal and external (dis)organization. But one doesn't need a PhD to understand intuitively and immediately how costly and ultimately ineffective that will end up being for their own constituents, and indeed for everyone else.

THE PROMISE OF COMPLEX FEDERALISM

The founding generations of existing national or regional federations understood in their own time the importance of nuanced political judgment and pragmatic compromise. Federalist experiments sometimes followed failed confederal experiments, which themselves had once seemed better than disorder within expanding societies defined by their diversity. Functionalist strategies promoted from the top down were rarely determinative. Commitments to non-violence necessitated the bottom-up search for practical methods of mutual accommodation. The quiet promise of subsidiarity – as much local autonomy as possible – often propelled that search. Again, as astute students of federalism have long pointed out, the form itself can at most help structure complex social relations only if there exists a will to eschew coercion and negotiate in good faith. What can unfold gradually in such contexts is a shared sense of legitimate rule based on a modicum of common social purposes.[12]

In line with an ancient tradition of political thought revived in the sixteenth century by Johannes Althusius and carried forward by Immanuel Kant, Otto von Gierke, and Carl Friedrich, the basic idea is still to develop the minimal level of social and political interaction essential for all individual lives to flourish.[13] Struggles generated by diverse perceptions of shared risks may be fraught. But they should not be expected magically to abate. Governmental arrangements that successfully manage those risks, even if imperfectly, hold the realistic promise of generating higher degrees of social cohesion over time. From the outset, trust might be ideal, but necessity may have to suffice.

Across today's globalizing society, with an incipient and partial set of such arrangements evolving from practical experiments in risk governance, postnationalism is not a prerequisite.[14] Exclusivist nationalism

[12] John G. Ruggie, "At Home Abroad, Abroad at Home," *Jean Monnet Chair Papers*, 20, The Robert Schuman Centre at the European University Institute, 1995; and Rawi Abdelal and John G. Ruggie, "The Principles of Embedded Liberalism and Global Capitalism," in *New Perspectives on Regulation*, edited by David Moss and John Cisternino (Cambridge, MA: Tobin Project, 2009), 151–162.

[13] Thomas O. Hueglin and Alan Fenna, *Comparative Federalism: A Systematic Inquiry*, 2nd ed. (Toronto: University of Toronto Press, 2015).

[14] Liberalism itself has not proven capable of transcending nationalism's success as an ideology of legitimation, but the promise of federalism and confederalism requires only partial success. The underlying tension has long motivated debate and critical reflection. See Ernst Haas, *Nationalism, Liberalism and Progress* (Ithaca, NY: Cornell University Press, 1997).

will have to give way, but ever since the dawn of this particular ideology pragmatic leadership has always been necessary to tip the balance in the civic direction. In existing multinational federations, at least those with an essentially democratic character allowing individuals a wide berth for social choices, frustrating negotiations are routine. So too are more pragmatic experiments focused on the mutualization of risks. Although specific experiments may fail, successful federations are driven forward by a shared sensibility: "Better in than out."

At the end of both world wars in the twentieth century, as well as at the end of the Cold War, high-profile debates explored what it might take to build and hold together a sustainable global federation. In the wake of the COVID-19 pandemic, and facing mounting environmental and technological risks, no nation-state on the planet can escape the need to open up its own policymaking frameworks. Although a world-state remains infeasible, it need not be considered utopian to contemplate serious moves beyond the current dominant paradigm of completely voluntary international cooperation. Some challenges and threats are beyond complicated. As they stretch beyond risk into uncertainty, the indeterminacy of their causes and effects renders them complex.[15] Again, top-down aspirations of control as well as bottom-up dreams of automaticity are frustrated by that complexity.

A "confederal" label for that dominant paradigm has long seemed appropriate when it comes to issues demanding collective action in a world able to muster only incomplete levels of cooperation.[16] It reemerges publicly, often in the aftermath of crises, whenever multilevel negotiations commence among established political authorities. More ambitious federal arrangements have sometimes also emerged in restricted geographic settings, but analogies drawn too directly from those experiences don't really come to grips with the complexity of the most difficult challenges currently facing us.

Scholars in the field of comparative federalism have long noted that many models for federal governing institutions exist in practice around the world. Despite their diversity, a pioneer in the field asserted that they

[15] Julia Kreienkamp and Tom Pegram, "Governing Complexity: Design Principles for the Governance of Complex Global Catastrophic Risks," *International Studies Review* 23, 2021, 779–806; and Andreas Thiel, William A. Blomquist, and Dustin E. Garrick, eds., *Governing Complexity* (Cambridge: Cambridge University Press, 2019).

[16] See, for example, Charles S. Maier, "Democracy and Its Discontents," *Foreign Affairs* 73, no. 4 (1994): 48–64; and by the same author, "Democratic Dangers beyond Borders," *Global Policy* 8, no. 6 (2017): 78–86.

were all marked by "underlying values of tolerance, recognition of the other, accommodating multiple and shared values, and peacefully debating difference."[17] Also emerging at their core, we might add, are officials authorized to act in the name of common interests.

Why should anyone believe that such experiments – in navigating uncertain pathways, managing shared risks, and trying to prevent future disasters – define the absolute limits of the collective capacity of all humankind? Why should the reciprocal and painstaking process of building enough trust to collaboratively design complex governing experiments fit for specific purposes be conceived as geographically or historically constrained in perpetuity?

THE FEDERALIZING LOGIC OF INSURANCE

The contemporary international order inclines toward deeper interdependence *and* more contentious political conflict. The political structures underpinning it reflect interacting macroeconomic and geostrategic policy choices. Again, not for the first time in history, common risks foreshadow the legitimation of governing capacity at more aggregated levels, despite persistent political tensions. Perceptions of shared fate can forge subtle compromises. New balances can be struck between the values of solidarity and autonomy, central control and subsidiarity, precautionary rules and disciplined discretion.

The differences in the character of global risks arrayed in Figure 3.1 in Chapter 3, as well as distinctions in feasible insurance practices and metaphors uncovered in Chapters 4 through 7, suggest specific kinds of global governing arrangements in the contemporary world. If we break them into their component parts, three distinct kinds of practical negotiations among existing governments are implicated. As noted throughout this book, they center on the politics of risk assessment, the politics of crisis prevention, and the politics of emergency management, resolution, and compensation if prevention fails. Along these same lines, we can begin to differentiate among the institutional innovations in risk governance already taking "public" or "private" forms in the overarching framework of global capitalism as it is currently evolving. Practices and metaphors drawn from the history of insurance help us to see those innovations.

[17] Richard Simeon, "Reflections on a Federalist Life," in *The Global Promise of Federalism*, edited by Grace Skogstad, David Cameron, Martin Papillon, and Keith Banting (Toronto: University of Toronto Press, 2013), 291.

Private insurance and reinsurance markets can and do generally already play vital roles in cross-border risk governance and resilience promotion when it comes to property damage from natural disasters, demographic change, population health, and certain kinds of accidents. Licensed and permitted to operate by existing governments, private insurers and reinsurers play key roles with regard to anticipated liabilities associated, for example, with industrial and energy production. They also routinely help manage short- to medium-term financial risks that naturally spill over territorial domains. Although they are set to do much more to help close what insurers call protection gaps, they remain inherently limited by profitability concerns. In the absence of public subsidies, private insurance and reinsurance providers must focus any innovative strategies on risks that can readily be pooled, diversified, and monetized.

Private firms have already proven themselves to be efficient assessors of at least some global risks meeting those requirements. Once insurance policies are in place, insurers and reinsurers are effectively delegated some responsibility for crisis prevention. It is in their interest to reduce prospective losses and moral hazards. Insurers thus do serve in some limited capacity as unofficial regulators, or quasi-governors. This is precisely where critiques of accountability and the potential maldistribution of benefits and costs often come in, thus requiring some official oversight that must logically now have a collaborative character. The case of nuclear liability provided a key case in point. If accidents occur, insurers and reinsurers supply compensation. They become useful if not central to the public purposes of emergency management, resolution, and recovery.

The constraints on all of these delegated governance roles become clear when uncertainty is elevated, and when risks become more complex and longer term in nature. Such limits can expose themselves in any of the four quadrants of Figure 3.1. For example, if advances in generative AI soon combine with biometric innovations to enable particular insurance providers to cherry-pick the risks they're willing to cover, the pooling necessary to maintain robust health insurance and reinsurance markets will break down. The same logic would indicate the erosion of viable and diversified property insurance markets if future natural disasters become less random and more widespread. In the wake of such developments, sustainable and adequate private insurance markets would not automatically revive themselves, but they might just be restored through joint governmental actions to prevent cherry-picking or to subsidize the pooling and transfer of risks.

The dilemmas posed by the limits of private insurability, however, arise most clearly and most intractably in arenas that are systemic, complex, and long term in their essential character. In the aftermath of the COVID-19 pandemic, for example, insurers and reinsurers were stumped by the challenge of imagining profitable risk pools akin to those associated with nuclear energy production. Imaginative rethinking in such cases may be contentious, but it is already underway. As they contemplate massive cybersecurity failures, terrorist attacks, and business continuity risks, for example, private insurers and reinsurers retain the ability to opt out and leave ultimate protection obligations to national governments.[18]

The most complex, global, and long-term risks, such as those outlined in Chapter 7, may engage private markets, but they clearly also require more integrated forms of collaborative public backstopping. At this moment in history, however, the prevention of crises associated with such risks and the management of emergencies they cause when prevention fails fall mainly or even exclusively on established governments. If they have the will and the capacity, some governments could offer public insurance facilities and post hoc compensation. Ideas for parallel club arrangements are proliferating, for example, in climate change negotiations. But the insurance metaphors being summoned really only mask the necessity of broader fiscal transfers. Relatively poor island nations threatened with inundation need direct foreign assistance, not insurance. Sometimes there is no substitute for solidaristic responses. They can be rationalized, justified, and elaborated with metaphors suggesting the sharing of risks, but they are finally demanded when uncertainty gives way to ever more certain threats to fundamentally shared interests.

Where unitary institutions remain infeasible or inefficient, institutions to govern unbounded risks and reduce sources of political uncertainty must rest on the acceptance of at least some mutual responsibilities. Successful institutions may sustain properly incentivized private markets and specialized kinds of insurance, such as insurance-linked securities targeted at specific natural disasters. But those markets must ultimately be supported by shared legal and financial backstops. The experience of the European Union in the development of common banking and securities markets over the past few decades both supports

[18] Tom Johansmeyer, "If Cyber Is Uninsurable, the United States Has a Major Strategy Problem," *Lawfare On-line*, July 26, 2023. www.lawfaremedia.org/article/if-cyber-is-uninsurable-the-united-states-has-a-major-strategy-problem, accessed on April 11, 2025.

that point and underlines the profoundly difficult political compromises that must in the end be negotiated.

Active members of the League of Nations, democratic and autocratic, tried to construct such arrangements in the aftermath of World War I. Within the basic structure of the League, an Economic and Financial Organization (EFO) evolved in just such a context. Its mandate developed over time, often in response to imminent disasters – such as prospective debt defaults in systemically significant regions. As a long-time member of the EFO staff later complained, however, "At the League, we were asked to catch fish, but we had no bait."[19]

After the next global war, an arguably more ambitious and better funded, if much more complicated, global governing apparatus emerged under the auspices of the United Nations and its affiliates. Although it did not become a federation, it did successfully, if often partially and unevenly, tackle myriad tasks delegated by its leading member-states. The IMF, for example, and the member-states controlling it, surely could have done much more as it tried to tackle various challenges. However, it's implausible to argue that the world as a whole would have been better off without the IMF during the past eight decades, or that the expanding capital markets complicating its original mandates could easily have been controlled.

When it comes to more complex risks such as those outlined in Chapter 7, the failures of international institutions and contentious debates over responsibility are impossible to ignore. Yet not a few policy proposals on global risk governance these days call for broader mandates for existing institutions, better agency funding, more technical assistance, redistributions of voting power, as well as larger, fairer, and better targeted funds. The World Bank, for example, seems a convenient vehicle for modest environmental loss and damage funds. While such ideas are well intended, however, few approach the scale and scope of the kinds of responses required to effectively and legitimately manage the most urgent and complex risks humanity currently faces.

The compelling logic of reliably collaborative public authority to back up global, reciprocal, and enforceable commitments to govern those risks ultimately points to the pragmatic need to build and strengthen successors to the international institutions constructed in the aftermath of

[19] Louis Rasminsky, quoted in Louis Pauly, "The League of Nations and the Foreshadowing of the International Monetary Fund," *Essays in International Finance*, no. 201, Princeton University, International Finance Section, December 1996, 7.

World War I and World War II. The serious question is whether systemic trauma on an even larger scale is actually required to move collaborating states beyond the status quo. Do the compromises necessary to forge new forms of co-insurance or ultimately reliable reinsurance actually require the catastrophes we are trying to avoid? Cynics believe it is so, and they cross their fingers that anyone will be left to resume the search for compromise. They may be right, but they do not have to be.

GLOBAL RISK POOLING AND THE PROBLEM OF DIVERSIFICATION

Before the disaster of 1861, the residents of Glarus probably couldn't anticipate all the dimensions of the "what should now be done" question facing them. Despite the fog of uncertainty surrounding all difficult political decisions, shared risks must in the end be perceived widely and borne mutually in the common interest. For the biggest challenges facing all of humanity today, the agenda for pragmatic leaders becomes clearer by the day. With respect to at least some risks, they and their constituents all live in Glarus in 1860. We know, however, that our homes are generally underinsured, and we know that the fundamental risks and uncertainties we now face are inextricably shared. We also know that we're depending on luck to avoid painful decisions on burden sharing. If there was any doubt on this score before the Glarus fire, it was surely gone afterwards. Experiments in risk governance that leave everything to chance, or retain wide scope for opting out, cannot succeed in the long run. Likewise, those who seek to leave nothing to chance will likely never find a politically feasible approach.[20]

Over the past five decades, moments of serious regional and systemic crises have sometimes stimulated innovative and promising policy experimentation. Insurance practices and their justifying metaphors have often proven useful, for example, in stabilizing volatile capital markets. Perceptions of mutual vulnerability have regularly collided with specific

[20] Thomas Schelling applied such reasoning in the arena of international security in *Strategy of Conflict* (Cambridge, MA: Harvard University Press, 1960), and *Arms and Influence* (New Haven, CT: Yale University Press, 1966). The approach was recently exemplified again in Reid B. C. Pauly and Rose McDermott, "The Psychology of Nuclear Brinkmanship," *International Security* 47, no. 3 (2023): 9–51. In political economy, the same reasoning applies to the psychological foundations of both insurance markets and federal systems featuring a significant role for market mechanisms in the distribution and redistribution of scarce economic and social resources.

issues of liability and compensation, and leading states have sometimes risen to their responsibilities as ultimate reinsurers and regulators. Again, this is what happened during the systemic crisis of 2008.

Rising global risks and the uncertainties surrounding transnational risk pooling across private and public sectors highlight the looming necessity to place an inchoate system of preventive governance on firmer normative and political foundations. Some risk societies emerging in seventeenth-century Europe gradually stumbled toward a viable compromise between state sovereignty and market liberalism. While similar experiments in global risk governance and burden sharing today hardly promise utopia, the insuring instinct continues to manifest itself. We know from history that it can readily be put to constructive use in the wake of systemic catastrophes, when the contentious politics of resource distribution and redistribution at least for a time gives way to emergency relief and efforts to prevent future crises. The core challenge today is to deploy that knowledge in anticipation of increasingly slow-moving global disasters. Enlightened self-interest justified hope when insurance and reinsurance systems were first developing. Why should it not do so again?

The social and political structures underpinning the world's economy and shaping its physical environment obviously generate profound debate. One worldview sees them necessarily reflecting the compound legacy of empires and the perennial competition among states descending from those empires. Another sees a relatively liberal but contested international regime evolving in the shadow of twentieth-century wars. Some observers depict an inevitably globalizing capitalism resting on the liberal internationalist foundation of sovereign but distinctly structured nation-states, with any coherence occasionally delivered by restricted, dominant, and elite-driven clubs. Others perceive a much more complex and adaptive system fluidly organized around nation-states and markets.

International relations scholar Tom Weiss eloquently framed the practical implications of this latter perspective a decade ago:

> State sovereignty remains the core of international relations. However, the meaning of that sovereignty is continually changing, and the leverage and significance of a host of non-state actors is growing in observable ways ... [P]arts of a world federal government are ideas that are both necessary and not impossible for today, and certainly not for the day after tomorrow.[21]

[21] Thomas Weiss, *Global Governance: Why? What? Whither?* (Cambridge: Polity, 2013), 169 and 184. Also see Raffaele Marchetti, "Global Governance or World Federalism?" *Global Society* 20, no. 3 (2006): 287–305.

The day after tomorrow is fast approaching. Persistent ideological differences over communal and individual rights as well as responsibilities must be acknowledged. But so must the promising history of pragmatic experiments in collaborative government in response to mounting risks and unavoidably shared sources of uncertainty. The insuring instinct pulls us forward, and the limits of insurability become ever less rigid. While outright fiscal transfers across political boundaries remain difficult as well as inadequate, practical ideas for mutual insurance and especially reliable reinsurance arrangements open up the realm of the possible.

In the interviews with analysts, executives, and government officials that informed this book, I heard diverse answers to the question of how global risks currently expanding might be governed in the future. There was a common core in most responses – a pragmatic one. Better to take two steps forward and one step back than to remain immobile. My interviewees acknowledged that we live today in a complex environment hardly immune from the kind of devastating intergroup rivalries marking all of human history. Even so, they often asserted that the global economy is now organizing itself loosely and uncertainly around the basic idea of state-supported markets intermediating ever larger shares of the demand for protection. Those markets are not "free," for they remain deeply reflective of the sometimes common and oftentimes competing interests of dominant states and societies. They are, however, more open and more difficult to control unilaterally than they once were.

Together with bilateral, regional, and global initiatives that states have directly undertaken, actual markets for insurance and reinsurance today may constitute key elements in an emerging system of risk governance. Yes, a widening gap exists between actual world losses from discrete disasters and the rising volume of losses covered by insurance. The latter reflects the rapid growth of the system within and across its Western base, while the gap testifies both to the increasing scale of potentially insurable losses and the still slow expansion of insurance markets in many countries. But rising great powers, from China to India, Indonesia, Nigeria, and Brazil, are not rejecting the ideas and practices that motivate and shape such markets. In fact, insurance and reinsurance markets are deepening rapidly in many emerging-market economies. And where markets grow, the need for political backstops and sustainable regulation increases as well. On this very point, Peter Borscheid takes us back to themes raised in the early chapters of this book when he summarizes a common perception of the contemporary situation.

Modern insurance, which started to expand as a European invention in the late eighteenth century, has now cast a dense safety net over the whole world; it may still have some substantial holes in it and it may well not be able to protect against every peril or risk, but, without it, there would surely be much more poverty, need, and fear in the world than there actually are.[22]

Over the past four decades, the term "complex interdependence" signified the consensus view among liberal internationalists on the political foundation of that safety net. It could all still literally blow up, of course, since ignorance and globalized military conflict have not been rendered obsolete. A better descriptor of the cases I've outlined in this book, though, is "complex integration." No serious plan for peaceful dis-integration is on offer for reliably coming to grips with the dangers pushing outward the frontier of insurability.

When it comes to challenges such as global warming, biodiversity loss, and pandemics, integrative strategies will require more fairness at both system and sub-system levels of governance. Of course, a sense of solidarity among as well as within unequal societies is difficult to build. States care a great deal about their relative positions, and theorists of social stratification suggest that similar concerns define the internal structures of many if not all societies. When such concerns are taken into account by leaders capable of looking over their own horizons, nevertheless, why should they not eventually agree to bear differentiated burdens in their own interest? Why should anyone assert that resolving a classic distributive dilemma at the global level, at least with regard to extreme risks and shared sources of uncertainty, is absolutely impossible? And why should Borscheid's observation be applicable only to the past? Private insurance instruments may play limited roles in resolving contemporary dilemmas, but insurance metaphors combined with a broadening sense of shared fate may help take the sting out of the necessary global redistribution of the burdens of adjustment.

Many of my interlocutors still viewed the United States and its main allies as the current leaders of a dynamic and evolving system for governing risks and coping with uncertainties. They assigned value to their evident power as well as to their liberal heritage, which they also saw as under mounting stress. But to what extent can governmental and civil

[22] Borscheid, "Introduction," in *World Insurance: The Evolution of a Global Risk Network*, edited by Peter Borscheid and Niels Viggo Haueter (Oxford: Oxford University Press, 2012), 32.

society actors within those states demonstrate prudent flexibility on the shared norms required to foster continuing negotiations and more durable forms of collaboration among themselves and ultimately with illiberal partners? Any sustainable crisis prevention and emergency management at the system level – indeed, any viable reinsurance and risk governance arrangements capable of pushing outward the limits of solidarity – must rest on such realism. Although analogies drawn from the history of insurance may remain useful in the cause of building confidence in such a context, the necessity of broader collaboration is being reinforced by a gathering sense not of uncertainty, but of the certainty of imminent catastrophes.

Two wise observers succinctly captured the conundrum that now faces all of us. "Uncertainty about the future, and the resulting hope that tomorrow can be radically different from today, are the hallmarks of the democratic idea. The question is whether uncertainty is still possible in our current age of emergency."[23] That thought needs to be combined with a more capacious sense of how liberal democratic norms have in fact developed and been explicitly enacted across time.

Debate on this point, especially on the balance between individual and collective autonomy, has evidently marked the seminal American experience. Even many progressives in the United States today would likely have little difficulty agreeing in principle with the view of a classic conservative of the early post-1945 period: "On the one hand, our culture does not really value the individual as much as it pretends; on the other hand, if justice is to be maintained and our survival assured, we cannot make individual liberty as unqualifiedly the end of life as our ideology asserts."[24] Surely accepting such a judgment today should not be hard in any liberal society.

Where individual claims now meet communal necessity, negotiations over the terms of global risk assessment, disaster prevention, and emergency management must now develop and deepen beyond the borders of the nation-state. In the common interest, ideological differences have to be defanged. If they aren't pushed too far, the logic and the metaphors of insurance might help in that process. Ultimately, there is nothing automatic about the politics lying at the base of the complex adaptive

[23] Ivan Krastev and Leonard Benardo, "Democracy Has Run Out of Future," *Foreign Policy Magazine*, (on-line, 27 April 2024). Also see Martin Wolf, *The Crisis of Democratic Capitalism* (London: Allen Lane, 2023).

[24] Reinhold Niebuhr, *The Irony of American History* (Chicago: University of Chicago Press, 1952), 8.

world system that optimists claim to discern at the present moment. Feasible policies still have to be constructed, realistic expectations of reciprocity rendered concrete, and difficult trade-offs confronted. But only some intrinsically shared interests, such as financial stability and climate sustainability, must be governed collaboratively, whether partly by impersonal market instruments or ultimately by joint assertions of authority. A global polity, like an integrated reinsurance system, may be emerging before our eyes. It does not have to take a unitary form.

AN UNCERTAIN BUT NOT HOPELESS FUTURE

Tragedy has decisively shaped the actual history of international organization. In the modern era, the League of Nations and the United Nations emerged out of global catastrophes. Perhaps the next great border-spanning innovation in the systemic governance of shared risks will only arise from the ashes of another and more devastating catastrophe. But are there other plausible possibilities?

The material I've covered in this book highlights feasible steps, if not toward utopia at least in a promising direction. Officially backstopped private insurance and reinsurance markets have proven functional and expansive, and more experiments along this line are underway. There are distinctions between liabilities arising from the production of nuclear energy and those arising from the long history of carbon-based development. Private insurance for natural disasters is also different from implicit reinsurance for systemically significant financial intermediaries. But lessons drawn from such cases are still worth comparing and contrasting. They might also provide useful metaphors to help rationalize and explain decisions that must soon be taken in the collective interest of our species.

Cross-border public insurance arrangements, often informal, are on the rise. So too are innovative public–private partnerships. To constrain implied moral hazards and preempt temptations to free-ride, leading states across open capital markets and shared physical environments are actively searching for minimally necessary coordinating mechanisms. The Basel Process, regular G20+ meetings, global climate and biodiversity conferences, and post-pandemic efforts to build up multilateral surveillance and preventive operations – all of these projects testify to a growing collective sense of shared interests that might at least partially be advanced through insurance-like arrangements. Insurance premiums may be easier to sell than tax payments. Governments need not directly take on all responsibilities, and private insurers and reinsurers can be motivated to share in the management of risks they would not normally take on their own. Experiments with more speculative sources of private support for public purposes, such as insurance-linked securities, are worth further study. But in the end, there is no substitute for the assertion of collaborative fiscal policies.

An adequate capacity for reliably collaborative risk governance and resilience promotion must soon exist across many but not all arenas of public policy. Adaptive technocratic facilities, even if limited, are essential. Checks and balances remain necessary. Ideological differences will persist, but parties, leaders, or super-empowered individuals seriously seeking to justify systemic disengagement must be contained. Routes leading toward the deepening of private as well as official relationships across economic, social, and political borders must be kept open, and this calls for a reasonable degree of transparency. Practical instruments are required to help preempt and manage clear, present, and common dangers. The insuring instinct and a shared sense of fate, which in principle combine the interests of "us" and "them" without insisting on ideological conformity or complete social integration, can guide an urgent search for feasible innovations in the basic machinery of collaborative government.[25]

Existing and aspiring federations conceived as macro-insurance arrangements provide an apt analogy. Not all are coherently "liberal," and not all are alike, but they all attempt to manage certain risks that simply need to be managed collaboratively.[26] Social solidarity, like political sovereignty, can be variable, negotiable, and divided. Their practical manifestations may well be subject to permanent negotiation. At base, however, they must simply provide an adequate enough base

[25] Dani Rodrik's image of a "light" economic governing system seeks the middle ground between overly ambitious cosmopolitan structures and the kind of voluntary intergovernmentalism that followed the breakdown of the Bretton Woods system. While I agree that the provision of global public goods can well be limited to selected domains, my own view is that the issue linkages already being experienced in complex domains require more ambition. Ideological conformity may not be required in the near term, but pragmatic instruments of limited government are necessary. See Dani Rodrik, "How to Smooth US-China Relations for the Benefit of the Global Economy: A Light Model of Global Economic Governance," *Journal of Government and Economics* 13 (2024), online/open access.

[26] On the strengths and weaknesses of such arrangements, see, for example, Jonathan Rodden, *Hamilton's Paradox: The Promise and Peril of Fiscal Federalism* (New York: Cambridge University Press, 2006); and John Erik Fossum, "Multiheaded Federations: The EU and Canada Compared," *Politics and Governance* 11, no. 3 (2023): 231–241.

to support the government of some risks. True, many actual federations are fragile. They nevertheless exist because the radical options of complete unification or complete separation are impractical. They also help their constituents cope with uncertainty.

At the system level today, we don't need a big leap of imagination to move beyond the kind of intergovernmental risk-governing institutions championed in the mid-1940s. The argument noted in Chapter 6 that the IMF evolved on the basis of a flawed and even biased public insurance model may be empirically well supported, but the Fund's mixed record in managing the mounting risks of a globalizing financial system mainly suggests that the model itself should be significantly improved, not abandoned. In this context, the inequitable consequences of open capital markets are easy to see, but so too are the drivers of resistance to capital controls at either individual or national levels. The logic of more ambitious multi-level regulation and supervision is harder to resist, especially when financial disintegration would be extravagantly costly and ad hoc official reinsurance so obviously benefits the well-off.

Informal structures, such as the Basel Process, the Financial Stability Board, and the G7 and G20 clubs, can kickstart innovative and necessary global initiatives, but they cannot ultimately replace more comprehensively effective and accountable collaborative institutions. International organizations must have essential mandates and be staffed by civil servants acting in the name of legitimate global authority – transcending without ignoring the separate states constituting it.[27] Most importantly, they are the keepers of historical memory, the main bulwark against the tendency of leaders and their constituents to forget, especially after moments of emergency have passed.[28] In the long run, the reasonable assessment of risks that cannot be managed locally, the feasible

[27] The idea is not new. It animated the Secretariat of the League of Nations as it developed and persists today at the organizational core of the United Nations and its main affiliates. Always controversial in settings caught between the logics of intergovernmentalism and supranationalism, the original vision saw a neutral civil service as the vital instrument for moving beyond "conference diplomacy." It is now past time to revive it. For background, see Dag Hammarskjöld, "The International Civil Servant in Law and in Practice," a reprint by the Dag Hammarskjöld Foundation of a lecture delivered at Oxford University on May 30, 1961 (Oxford: Oxford University Press, 2021). For a sophisticated defense of the concert model, see Andrew Cooper, *The Concertation Impulse in World Politics* (Oxford: Oxford University Press, 2024).

[28] The phenomenon has various names, like disaster myopia. See, for example, Jack M. Guttentag and Richard Herring, "Disaster Myopia in International Banking," *Essays in International Finance*, 164 (Princeton, NJ: International Finance Section, Department of Economics, 1986).

negotiation of the burden-sharing arrangements required to implement sustainable prevention strategies, and deliver emergency and recovery services where they are needed – all depend on gradually moving away from informality.[29] The same logic already applies to governing many markets – for essential commodities, vital services, leading-edge technologies, and renewable energy.

The idea that much of the world drifted into a "weakly confederal" system during the turbulent twentieth century is hardly novel or controversial.[30] Nor should it be difficult to acknowledge that this system is adapting today as it confronts complex challenges that stretch political imaginations beyond conventional assessments of risk and beyond traditional notions of state sovereignty. Only the details of the intricate but essential political negotiations thereby required should stoke serious argument. Their main objective must be functional, sustainable, and limited governing instruments.

Again, this is not a utopian vision. Inside the United States and other liberal democracies, grassroots and public education campaigns in support of variegated multilateral governing structures – in the national interest – were on the rise in the mid-twentieth century. The Cold War soon put a damper on forward movement but did not entirely stop it.[31] In 1968, it was considered unusual but not ridiculous that Supreme Court Justice William O. Douglas would publish a monograph in support of world federalism.[32] Of course, less open minds, in the United States and elsewhere, stayed attached to the free-riding ideologies of nationalism and self-reliance. Their inevitable frustrations only grew during subsequent decades.

[29] Charles B. Roger, *The Origins of Informality: Why the Legal Foundations of Global Governance Are Shifting, and Why It Matters* (Oxford: Oxford University Press, 2020).

[30] Arthur A. Stein, "Incentive Compatibility and Global Governance: Existential Multilateralism, a Weakly Confederal System, and Hegemony," in *Can the World Be Governed? Possibilities for Effective Multilateralism*, edited by Alan Alexandroff (Waterloo, ON: Wilfrid Laurier University Press, 2008), 17–84. Paul Tucker alludes to something similar when he highlights the "constrained pluralism" existing in the background when liberal states came to the fore. See Tucker, *Global Discord: Values and Power in a Fractured World Order* (Princeton, NJ: Princeton University Press, 2024).

[31] Joseph Preston Baratta, "The International Federalist Movement," *Peace and Change* 24, no. 3 (1999): 340–372; For context, see Mark Mazower, *Governing the World: The History of an Idea* (New York: Penguin, 2013), and Bob Reinalda, "The History of International Organization(s)," in the *Oxford Research Encyclopedias: International Studies* (2019): 1–25.

[32] William O. Douglas, *Towards a Global Federalism* (New York: New York University Press, 1968).

Careful observers can discern signals of at least limited receptivity to Douglas's idea much further afield. In fact, a rich literature explores the place of federal principles in China's own history.[33] Sun Yat-sen raised the subject explicitly in the late nineteenth century. Related debates followed the collapse of the Qing dynasty, and even carried over through the years following the end of a long civil war in 1949. The idea of diffusing powers receded in later years, when the victors sought to counter traditional fears of the country's fragmentation. In India, federalist ideas are even more deeply rooted, as is the daily contest between centralizing governmental tendencies and local resistance. The same tension, but also the possibilities of risk-driven movement toward collaboration, sparks imaginations and stimulates political experiments inside and across the borders of many other complicated states around the world.

If one opens one's eyes and travels around the world just a bit, one can observe that a global society is already emerging. A reasonable and pragmatic observer must then face the obvious question. When it comes to certain problems faced across the vast sweep of that society, what serious alternatives exist to the development of some minimal level of collaborative and binding risk and burden sharing capacity? What is the alternative to pushing insurance-like experiments to the next level? To close one's mind to that question – drawn to unrealistic dreams of less ambiguous structures of consolidated global power, to fantasies of complete political autonomy, or to fixations concerning the inexorable balancing role of interstate war in the nuclear age – is to offer no hope. The evident requirement of our time is to remain open to the prospect of effective collaborative government when it comes to complex risks that lie just beyond the zone of conventional insurance underwriting. Call it risk pooling entirely covered by official, comprehensive, and shared reinsurance, offered only when disaggregated forms of coverage and incentives for crisis prevention are not more efficient.

In sum, sustainable solutions to inextricably shared problems that must be addressed collectively do not require abandoning ideas of political independence or pragmatic policy variation across the board. They do, however, require imaginative rethinking aimed at much deeper forms of authoritative collaboration in policy arenas irrevocably

[33] Gabriella Montinola, Yingyi Qian, and Barry R. Weingast, "Federalism, Chinese Style: The Political Basis for Economic Success in China," *World Politics* 48, no. 1 (1995): 50–81; Alexander Libman and Michael Rochlitz, *Federalism in China and Russia* (Northampton, MA: Edward Elgar, 2019).

reshaped by the complexity and differential time horizons of unavoidable cross-border, systemic, and global dangers. And they must extend far beyond the members of exclusive, self-appointed clubs to the whole of an emerging world society.

Three years after the Manhattan Project he led culminated in the use of atomic weapons, Henry Stimson, the conservative American statesman – and political realist – who served as Secretary of State and Secretary of War during administrations extending from William Howard Taft to Harry Truman, made a famous appeal to his nation. Despite persistent military and ideological threats, he thought that forever abandoning the national dream of self-reliance across the board was now essential in the cause of building world peace. Not only because of the dawn of the nuclear era, he clearly saw rising technological challenges demanding a practical statecraft aligning long-term global objectives with his country's traditional liberal aspirations. The implication was straightforward. "In counseling against policies which ignore the facts of the world as it is, I do not, of course, mean to argue that we can for a moment forget the nature of our final goal. Lasting peace and freedom cannot be achieved until the world finds a way toward the necessary government of the whole."[34]

Anticipating the criticism that the level of cooperation required to form such a government depended fundamentally on a prior sense of trust, Stimson had earlier written (in the inadequately inclusive style of the day):

> The chief lesson I have learned in a long life is that the only way to make a man trustworthy is to trust him; and the surest way to make him untrustworthy is to distrust him and show your distrust. And it is from this lesson that I draw the conviction that only a direct and open dealing on this [the unlocking of atomic energy], the most pressing problem of our time, can bring us enduring cooperation and an effective community of purpose among the nations of the earth.[35]

In arenas of complex and long-term risks including but now extending far beyond those involved in harnessing nuclear energy, Stimson's conviction remains compelling, and not only for the United States. His deeper insight, applicable to the cases discussed in this book, was that

[34] Henry L. Stimson, "The Challenge to Americans," *Foreign Affairs* 26, no. 1 (October 1947), 12. Also see Henry Stimson and McGeorge Bundy, *On Active Service in Peace and War* (New York: Harper and Brothers, 1947), especially pages 652–654.

[35] Henry L. Stimson, "The Bomb and the Opportunity," *Harper's Magazine*, March 1, 1946, 192.

nuclear energy constituted only a "first step in a new control by man over the primal forces of nature too revolutionary and too dangerous to fit into the old patterns."[36]

New patterns of governing in our time must reflect a new consensus: Complex integration is a fact of life. Orthodox approaches to global policymaking must be transcended, at least in part.[37] Market-based practices can help manage some risks that can't be readily contained within established political boundaries, but today they ultimately depend on the assurances provided by collaborative public authority. In certain policy arenas, private insurance and risk-management systems increasingly play functional and broadly accepted roles. When border-spanning burden-sharing arrangements must be negotiated outside such systems, rationalizing and explaining them by drawing (however imperfectly) on insurance and reinsurance metaphors may be helpful in the essential process of building support across the frontiers of nationality.

Other lessons from modern history remain available in the search for a sustainable global consensus on collaboratively governing risks that cross conventional political boundaries. Agreements based on a sense of diffuse reciprocity – that is, reasonable expectations of fair treatment and mutual assistance in the long run and not necessarily immediately enforceable – are feasible among like-minded parties. But setting the stage for "direct and open dealing" beyond them is required and might not always be as straightforward as Stimson implied. For a time, confidence-building measures based on a stricter sense of reciprocity may have to be made explicit in some cases.[38] Differences in economic and political cultures – distinct from the temptations of populist nationalism – may erode over time. A sense of empathy for the reasons lying behind those differences, however, will surely help accelerate that process.

It obviously remains in everyone's self-interest to maintain a habitable planet, but traditional conflicts over dominance and control still

[36] Ibid. Also see Edward Farley Aldrich, *The Partnership: George Marshall, Henry Stimson, and the Extraordinary Collaboration That Won World War II* (Guilford, CT: Stackpole Press, 2022), 456–468. On trust building in international relations, see Brian Rathbun, *Trust in International Cooperation: International Security Institutions, Domestic Politics, and American Multilateralism* (Cambridge: Cambridge University Press, 2012); and Nicholas J. Wheeler, *Trusting Enemies: Interpersonal Relationships in International Conflict* (Oxford University Press, 2018).

[37] Edgar Grande and Louis Pauly, eds., *Complex Sovereignty: Reconstituting Political Authority in the Twenty-First Century* (Toronto: University of Toronto Press, 2005).

[38] Robert O. Keohane, "Reciprocity in International Relations," *International Organization* 40, no. 1 (1986): 1–27.

threaten to undermine that very objective. The chimera of autonomy retains its allure. In such a context, a tightly bound global federation remains similarly unrealistic. But on existential challenges, we cannot escape entangled politics across integrating societies. We are left with the objective necessity of pooling and diversifying risks to the extent possible and sharing of inevitable burdens of disaster prevention and emergency management where global risks slide into the common realm of uncertainty. As Stimson knew, dramatic technological change calls for imaginative political experiments in the face of readily understandable resistance. In policy arenas such as those outlined here, pragmatic and flexible judgments must underpin practical experiments aimed necessarily at rebalancing individual and collective values at the necessary scale. Today's impossible dream may then gradually become tomorrow's shared strategic vision.

Insurance practices and metaphors evoking the rights and responsibilities of individuals in burden-sharing systems have long had observably transformative social and political effects at local, national, and regional levels. Again, private capital has often been successfully gathered and productively deployed through market mechanisms that ultimately serve public purposes. Nonmarket collective capacities, as we have seen, have also then proven essential to safeguard vital and expanding markets. In key arenas of risk and policy, reinsuring the reinsurers has become an unavoidably collaborative public function.

Although the insurance and reinsurance experiments examined in this book have not promised complete fairness or unlimited opportunity, they have begun elaborating globally the kind of jerry-built structures of public and private insurance that Thomas Morawetz described in Chapter 1. They have effectively pushed political frontiers outward, strengthened societal resilience, and expanded the potential scope of future burden sharing. They have given practical and legitimate expression to interest-based forms of cross-national risk mutualization and political collaboration. Their most ambitious forms involve states and societies taking steps beyond intergovernmental voluntarism. The safety net evolving beneath European capital markets serves as a mundane and still-dynamic example. More expansive is the evolving regime covering third-party liability in the wake of accidents at nuclear plants and the less formal commitments on international financial stabilization signified by the Basel Process. To be sure, however, existing and proposed international arrangements leave widening gaps in the coverage of many global risks, especially in the developing world.

With the kinds of risks and gathering uncertainties outlined in Chapter 7 in mind, turning back from expanding experiments informed by the history and logic of insurance and reinsurance and retreating from the agenda of collaborative risk governance remains possible. The populist and nationalist backlash to global economic and social pressures so evident in our world cannot be denied. Of course, our species could circle back to Hobbes's state of nature. But we can readily anticipate the consequences of catastrophes foreseen. Even if easily imaginable systemic disasters are avoided, the fog of uncertainty may thicken again as the reality of global integration meets the momentary limits of political possibility. Last-ditch efforts to obscure the dimensions of many risks and to bolster the illusion of national autonomy are hardly in short supply. But they offer no hope for the future.

Among and beyond leading states and societies fundamental strategic reconsiderations are stimulating change in the assessment of unbounded risks, the prevention of cross-border disasters, and the management of global emergencies. Unwise choices remain conceivable, but promising experiments are already underway. Just as it did in the aftermath of the Glarus fire in 1861, the insuring instinct can drive a pragmatic reimagining in forms of deepening social and political collaboration. The regional and global arrangements it has already inspired testify to the possibilities of human ingenuity under pressure. They justify a realistic sense of hope.

Selected Bibliography

Full references are provided in the notes. For readers interested in exploring specific themes more deeply, I highlight here key books and articles.

ON THE HISTORY, PSYCHOLOGY, AND SOCIOLOGY OF RISK AND UNCERTAINTY

Adams, John. *Risk*. London: UCL Press, 1995.

Arnoldi, Jakob. *Risk: An Introduction*. Cambridge: Polity, 2009.

Beck, Ulrich. *Risk Society: Toward a New Modernity*. London: Sage, 1992.

Beck, Ulrich. *World Risk Society*. Cambridge: Polity, 1999.

Bernstein, Peter L. *Against the Gods: The Remarkable Story of Risk*. New York: John Wiley, 1998.

Daston, Lorraine. *Classical Probability in the Enlightenment*. Princeton: Princeton University Press, 1988.

Douglas, Mary and Aaron Wildavsky. *Risk and Culture: An Essay on the Selection of Technical and Environmental Dangers*. Berkeley: University of California Press, 1982.

Ericson, Richard V. and Aaron Doyle, eds. *Risk and Morality*. Toronto: University of Toronto Press, 2003.

Hacking, Ian. *The Emergence of Probability*. Cambridge: Cambridge University Press, 1975, 2006.

Hacking, Ian. *The Taming of Chance*. Cambridge: Cambridge University Press, 1990.

Katzenstein, Peter J., ed. *Uncertainty and Its Discontents*. Cambridge: Cambridge University Press, 2022.

Katzenstein, Peter J. and Lucia Seybert, eds. *Protean Power: Exploring the Uncertain and Unexpected in World Politics*. Cambridge: Cambridge University Press, 2018.

Kay, John and Mervyn King. *Radical Uncertainty: Decision-Making Beyond the Numbers*. New York: W. W. Norton, 2020.

Klaas, Brian. *Fluke: Chance, Chaos, and Why Everything We Do Matters*. New York: Simon & Schuster, 2024.
Knight, Frank. *Risk, Uncertainty, and Profit*. Boston: Houghton, Mifflin, 1921.
Lindley, Dennis V. *Understanding Uncertainty*. Hoboken: John Wiley & Sons, 2006.
Marchau, Vincent A.W. J. et al., eds. *Decision-Making under Deep Uncertainty*. Cham, CH: Springer, 2019.
Renn, Ortwin. *Risk Governance: Coping with Uncertainty in a Complex World*. Abingdon: Routledge, 2006.
Skidelsky, Robert. *Keynes: The Return of the Master*. New York: Public Affairs, 2009.
Slovic, Paul, ed. *The Perception of Risk*. London: Earthscan, 2000.
Taleb, Nassim Nicholas. *The Black Swan: The Impact of the Highly Improbable*. New York: Random House, 2007.
Tversky, Amos, Paul Slovic, and Daniel Kahneman, eds. *Judgment under Uncertainty*. New York: Cambridge University Press, 1982.

ON THE HISTORY, PRACTICE, AND LIMITS OF INSURANCE AND REINSURANCE

Berliner, Baruch. "Large Risks and Limits of Insurability," *The Geneva Papers on Risk and Insurance* 10, no. 37 (1985): 313–329.
Burchell, Graham, Colin Gordon, and Peter Miller, eds. *The Foucault Effect: Studies in Governmentality*. London: Harvester Wheatsheaf, 1991.
Clark, Geoffrey. *Betting on Lives*. Manchester: Manchester University Press, 1999.
Clark, Geoffrey et al., eds. *The Appeal of Insurance*. Toronto: University of Toronto Press, 2010.
Ericson, Richard V. and Aaron Doyle. *Uncertain Business: Insurance and the Limits of Knowledge*. Toronto: University of Toronto Press, 2004.
Ericson, Richard V., Aaron Doyle, and Dean Barry. *Insurance as Governance*. Toronto: University of Toronto Press, 2003.
Farber, Hannah. *Underwriters of the United States: How Insurance Shaped the American Founding*. Chapel Hill: University of North Carolina Press, 2021.
Faure, Michael G. and Ton Hartlief. *Insurance and Expanding Systemic Risks*. Paris: OECD, 2003.
Friedman, Rachel. *Probable Justice: Risk, Insurance, and the Welfare State*. Chicago: University of Chicago Press, 2020.
Haueter, Niels Viggo. *A History of Insurance*. Zurich: Swiss Re, 2013.
Haueter, Niels Viggo and Geoffrey Jones, eds. *Managing Risk in Reinsurance*. Oxford: Oxford University Press, 2017.
Haufler, Virginia. *Dangerous Commerce* (Ithaca, NY: Cornell University Press, 1997).
James, Harold et al. *The Value of Risk: Swiss Re and the History of Reinsurance*. Oxford: Oxford University Press, 2013.
Jarzabkowski, Paula, Rebecca Bednarek, and Paul Spee. *Making a Market for Acts of God: The Practice of Risk-trading in the Global Reinsurance Industry*. Oxford: Oxford University Press, 2015.

Kunreuther, Howard et al. *The Future of Risk Management*. Philadelphia: University of Pennsylvania Press, 2020.
Lobo-Guerrero, Luis. *Insuring Life*. Abingdon: Routledge, 2016.
Lobo-Guerrero, Luis. *Insuring Security*. Abingdon: Routledge, 2011.
Lobo-Guerrero, Luis. *Insuring War*. Abingdon: Routledge, 2012.
Morawetz, Thomas. "Insurance: How It Matters as Psychological Fact and Political Metaphor," *Connecticut Law Journal* 6 no. 1 (1999): 9.
Nacol, Emily. *An Age of Risk*. Princeton: Princeton University Press, 2016.
Power, Michael. *Organized Uncertainty: Designing a World of Risk Management*. Oxford: Oxford University Press, 2007.
Schanz, Kai-Uwe and Fabian Sommerrock. *Harnessing Technology to Narrow the Insurance Protection Gap*. Zurich: The Geneva Association, 2016.
Schanz, Kai-Uwe. *The Value of Insurance in a Changing Risk Landscape*. Zurich: The Geneva Association, November 2023.
Trebilcock, Clive. *Phoenix Assurance and the Development of British Insurance*, vol. 1. Cambridge: Cambridge University Press, 1985.
van der Heide, Arjen. *Dealing in Uncertainty: Insurance in the Age of Finance*. Bristol, UK: Bristol University Press, 2023.
Zhang, Vicki. *Uncalculated Risks: The Transformation of Insurance, the Erosion of Regulation, and the Economic and Social Consequences*. Toronto: Canadian Scholars' Press, 2015.

ON SYSTEMIC RISK IN INTERNATIONAL CAPITAL MARKETS

Abdelal, Rawi. *Capital Rules: The Construction of Global Finance*. Cambridge, MA: Harvard University Press, 2007.
Angeloni, Ignazio et al. *Geneva 27: Much Money, Little Capital, and Few Reforms: The 2023 Banking Turmoil*. Paris and London: CEPR Press, 2024.
Bell, Stephen and Andrew Hindmoor. *Masters of the Universe, Slaves of the Market*. Cambridge, MA: Harvard University Press, 2015.
Best, Jacqueline. *The Limits of Transparency: Ambiguity and the History of International Finance*. Ithaca, NY: Cornell University Press, 2005.
Bremmer, Ian. *The Power of Crisis*. New York: Simon & Schuster, 2022.
Brummer, Chris. *Soft Law and the Global Financial System: Rule Making in the Twenty-first Century*. Cambridge: Cambridge University Press, 2012.
Brunnermeier, Marcus, Harold James, and Jean-Pierre Landau. *The Euro and the Battle of Ideas*. Princeton: Princeton University Press, 2016.
Callon, Michel ed. *The Laws of the Markets*. Oxford: Blackwell, 1998.
Calomiris, Charles and Stephen Haber. *Fragile by Design: The Political Origins of Banking Crises and Scarce Credit*. Princeton: Princeton University Press, 2014.
Cohen, Benjamin J. *The Geography of Money*. Ithaca, NY: Cornell University Press, 1998.
Copelovitch, Mark and David Singer. *Banks on the Brink: Global Capital, Securities Markets, and the Political Roots of Financial Crises*. Cambridge: Cambridge University Press, 2020.

Danielsson, Jon. *The Illusion of Control: Why Financial Crises Happen, and What We Can (and Can't) Do About It*. New Haven: Yale University Press, 2022.
Drezner, Daniel. *The System Worked: How the World Stopped Another Great Depression*. Oxford: Oxford University Press, 2014.
Eich, Stefan. *The Currency of Politics*. Princeton: Princeton University Press, 2022.
Eichengreen, Barry. *Capital Flows and Crises*. Cambridge, MA: MIT Press, 2003.
Farrell, Henry and Abraham Newman. *Underground Empire: How America Weaponized the World Economy*. New York: Henry Holt, 2023.
Frieden, Jeffry A. *Global Capitalism*. New York: W. W. Norton, 2020.
Geithner, Timothy. *Stress Test: Reflections on Financial Crises*. New York: Crown, 2014.
Goodhart, Charles. *The Basel Committee on Banking Supervision: A History of the Early Years 1974–1997*. Cambridge: Cambridge University Press, 2011.
Goodhart, Charles and Gerhard Illing, eds. *Financial Crises, Contagion, and the Lender of Last Resort*. Oxford: Oxford University Press, 2002.
Gorton, Gary. *Misunderstanding Financial Crises: Why We Don't See Them Coming*. Oxford: Oxford University Press, 2012.
Grabel, Ilene. *When Things Don't Fall Apart: Global Financial Governance and Developmental Finance in an Age of Productive Incoherence*. Cambridge, MA: MIT Press, 2017.
Helleiner, Eric. *States and the Reemergence of Global Finance*. Ithaca, NY: Cornell University Press, 1994.
Helleiner, Eric. *The Status Quo Crisis: Global Financial Governance After the 2008 Meltdown*. Oxford: Oxford University Press, 2014.
Helleiner, Eric, Stefano Pagliari and Hubert Zimmerman, eds. *Global Finance in Crisis*. London: Routledge, 2009.
James, Harold. *Seven Crashes: The Economic Crises That Shaped Globalization*. New Haven: Yale University Press, 2023.
Kindleberger, Charles and Robert Aliber. *Manias, Panics, and Crashes: A History of Financial Crises*. New York: John Wiley & Sons, 1978.
MacKenzie, Donald A. *An Engine, Not a Camera: How Financial Models Shape Markets*. Cambridge: MIT Press, 2006.
Minsky, Hyman. *Stabilizing an Unstable Economy*. New Haven: Yale University, 1986.
Nathan, Marcus. *Austrian Reconstruction and the Collapse of Global Finance, 1921–1931*. Cambridge, MA: Harvard University Press, 2018.
Nelson, Stephen C. and Peter J. Katzenstein. "Uncertainty, Risk, and the Financial Crisis of 2008," *International Organization* 68, no. 2 (2014): 361–392.
Palan, Ronen. *The Offshore World: Sovereign Markets, Virtual Places, and Nomad Millionaires*. Ithaca, NY: Cornell University Press, 2006.
Reinhart, Carmen and Kenneth Rogoff. *This Time is Different: Eight Centuries of Financial Folly*. Princeton: Princeton University Press, 2011.
Schoenmaker, Dirk. *Governance of International Banking: The Financial Trilemma*. Oxford: Oxford University Press, 2013.
Schwartz, Herman. *Subprime Nation: American Power, Global Capital, and the Housing Bubble*. Ithaca, NY: Cornell University Press, 2009.
Singer, David. *Regulating Capital*. Ithaca, NY: Cornell University Press, 2007.

Strange, Susan. *Mad Money*. Manchester: Manchester University Press, 1998.

Subacchi, Paola. *The Cost of Free Money: How Unfettered Capital Threatens Our Economic Future*. New Haven: Yale University Press, 2020.

Tooze, Adam. *Crashed: How a Decade of Financial Crises Changed the World*. New York: Viking, 2018.

Trivellato, Francesca. *The Promise and Peril of Credit*. Princeton: Princeton University Press, 2019.

Underhill, Geoffrey and Erik Jones. "Optimum Financial Areas: Retooling the Governance of Global Finance," *The World Economy* 46, no. 6 (2023): 1582–1608.

ON RISK AND INSURANCE IN THE NUCLEAR ENERGY SECTOR

Ferguson, Charles D. *Nuclear Energy: Balancing Benefits and Risks*. CSR no. 28. New York: Council on Foreign Relations, 2007.

Fischer, David. *History of the International Atomic Energy Agency*. Vienna: IAEA, 1997.

Hephron, Raphael, Stephen Ashley, and William Nuttall. "The Global Nuclear Liability Regime post-Fukushima Daiichi," *Progress in Nuclear Energy* 90 (2016): 1–10.

Jacobs, Robert A. *Nuclear Bodies: The Global Hibakusha*. New Haven: Yale University Press, 2022.

Pelzer, Norbert. "Nuclear Accidents: Models of Reparation," in *Nuclear Non-Proliferation in International Law*, 3, edited by Jonathan Black-Branch and Dieter Fleck (The Hague, NL: T.M.C Asser Press, 2016), 355–401.

Schwartz, Julia A. "International Nuclear Third Party Liability Law: The Response to Chernobyl," in OECD, *International Nuclear Law in the Post-Chernobyl Period*. Paris: OECD, 2006.

Schwartz, Julia A. "Liability and Compensation for Third Party Damage Resulting from a Nuclear Incident," in *Principles and Practice of International Nuclear Law*, edited by Kimberly Sexton Nick and Stephen G. Burns. Paris: Nuclear Energy Agency/OECD, 2022), 409–444.

ON FINANCIAL RISK GOVERNANCE IN THE EUROPEAN UNION

Dallara, Charles H. *Euroshock: How the Largest Debt Restructuring in History Helped Save Greece and Preserve the Eurozone*. New York: Rodin Books, 2024.

European Stability Mechanism. *Safeguarding the Euro in Times of Crisis*. Luxembourg: Publications Office of the European Union, 2019.

Ferreiro, Jesús, Giuseppe Fontana, and Felipe Serrano, eds. *Fiscal Policy in the European Union*. London: Palgrave Macmillan, 2008.

Goodhart, Charles and Dirk Schoenmaker. "Burden Sharing in a Banking Crisis in Europe," *Sveriges Riksbank Economic Review* 2 (2006): 34–57.

Henning, C. Randall. *Tangled Governance: International Regime Complexity, the Troika, and the Euro Crisis*. Oxford: Oxford University Press, 2017.

Howarth, David and Lucia Quaglia. "Failing Forward in Economic and Monetary Union: Explaining Weak Eurozone Financial Support Mechanisms," *Journal of European Public Policy* 28, no. 10 (2021): 1555–1572.
Howarth, David and Lucia Quaglia. "The Difficult Construction of a European Deposit Insurance Scheme," *Journal of Economic Policy Reform* 21, no. 3 (2018): 190–209.
James, Harold. *The IMF and the European Debt Crisis*. Washington, DC: International Monetary Fund, 2024.
Mody, Ashoka. *Euro Tragedy: A Drama in Nine Acts*. Oxford: Oxford University Press, 2018.
Quaglia, Lucia. *The European Union and Global Financial Regulation*. Oxford: Oxford University Press, 2014.
Risse, Thomas and Tanja A. Börzel, eds. *From Europeanisation to Diffusion*. London: Routledge, 2014.
Schelkle, Waltraud. *The Political Economy of Monetary Solidarity: Understanding the Euro Experiment*. Oxford: Oxford University Press. 2017.
Schimmelfennig, Frank. "European Integration in the Euro Crisis: The Limits of Postfunctionalism," *Journal of European Integration* 36, no. 3 (2014): 321–337.

ON INSURANCE, GOVERNMENT, AND COMPLEX GLOBAL CHALLENGES

Allan, Jen Iris et al. "Making the Paris Agreement: Historical Processes and the Drivers of Institutional Design," *Political Studies* 71, no. 3 (2021): 914–934.
Bernstein, Steven. "IR, Climate Politics and Change," *International Relations* 38, no. 3 (2024): 349–368.
Best, Eric, Pedro Robles, and Daniel J. Mallinson. "The Future of AI Politics, Policy, and Business," *Business and Politics* 26, no. 2 (2024): 171–179.
Boin, Arjen, Magnus Ekengren, and Mark Rhinard. "Hiding in Plain Sight: Conceptualizing the Creeping Crisis," *Risks, Hazards and Crisis in Public Policy* 11, no. 2 (2020): 116–138.
Christophers, Brett, Patrick Bigger, and Leigh Johnson. "Stretching Scales? Risk and Sociality in Climate Finance," *Environment and Planning A: Economy and Space* 52, no. 1 (2020): 88–110.
Colgan, Jeff, Jessica Green and Thomas Hale. "Asset Revaluation and the Existential Politics of Climate Change," *International Organization* 75, no. 2 (2021): 586–610.
Dasgupta, Partha. *The Economics of Biodiversity: The Dasgupta Review*. London: HM Treasury, 2021.
Dewulf, Art and Robbert Biesbroek. "Nine Lives of Uncertainty in Decision-making: Strategies for Dealing with Uncertainty in Environmental Governance," *Policy and Society* 37, no. 4 (2018): 441–458.
Falkner, Robert. *Environmentalism and Global International Society*. Cambridge: Cambridge University Press, 2021.
Golnaraghi, Maryam et al. *Bringing Climate Tech to Market: The Powerful Role of Insurance*. Zurich: The Geneva Association, 2024.
Hale, Thomas. *Long Problems: Climate Change and the Challenge of Governing Across Time*. Princeton: Princeton University Press, 2024.

Levin, Kelly et al. "Overcoming the Tragedy of Super Wicked Problems: Constraining Our Future Selves to Ameliorate Global Climate Change," *Policy Sciences* 45, no. 2 (2012): 123–152.

Loreau, Michel, Matthieu Barbier, Elise Filotas, et al. "Biodiversity as Insurance: From Concept to Measurement and Application," *Biological Reviews* 96, no. 5 (2021): 2333–2354.

Manulak, Michael. *Change in Global Environmental Politics: Temporal Focal Points and the Reform of International Institutions*. Cambridge: Cambridge University Press, 2022.

McCarthy, Michae. "A Brief History of the World Health Organization," *The Lancet* 360, no. 9340 (2002).

Noordhoek, Dennis. *Regulation of Artificial Intelligence in Insurance*. Zurich: The Geneva Association, 2023.

Paterson, Matthew. "Climate Change and International Political Economy: Between Collapse and Transformation," *Review of International Political Economy* 28, no. 2 (2021): 394–405.

Pompella, Maurizio and Nicos A. Scoridis. *The Palgrave Handbook of Unconventional Risk Transfer*. Cham, CH: Palgrave, 2017.

Price-Smith, Andrew. *Contagion and Chaos: Disease, Ecology, and National Security in the Era of Globalization*. Cambridge, MA: MIT Press, 2009.

Sabel, Charles F. and David G. Victor. *Fixing the Climate: Strategies for an Uncertain World*. Princeton: Princeton University Press, 2022.

Schanz, Kai-Uwe. *The Global Risk Landscape after COVID-19*. Zurich: Geneva Association, 10 June 2021.

Sears, Nathan. "International Politics in the Age of Existential Threats," *Journal of Global Security Studies* 6, no. 3 (2021): 1–23.

Sustainable Insurance Forum. *Nature-related Risks in the Global Insurance Sector*. United Nations Development Program, November 2021.

Swiss Re Institute. *Biodiversity and Ecosystem Services: A Business Case for Reinsurance*. Zurich: Swiss Re Institute, 2021.

Thiel, Andreas, William A. Blomquist, and Dustin E. Garrick, eds. *Governing Complexity*. Cambridge: Cambridge University Press, 2019.

University of Cambridge Institute for Sustainability Leadership. *Risk Sharing in the Climate Emergency: Financial Regulation for a Resilient, Net Zero, Just Transition*. Cambridge: University of Cambridge Institute for Sustainability Leadership, 2021.

World Bank/Disaster Risk Financing & Insurance Program. *Insuring Nature's Survival: The Role of Insurance in Meeting the Financial Need to Preserve Biodiversity*. Washington, DC: World Bank Group, 2022.

Wright, Lawrence. *The Plague Year: America in the Time of COVID*. New York: Knopf, 2021.

ON THE CHANGING POLITICS OF GLOBAL ORDER UNDER CONDITIONS OF RISK AND UNCERTAINTY

Abbott, Kenneth et al., eds. *International Organizations as Orchestrators*. Cambridge: Cambridge University Press, 2015.

Adler, Emanuel. *World Ordering*. Cambridge: Cambridge University Press, 2019.

Albert, Mathias. *A Theory of World Politics*. Cambridge: Cambridge University Press, 2016.

Beck, Ulrich. *The Metamorphosis of the World*. Cambridge: Polity Press, 2016.

Beck, Ulrich. *World at Risk*. Cambridge: Polity, 2009.

Blyth, Mark. *Great Transformations: Economic Ideas and institutional Changes in the Twentieth Century*. Cambridge: Cambridge University Press, 2002.

Boughton, James. *Silent Revolution: The International Monetary Fund 1979–1989*. Washington, DC: International Monetary Fund, 2001.

Büthe, Timothy and Walter Mattli. *The New Global Rulers: The Privatization of Regulation in the World Economy*. Princeton: Princeton University Press, 2011.

Buzan, Barry and Robert Falkner. *The Market in Global International Society* Oxford: Oxford University Press, 2025.

Buzan, Barry and George Lawson. *The Global Transformation*. Cambridge: Cambridge University Press, 2015.

Chwieroth, Jeffrey. *Capital Ideas: The IMF and the Rise of Financial Liberalization* Princeton: Princeton University Press, 2010.

Clavin, Patricia. *Securing the World Economy*. Oxford: Oxford University Press, 2013.

Cooper, Andrew. *The Concertation Impulse in World Politics*. Oxford: Oxford University Press, 2023.

Davis, Christina. *Discriminatory Clubs: The Geopolitics of International Organizations*. Princeton: Princeton University Press, 2023.

Deudney, Daniel. *Bounding Power: Republican Security Theory from the Polis to the Global Village*. Princeton: Princeton University Press, 2007.

Germain, Randall, ed. *Susan Strange and the Future of Global Political Economy: Power, Control and Transformation*. Abingdon, UK: Routledge, 2016.

Goldin, Ian. *Divided Nations*. Oxford: Oxford University Press, 2013.

Grande, Edgar and Louis Pauly, eds. *Complex Sovereignty: Reconstituting Political Authority in the Twenty-First Century*. Toronto: University of Toronto Press, 2005.

Graz, Jean-Christophe. *The Power of Standards: Hybrid Authority and the Globalisation of Services*. Cambridge: Cambridge University Press, 2019.

Green, Jessica F. *Rethinking Private Authority*. Princeton: Princeton University Press, 2014.

Hayek, Friedrich. *Individualism and Economic Order*. Chicago: University of Chicago Press, 1948.

Henning, C. Randall. *Regional Financial Arrangements and the International Monetary Fund*. Waterloo, ON: Centre for International Governance Innovation, 2020.

Hooghe, Liesbet, Tobias Lenz and Gary Marks. *A Theory of International Organization*. Oxford: Oxford University Press, 2019.

Ikenberry, G. John. *A World Safe for Democracy: Liberal Internationalism and the Crises of Global Order*. New Haven: Yale University Press, 2020.

Independent Evaluation Office. *The Evolving Application of the IMF's Mandate*. Washington, DC: International Monetary Fund, June 2024.

James, Harold. *International Monetary Cooperation since Bretton Woods*. New York: Oxford University Press, 1996.

Kirshner, Jonathan. *An Unwritten Future: Realism, Uncertainty, and World Politics*. Princeton: Princeton University Press, 2022.

Koenig-Archibugi, Mathias and Michael Zürn. *New Modes of Governance in the Global System*. Basingstoke: Palgrave Macmillan, 2006.

Kreienkamp, Julia and Tom Pegram. "Governing Complexity: Design Principles for the Governance of Complex Global Catastrophic Risks," *International Studies Review* 23 (2021): 779–806.

Lake, David A. *Hierarchy in International Relations*. Ithaca, NY: Cornell University Press, 2009.

Lake, David A. *Indirect Rule: The Making of U.S. International Hierarchy*. Ithaca, NY: Cornell University Press, 2024.

Lipscy, Phillip Y. and Haillie Na-Kyung Lee. "The IMF As a Biased Global Insurance Mechanism," *International Organization* 73, no. 1 (2019): 35–64.

Mazower, Mark. *Governing the World: The History of an Idea*. New York: Penguin, 2013.

Patomaki, Heikki. *World Statehood*. Cham, CH: Springer, 2023.

Pauly, Louis W. *Who Elected the Bankers? Surveillance and Control in the World Economy*. Ithaca, NY: Cornell University Press, 1997.

Rathbun, Brian. *Trust in International Cooperation: International Security Institutions, Domestic Politics, and American Multilateralism*. Cambridge: Cambridge University Press, 2012.

Renckens, Stefan. *Private Governance and Public Authority: Regulating Sustainability in a Global Economy*. Cambridge: Cambridge University Press, 2020.

Reus-Smit, Christian. *On Cultural Diversity: International Theory in a World of Difference*. Cambridge: Cambridge University Press, 2018.

Rixen, Thomas, Lora Anne Viola, and Michael Zürn, eds. *Explaining Institutional Development in World Politics*. Oxford: Oxford University Press, 2016.

Roger, Charles B. *The Origins of Informality: Why the Legal Foundations of Global Governance Are Shifting, and Why It Matters*. Oxford: Oxford University Press, 2020.

Rosenau, James N. and Ernst-Otto Czempiel, eds. *Governance without Government*. Cambridge: Cambridge University Press, 1992.

Ruggie, John G. *Constructing the World Polity*. London: Routledge, 1998.

Sabel, Charles F. and Jonathan Zeitlin. *Experimentalist Governance in the European Union* Oxford: Oxford University Press, 2010.

Sandler, Todd. *Global Collective Action*. Cambridge: Cambridge University Press, 2004.

Scoones, Ian and Andy Stirling, eds. *The Politics of Uncertainty: Challenges of Transformation*. London: Routledge, 2020.

Suganami, Hidemi. *The Domestic Analogy and World Order Proposals*. Cambridge: Cambridge University Press, 1989.

Truman, Edward, ed. *Reforming the IMF for the Twenty-first Century*. Washington, DC: Peterson Institute for International Economics, 2006.

Tucker, Paul. *Global Discord: Values and Power in a Fractured World Order.* Princeton: Princeton University Press, 2024.

Weiss, Thomas. *Global Governance: Why? What? Whither?* Cambridge: Polity, 2013.

Wendt, Alexander. *Social Theory of International Politics.* Cambridge: Cambridge University Press, 1999.

Wheeler, Nicholas J. *Trusting Enemies: Interpersonal Relationships in International Conflict.* Oxford: Oxford University Press, 2018.

Zürn, Michael. *A Theory of Global Governance.* Oxford: Oxford University Press, 2018.

Index